11-20-21

D1053086

LOVE'S HIDDEN BLESSINGS

LOVE'S HIDDEN BLESSINGS

God Can Touch Your Life When You Least Expect It

Sue Monk Kidd

Carmel, New York 10512

Material from *Guideposts* magazine is used with permission.
Copyright © 1979, 1980, 1981, 1982, 1983, 1984, 1985, 1986,
1987, 1988, 1989 by Guideposts Associates, Inc., Carmel, New
York, 10512.
All rights reserved.

Copyright © 1990 by Sue Monk Kidd for compilation,
arrangement, Introduction, and piece entitled "Crumbling
Sandcastles".
All rights reserved.

"Crumbling Sandcastles" first appeared in July/August 1989
issue of *Today's Christian Woman*, published by Christianity
Today, Inc., Carol Stream, Illinois.

This Guideposts edition published by special
arrangement with Servant Publications.

90 91 92 93 94 10 9 8 7 6 5 4 3 2

Printed in the United States of America
ISBN 0-89283-686-5

Library of Congress Cataloging-in-Publication Data

Kidd, Sue Monk.
   Love's hidden blessings : God can touch your life when you
least expect it / Sue Monk Kidd.
      p.   cm.
   ISBN 0-89283-686-5
   1. Kidd, Sue Monk.   2. Christian biography—United
States.   3. Spiritual life.   I. Title.
BR1725.K47A3   1990
248'.092—dc20   90-34171
                                                          CIP

Dedication

To my grandmother, Sue,
who gave me not only her name,
but an example to emulate.

CONTENTS

INTRODUCTION

THIS BOOK is a collection of stories from my life, spanning many years. If there is an underlying theme to them, it is surely this: God's presence can be known through the ordinary (and not so ordinary) events of our lives. Even the simplest happening can be full of holy sounds.

I first learned this truth one windy night, when I was no more than four. A sound slipped quietly into my bedroom and woke me. It was a soft scratching on my window screen. I remember lying in bed in my pink flannel gown with the white bow on it, trying to imagine what the sound could be, unaware that I was about to stumble into a mystery that would in some way linger with me the rest of my life.

Scratch, scratch. It didn't occur to me to be afraid. I felt protected in my little room. I was struck only with curiosity. Every child has an imaginary box of "what-ifs," and lying there in the dark, I opened mine.

Accessible to wonder, lifted into the space between possibility and expectation, I listened to the sound. Finally, I crept through the shadows to my parents' bed. I shook my mother's shoulder. I smile now when I think of it, but here's what I said: "Mama, I can hear an angel brushing against my window." Then I waited to see what she would say.

My mother was wise. She didn't say, "Don't be silly. The scratching is only the wind dragging a branch across the window. Go back to bed." She knew that the ability to let go and listen creatively to the world with faith and wonder, the power to look at the humdrum and familiar and see the sacred possibility inside it, is a fragile thing, easily lost, the sort of thing we leave at our childhood windows when we cross over into adulthood. So rather than douse my tiny flame of childlike imaginings, she put her blessing upon it. "An angel?" she said rather sleepily. "How wonderful! Do say hello for me."

I never forgot that small and whimsical fragment of my childhood. It was the beginning of an awareness that has shaped much of my life ever since: common happenings are not always what they appear to be. Epiphanies of God, manifestations of divine presence, can break in upon us from the least likely places. And if we take out our box of holy wonderings—if we keep alive our childlike ability to look past the obvious and see deeply into the heart of familiar things, who knows what sacred light we might glimpse? If we listen to life with more than our ears, who knows when everyday noise might become the eloquent voice of God speaking? Who knows?

"If God speaks anywhere," writes Frederick Buechner, "it is into our personal lives that he speaks." Yes, I believe this. I believe the voice of God comes out of the thick of our days, out of the small scratchings of life upon our window.

The language of God is life itself, and I live with the unquenchable need to take my life in my hands and try to read the divine alphabet written upon it. I am devoted to the notion that life is not a random jumble of commonplace events, but a sacred tale. Hidden within the repertoire of problems, delights, crises, and familiarities that fill our days, are the veiled comings of God, divine disclosures unraveling in unlikely ways and from unexpected places.

The challenge is to open ourselves to them, to discover the mystery of the ordinary, the sacred buried in our midst. Unfortunately, the touch and message of God tend to go unnoticed in our daily story; they are often lost between the lines of life. Why is it so hard to grasp that the kingdom of God really *is* in our midst?

Many times I miss the unique ways that God turns up in my life because I am simply too busy to take note. Moses never would have seen the burning bush if he hadn't "turned aside" from his busy shepherding. To lift my life to the realm of a sacred tale, I will have to pause and ponder the sudden places where God and life intersect. I will have to take time to reflect on the configuration of events in my life and discover the puzzle of meaning.

A few months ago I was driving through the mountains of North Carolina, returning from an appointment. I was in a hurry, feeling pressured by all the "important stuff" waiting back home for my attention. Suddenly I saw a car stopped in the road ahead of me. I braked behind it, fuming a little, wondering what the problem could be. Then I saw one of those big, silent turtles crossing the road at an unbearably slow pace. So there we sat, waiting for this creature to pass.

I observed it casually at first, then with great and particular care, reflecting upon its movements, and then upon my own. The comparison startled me. What was I missing by racing through life at breakneck speeds? I looked from the turtle to the sweep of the mountains in the distance and the rich colors of the trees. I rolled down the car window and felt the breeze of autumn lift my hair. I sniffed mountain laurel. I felt God's contemplative peace enter my heart.

It's easy for us adults to operate under the illusion that what we are doing is so important we cannot stop doing it. We think we cannot slow down, especially for something so trifling as a turtle. But that is exactly the sort of thing we must never be too busy for. That was God's turtle. It was the angel at my window.

Along with our busyness, it seems we adults have also built up a veneer of "grown-up" cynicism around ourselves, an unwillingness to believe that God can really be found in the helter skelter routine of our lives—in the quarrel with our spouse, the commute to work, a child's whimper in the night, the death of a pet, a sudden hospitalization, a bird's nest that falls out of a tree.

Perhaps we have been told too often that there is no angel at the window. Certainly when I grew up, I often lost touch with what Madeleine L'Engle calls, "the child's creative acceptance of the realities moving on the other side of the everyday world." We are conditioned to depend solely on our intellect and pragmatism, and ignore symbolic, intuitive thinking that opens us to the creative realm of still, small voices, inner nudges, metaphoric images, turning points, and forays into wonder. We tend to lose the child's heart with its uninhibited willingness to see a divine spark in the ordinary stuff of life.

The culture in which we live does not give us "permission" to look and listen to the world as a place where holy happenings unfold. So as adults we fall prey to a pseudosophistication that does not allow us to carry on a creative dialogue with our own lives. We are apt to abandon storied approaches and adopt only rational, dogmatic ways of making sense of our lives. And before long we lose the vivid sense of God speaking through our days. We grow spiritually deaf.

Henri Nouwen has spoken of the spiritual life as a movement from absurdity to listening. The word, absurd comes from the word, *surdus* which means, deaf. To live a life of absurdity is to remain deaf to the voice of God calling to us from every moment, within all places.

Once I went to visit a friend in the hospital who was a poet and retired music teacher. When I arrived I asked her about her day. Her answer surprised me. She said, "Today I've been listening, really listening to my life. Through the cards that arrive in the mail, I hear God cheering me to get well. Through the flowers, I hear him remind me there is still beauty in the world. In the cry of the woman in the next bed, I feel God open my small heart to a new depth of compassion. When the nurse rubbed my back, I felt the caress of God's hand upon my life. In all of this God sang to me. It was like music. There is a symphony to be heard here, my friend!"

Yes, a symphony. Is there any place from which God

cannot sing to us? Is there anything that crosses our paths that God cannot use to teach, heal, guide, and nourish us? God's messages are everywhere, written in the language of raindrops winding down a window and teardrops winding down a face. The question is whether we will break through our "absurdity" and refine our awareness of holy sounds amid the daily static.

Jesus said, "He who has ears to hear, let him hear" (Matt. 11:15). In these pages I try to hear what God is saying to me through a redwood tree, a child on crutches, even the feelings I got when I approached my fortieth birthday. Incarnate words are different and unique for each listener's life. It's up to each of us to hear our own lives and translate for ourselves.

But listening is not easy. When my son was eight, I took him to the pediatrician for a hearing test. "He doesn't seem to hear half of what I say to him," I complained. A knowing smile appeared on the doctor's face. After the test he said, "Your son's hearing is perfect. He's merely like the rest of us. He hears only what he chooses to hear. The rest he filters out."

I left, wondering how selective I was with my own hearing, especially when it came to holy sounds. What was I filtering out? Did I "choose" to hear the voice of the Spirit in obvious places, like the Bible or church, but screen it out of my everyday surroundings? It is so like us to believe that God strikes music somewhere other than where we are—in faraway places, in other people's lives, but not in the familiar confines of our own.

Years ago, I read a fanciful story about a man named

❦

Eizik, who lived an ordinary life in Cracow, Poland. He was not a wealthy man, and one could guess that his days were an unending cycle of mundane tasks.

One night Eizik went to sleep and dreamed there was a treasure in Prague, buried under a bridge which led to the King's palace. After he dreamed this same dream three times, he decided God was trying to tell him something. So even though Prague was far away, and it meant a long and difficult journey, Eizik set out in search of the treasure.

When he arrived at the bridge in Prague, he discovered that it was guarded night and day by a soldier, so he dared not start digging. Every morning he came to the bridge and walked around it until evening, trying to figure out what to do.

Finally the soldier, a kindly man, asked Eizik why he was there. Eizik told him about the dream of treasure that had brought him from so far.

The guard began to laugh. "You poor fellow," he exclaimed. "You wore out your shoes to come here because of that! Why, if I believed in such nonsense, I would have gone to Cracow, when I dreamed three times that there was a treasure buried under the stove in the house of a man named Eizik." At that Eizik traveled home and dug up the treasure buried under the stove in his own house.

I like this story because it reminds me of an illusive truth that most of us stalk all our lives but rarely seem to net: while our inclination is to dream of treasure in far-off places, and even spend our entire lives searching for it there, the real treasure always lies right under our noses, in the simple and ordinary landscape of our own lives.

We hear the music of God where we choose, the rest we filter out. In her poem, "Aurora Leigh," Elizabeth Barrett Browning conveys the same truth:

Earth's crammed with heaven,
And every common bush afire with God;
But only he who sees take off his shoes—
The rest sit round it and pluck blackberries.

Common bushes. The stove in our own house. These are the things I write about in these pages. For these are the places the divine music plays—the places our most precious blessings are hidden.

When the idea to put together this collection of personal stories was presented to me, I didn't hesitate. I believe in stories. The world has enough dogma. It's stories we need more of, stories that reverence the still, small voice that sings our life. As Anthony de Mello observed, "The shortest distance between a human being and Truth is a story." Jesus, himself, told stories about the most common things in the world—a lost sheep, a seed that falls on rocky ground, a woman who sweeps her house in search of a coin, a man whose son runs away from home.

All personal theology should begin with the words— "let me tell you a story." For you and I were not made to subscribe to a story, but to *be* a story. Our souls are story-shaped.

My hope is that the simple stories in this book will be an invitation to listen anew to your own life and hear the sounds of a sacred tale. For when it comes right down to it, that's what matters—coming to know in the deep of our hearts that God speaks to us from our own experiences, both large and small, fierce and tender. What matters is beholding the mystery brushing upon our windows.

There is a symphony to be heard here, my friend.

CHAPTER ONE

ALWAYS END WITH LOVE

Don't Let It End This Way

HE HOSPITAL was unusually quiet that bleak January evening, quiet and still like the air before a storm. I stood in the nurses' station on the seventh floor and glanced at the clock. It was nine p.m.

I threw a stethoscope around my neck and headed for room 712, last room on the hall. 712 had a new patient. Mr. Williams. A man all alone. A man strangely silent about his family.

As I entered the room, Mr. Williams looked up eagerly, but dropped his eyes when he saw it was only me, his nurse. I pressed the stethoscope over his chest and listened. Strong, slow, even beating. Just what I wanted to hear. There seemed little indication he had suffered a slight heart attack a few hours earlier.

He looked up from his starched white bed. "Nurse,

would you . . ." He hesitated, tears filling his eyes. Once before he had started to ask me a question, but had changed his mind.

I touched his hand, waiting.

He brushed away a tear. "Would you call my daughter? Tell her I've had a heart attack. A slight one. You see, I live alone and she is the only family I have." His respiration suddenly speeded up.

I turned his nasal oxygen up to eight liters a minute. "Of course I'll call her," I said, studying his face.

He gripped the sheets and pulled himself forward, his face tense with urgency. "Will you call her right away—as soon as you can?" He was breathing fast—too fast.

"I'll call her the very first thing," I said, patting his shoulder. "Now you get some rest."

I flipped off the light. He closed his eyes, such young blue eyes in his 50-year-old face.

712 was dark except for a faint night light under the sink. Oxygen gurgled in the green tubes above his bed. Reluctant to leave, I moved through the shadowy silence to the window. The panes were cold. Below a foggy mist curled through the hospital parking lot. Above snow clouds quilted the night sky. I shivered.

"Nurse," he called, "Could you get me a pencil and paper?"

I dug a scrap of yellow paper and a pen from my pocket and set it on the bedside table.

"Thank you," he said.

I smiled at him and left.

I walked back to the nurses' station and sat in a squeaky

swivel chair by the phone. Mr. Williams' daughter was listed on his chart as the next of kin. I got her number from information and dialed. Her soft voice answered.

"Janie, this is Sue Kidd, a registered nurse at the hospital. I'm calling about your father. He was admitted tonight with a slight heart attack and . . ."

"No!" she screamed into the phone, startling me. "He's not dying, is he?" It was more a painful plea than a question.

"His condition is stable at the moment," I said, trying hard to sound convincing. In silence I bit my lip.

"You must not let him die!" she said. Her voice was so utterly compelling that my hand trembled on the phone.

"He is getting the very best care."

"But you don't understand," she pleaded. "My daddy and I haven't spoken in almost a year. We had a terrible argument on my twenty-first birthday, over my boyfriend. I ran out of the house. I . . . I haven't been back. All these months I've wanted to go to him for forgiveness. The last thing I said to him was, 'I hate you.'"

Her voice cracked and I heard her heave great agonizing sobs. I sat, listening, tears burning my eyes. A father and a daughter, so lost to each other. Then I was thinking of my own father, many miles away. It had been so long since I had said, I love you.

As Janie struggled to control her tears, I breathed a prayer. "Please God, let this daughter find forgiveness."

"I'm coming. Now! I'll be there in thirty minutes," she said. *Click.* She had hung up.

I tried to busy myself with a stack of charts on the desk.

I couldn't concentrate. Room 712. I knew I had to get back to 712. I hurried down the hall nearly in a run. I opened the door.

Mr. Williams lay unmoving. I reached for his pulse. There was none.

"Code 99. Room 712. Code 99 . Stat." The alert was shooting through the hospital within seconds after I called the switchboard through the intercom by the bed.

Mr. Williams had had a cardiac arest.

With lightning speed I leveled the bed and bent over his mouth, breathing air into his lungs. I positioned my hands over his chest and compressed. One, two, three. I tried to count. At 15 I moved back to his mouth and breathed as deeply as I could. Where was help? Again I compressed and breathed. Compressed and breathed. He could not die!

"Oh God," I prayed, "His daughter is coming. Don't let it end this way."

The door burst open. Doctors and nurses poured into the room pushing emergency equipment. A doctor took over the manual compression of the heart. A tube was inserted through his mouth as an airway. Nurses plunged syringes of medicine into the intravenous tubing.

I connected the heart monitor. Nothing. Not a beat. My own heart pounded. "God, don't let it end like this. Not in bitterness and hatred. His daughter is coming. Let her find peace."

"Stand back," cried a doctor. I handed him the paddles for the electrical shock to the heart. He placed them on Mr. Williams' chest. Over and over we tried. But nothing. No response. Mr. Williams was dead.

A nurse unplugged the oxygen. The gurgling stopped. One by one they left, grim and silent.

How could this happen? How? I stood by his bed, stunned. A cold wind rattled the window, pelting the panes with snow. Outside—everywhere—seemed a bed of blackness, cold and dark. How could I face his daughter?

When I left the room, I saw her against the wall by a water fountain. A doctor, who had been inside 712 only moments before, stood at her side, talking to her, gripping her elbow. Then he moved on, leaving her slumped against the wall.

Such pathetic hurt reflected from her face. Such wounded eyes. She knew. The doctor had told her her father was gone.

I took her hand and led her into the nurses' lounge. We sat on little green stools, neither saying a word. She stared straight ahead at a pharmaceutical calendar, glass-faced, almost breakable-looking.

"Janie, I'm so, so sorry," I said. It was pitifully inadequate.

"I never hated him, you know. I loved him," she said.

God, please help her, I thought.

Suddenly she whirled toward me. "I want to see him."

My first thought was, why put yourself through more pain; seeing him will only make it worse. But I got up and wrapped my arm around her. We walked slowly down the corridor to 712. Outside the door I squeezed her hand, wishing she would change her mind about going inside. She pushed open the door.

We moved to the bed, huddled together, taking small steps in unison. Janie leaned over the bed and buried her face in the sheets.

I tried not to look at her, at this sad, sad good-bye. I backed against the bedside table. My hand fell upon a scrap of yellow paper. I picked it up. I read.

"My dearest Janie. I forgive you. I pray you will also forgive me. I know that you love me. I love you, too. Daddy."

The note was shaking in my hands as I thrust it toward Janie. She read it once. Then twice. Her tormented face grew radiant. Peace began to glisten in her eyes. She hugged the scrap of paper to her breast.

"Thank You, God," I whispered, looking up at the window. A few crystal stars blinked through the blackness. A snowflake hit the window and melted away, gone forever.

Life seemed as fragile as a snowflake on the window. But thank You, God, that relationships, sometimes fragile as snowflakes, can be mended together again ... but there is not a moment to spare.

I crept from the room and hurried to the phone. I would call my father. I would say, I love you.

7

THE LOVE-ME-NOT
PETAL

NE LATE summer day far back in my childhood, Granddaddy and I picked the last of the blackberries along a country fence. Now and then he would hold a berry up to the sun and say, "This one should be eaten right away." With that I would whisk the berry from his fingers and gobble it up while he pretended great exasperation over losing it.

We picked and ate and laughed. Then all of a sudden I saw a wild sunflower growing alone among the berries. I picked it from the fence and, casting a look at Granddaddy, began to pluck away the petals. "Granddaddy loves me . . . loves me not . . . loves me . . . loves me not . . ." I was feeling the magic of a late summer kingdom, where blackberries and grandfathers and love would never end. "Loves me . . . loves me not . . . loves me . . ." Only one more petal. I stared at it, unable to say the final "loves me not."

Somehow the magic had vanished. A few moments later I scratched my hand on a brier and broke into tears. "That's a little scratch for such big tears," Granddaddy said. "Must have been a stinging thorn."

"Yessir, it was," I told him. But I wasn't only crying over the scratch. I was crying because there were no more petals. I didn't want it to end that way.

We got into his old black truck and jostled down the dirt road. Granddaddy peered through the windshield, looking side to side. Finally the truck stopped. Granddaddy stepped out, calling me to follow. There on the side of the road was a row of sunflowers! I reached for a blossom and once again plucked the petals from the brown button center and within moments I was able to exclaim, "*Loves me!*" as the last petal fell away. Granddaddy nodded and climbed back in the truck, his straw hat tilted over his glasses, I climbed in beside him, and the magic was once again with us. And away we went, laughing again, the red dust of summer billowing up behind us.

Of course, there was never any "interruption" of love between us that day. It existed only in the imagination of a little girl who still believed in the fancy of love-me-not flowers. But since then I've had lots of *real* "love-me-not" moments in my life—moments when I allow myself to believe that love has been denied me. Times when love for my husband or children or friends becomes over-shadowed by anger, pride, bitterness, fear, or plain old apathy. But fortunately I've learned that the presence of bad feelings doesn't have to mean the absence of love.

When these dark moments come, I am still tempted to sit quietly and nurse my little wounds, pridefully refusing to seek a brighter prospect. But, as my grandfather taught me, the secret to restoring the kingdom is never to let the "love-me-not" petal be the last one you touch. You keep on searching and trying until somehow, some way, you end with love.

CHAPTER TWO

CHILDLIKE FAITH

THE FINGER-PAINTED PRAYER

T CERTAINLY didn't seem like the kind of morning for a crisis. I sat in the kitchen where the May sun reclined against the windows, geraniums bloomed red on the sill, and finger paintings trimmed the refrigerator door. With husband off to work and children off to play, I lingered over a late breakfast, savoring a moment of quiet and a mug of coffee.

I propped my feet on my son's soccer ball that rolled around under the table, and smiled at his paintings plastered across the refrigerator. Such an artist, my four-year-old! I loved his bright, bold pictures—a tall house on a green hill, a smiling stick figure in a rocket ship, a line of giant-sized daisies, an orange butterfly. They brought out the picnic in me.

Picnic! The idea brought a wiggle to my toes. An hour with nothing but a grassy knoll, a spring breeze and a peanut butter and jelly sandwich. That was just what my husband, Sandy, needed. He had been so tired and pale lately. A month ago the doctor had noticed a small patch of pneumonia in his lungs. Sandy had never really got over it. In fact, I'd been badgering him to have another checkup. If he wouldn't have a checkup, he'd at least have a picnic.

I was trying to remember where I had stashed the picnic basket, when the phone rang. I reached up to the phone on the wall. It was Sandy.

"Hey! Let's have a picnic for lunch," I blurted out before he could say why he had called. "I'll bring the kids and meet you in the park. Deal?"

There was an interminably long silence on the other end—so long, I became uneasy.

His voice was subdued, almost a whisper. "The picnic sounds nice . . . but not possible."

Somehow I knew that what came next would be painful. It was all there in the strange quietness of his voice.

"I dropped by the doctor's on the way to work," he said. "You'll never believe this. He just admitted me to the hospital. My chest X-ray looks suspicious."

"Suspicious?" I said weakly.

"That little spot he thought was pneumonia has advanced rapidly. He thinks it could be a malignancy."

I sucked in my breath, stunned.

"Don't worry. Just concentrate on getting pajamas over here. I don't look so charming in this little white gown." He laughed. It was strained, somebody else's laugh.

We hung up. I sagged in the chair, gripping the sides till my knuckles hurt. A mental picture flashed in my mind with such terrible clarity that I could hardly get my breath. My husband, 30 years old, taken away by some dreadful disease.

"Oh, God!" I cried. "Please not this!" But even as I said the words, waves of fear from that grim picture washed over me. I stumbled on through a prayer for my husband's life, his health. But deep inside something had already knotted in my stomach. It was doubt.

I called a baby-sitter and began to straighten the kitchen at a near frenzied pace. All the while I prayed, prayed while the knots tightened in my stomach and that terrible picture left spots before my eyes.

I picked up the grape jelly from the table, bent down and scooped up the soccer ball from the floor. Then I did something so absurd, so preposterous, I still can't fathom it. In all that rushing about and frantic praying, I mixed up the simple matter of putting away the jelly and putting up the ball. Before I knew it, I was standing in my son's room, blinking at the grape jelly sitting on his closet shelf. It sat between a yellow dump truck and a space patrol helmet, in a spot usually reserved for the soccer ball. Naturally I wondered if the ball was in the refrigerator.

I plopped back on Bob's tiny tot table, leveled by this silly blunder, finally forced to sit down and take stock. Tears spattered down my face. I was in a deplorable state of distraction—putting jelly in the closet, a ball in the refrigerator, knots in my stomach and that picture, that dreadful picture in my mind. I had always hoped when problems came, I would meet them with steady, reassuring faith.

"But look at me!" I said out loud. "Just look at me. All this praying, and I'm going in feverish little circles of doubt and fear. Where is my faith?"

I looked toward the shuttered windows splintered with sunlight, as if some answer might materialize. But I saw only that same silent image of losing my husband. It swamped me with fear.

I couldn't face Sandy like this. I wiped my eyes and prayed a desperate prayer. "God, show me how to find faith."

I retrieved the jelly from the closet and plodded back to the kitchen. Bob ran ahead of me, a streak of flushed cheeks and blond, wind-blown hair. He went straight for the refrigerator and swung open the door.

"What's my soccer ball doing in here?" he asked.

"Never mind."

"But what's it DOING in here?"

"Don't ask silly questions," I said, peering in at it. The thing was bigger than a ten-pound ham. I picked it up—ice cold. I dropped it in his hands and led him to a chair.

"Daddy's in the hospital," I said.

Bob turned the ball over and over in his hands, silent. His daddy had given him that ball. They had often played on the lawn, kicking and catching. I wondered if Bob was thinking of those times.

Bob and I had prayed together when his dog got sick and it seemed only right to do so when his daddy was ill. But I wasn't sure I had any prayers left. They had all run aground in doubt. But I looked at Bob hugging the ball and heard myself ask, "Shall we pray for Daddy?"

He nodded and bowed his head. "Let Daddy get well and play soccer ball with me. Amen."

I ruffled his hair and bit my lip. He skipped happily to his room, leaving me more fearful than ever.

When the baby-sitter arrived, I stopped by Bob's room to say good-bye. He sat at his table under the shuttered windows, up to his elbows in finger paint.

"I made a picture of me and Daddy," he said, proudly.

I peered over his shoulder. "Very nice." Suddenly I stopped cold and bent closer.

An over-sized ball of yellow sun hovered in the upper corner of his paper. It was wedged in a wobbly strip of blue sky. On a green hill stood a tall stick man and short stick boy. The stick man held an unmistakable soccer ball. The stick boy held up his hands for a catch. On their faces were gigantic red smiles.

I knelt beside the table, my heart beating strangely. This was his prayer! His prayer in a picture.

It was as if God was saying to me, "You wanted a way to find faith? Here it is. Put your prayer into a picture, a mental picture so bright and bold, there can be no room for doubt and fear." It seemed logical. To rid myself of the unyielding, frightening picture, I must replace it with one more vivid.

Bob shoved the picture in my hands and zoomed off to play. Holding that tangible bit of childlike faith, I prayed. It was a small prayer, but had a vivid new image to go with it. I simply looked at Bob's painting and whispered, "Yes, God. Make it happen . . . just like this." I closed my eyes. I concentrated. I pictured my husband on a green hill,

16

under an enormous yellow sun and brilliant blue sky, playing ball with Bob. Nothing more. Nothing less.

The knots in my stomach seemed better. Definitely better.

For the next two weeks my husband lay in the hospital undergoing surgery and tests in an exhausting search for a diagnosis. Each day I clung to my picture.

One afternoon in the hospital room, the doctor brought us the diagnosis. A progressive fungal disease had invaded Sandy's lungs. It could spread to other organs, destroying vital tissue as it had in his chest. There was one possible cure. Only one. It was a precarious drug to be dripped into my husband's veins for six weeks. But would it work for him? Was it in time?

I looked at my husband, so thin, pale, and weak. A surge of fear threatened. I closed my eyes. It was there, rooted in my mind. Green hill, blue sky, golden sun, and Sandy, smiling and healthy, romping on the lawn with his son. The fear subsided. A steady, reassuring faith filled me. I believed it!

That evening I taped my son's finger painting front and center on the refrigerator as sort of an exclamation point to the faith God had brought blooming into my life.

Then one shiny July morning, soon after my husband came home from the hospital, I looked out the patio door. I caught my breath. It was happening.

Bob and his daddy stood on the green hill in our back yard, smiling gigantic smiles and holding, what else, a soccer ball. I craned my eyes to the sky. A tremendous yellow sun sat snugly in a corner of the bluest sky I'd ever seen. Bob lifted his hands for the catch. His daddy kicked the ball. It sailed through the air.

I stood at the door, awed by this tender little moment in time, when God seemed to pause in our backyard and put the finishing touches on a four-year-old's finger-painted prayer. In that moment, I knew that with God and a bright, bold prayer in my mind, anything was possible. Anything.

KEEP THESE THINGS

E MADE HIS way slowly down the long aisle of the church with the stained glass gleaming and the big organ booming and everyone singing the invitation hymn. I noticed his shoe was untied, the lace flopping in the gold carpet. My son Bob, nine years old, was joining the church. And, watching him, my mind flashed back along a particular corridor of memories.

I could see him at age three, March clouds blowing over his head like big white kites, and his eyes wondering after them. "Mama, can God fly?" That was his first question about God. But there were more. When he was five and his sister was two, he asked, "Does God love boys who hit their sisters?" That was an easy one. "Yes," I said. "God doesn't love hitting, but He loves *you* always."

Then there was a tough question when his Little League

baseball game was rained out: "If God cares so much, how come He let it rain today?"

"I'm not sure why," his daddy said. "We don't always understand what He does, but we know God still cares."

Bob was reaching for the minister's hand now. He shook it very grown-up-like and sat down in the front pew. The organ went on playing. And I was back among the memories. On a February day, Bob came home from church with a lopsided valentine he had made and addressed to God. "Be Mine," it said. I saved it along with his other Sunday school work—all those paper bookmarks decorated with gold stars and Bible verses like "God is love."

I thought of all the little prayers that had woven in and out of Bob's life. The blessings he had stumbled through at mealtime. The bedtime thank-Yous. The time he prayed so hard for his dog to get well.

The hymn was almost over. Bob looked around at me, his face brimming with a grin. It broke across his face just as it had one golden November day in the swing beneath the oak. "Mama, I want to become a Christian," he'd said.

"Do you know what that means?"

"It means I believe in Jesus and that I accept Him into my heart." His eyes were serious blue. So we prayed. And then, as now, the same grin had come.

The memories faded with the organ music. Bob stood before the church, looking up into the minister's face. "Welcome into our church family," said Dr. Craine. He smiled down at Bob. I smiled, too, and squeezed my husband's hand.

❧

"Let the little children come unto Me," Jesus once said. And here in this big, warm church my son had come forward. How had we arrived at this moment?

I knew it had somehow evolved out of all the childlike questions, the little prayers, the Sunday school bookmarks, the sessions in the swing. How important little threads of experience are to the fabric of a child's life!

I looked at Bob with the altar behind him and the world before him. Then I tucked the moment away with all the others. Like Mary, I would keep these things, and ponder them in my heart.

CHAPTER THREE

THE HEART OF CHRISTMAS

THE GIFT OF LIFE

T WAS THE NIGHT before Christmas and not a creature was stirring on the pediatric floor of the hospital. I was the nurse scheduled to work. I sat at the desk, staring at a piece of plastic holly on the wall, feeling miserable. I thought about the last-minute shopping I'd wanted to do, the cookies that hadn't been decorated, the caroling, the Bowl game on television. *It isn't fair*, I thought, *I'm missing Christmas Eve!*

I stood up and dragged my feet down the deserted corridor. I stopped at the sick nursery and sighed. There was that tacky plastic holly again, taped over the door. I pushed open the door and went in. There was only one child in the nursery, a tiny baby, a few weeks old. He had a respiratory infection but seemed to be improving. Still, a nursing assistant observed him around the clock. I noticed her standing by his crib as I came in.

"Merry Christmas," she said.

"Some way to spend Christmas Eve," I muttered. I began to scan the temperature chart across the room, when I heard an almost inaudible little gasp.

"My God! He's stopped breathing!" cried the nursing assistant.

I raced for the crib and leaned over the baby. He was limp, turning dusky blue around the mouth. I found a thready heartbeat but practically no respirations. "Get a doctor and a respiratory therapist," I said. "FAST!"

Seconds ticked. I cleared the baby's throat with suction, pulled back his chin and inserted a tiny plastic airway. *Hurry*, I kept thinking. I placed the black resuscitation bag over his nose and mouth, and began to squeeze. In and out, in and out, breathing air into his lungs. My other hand held the stethoscope over his chest and listened to his heart patter like a faint little clock winding down.

The nursery door crashed open. In poured two doctors, another nurse, a laboratory technician and a respiratory therapist. We worked frantically in a circle around his crib in a maddening blur of emergency drugs, hissing oxygen, and the blip of a heart monitor. Gradually the activity began to slow. Everything that medicine could do had been done. The baby lay unmoving, except for the mechanical rise and fall of his chest by a respirator.

The room grew quiet. Now it seemed every heart focused on the baby. Nothing seemed to matter except that the limp baby boy breathe again on his own. *Lord, help him*, I thought.

"Breathe," said a doctor. "Come on, little fellow, breathe!"
"Please, God," whispered the nurse beside me.

I saw the same plea in every face as the prayer seemed to move around the crib like a circle of hope.

Suddenly a gurgle drifted up from the crib. Next, a cough . . . and then a tiny cry! Deep silence gripped the nursery. Then the respirator was removed. Everyone waited, all eyes on the baby. He curled his fingers and waved his arms in the air. And then he breathed . . . breathed all by himself.

I turned and fumbled with the drug tray, hiding the tears that filled my eyes. I couldn't help but believe that I was standing on the rim of a magnificent miracle. It was Christmas Eve and a baby boy was alive! The extraordinary and precious gift of life had been laid at his feet by Someone other than the little band of people who surrounded his crib. The presence of Christ seemed to fill the nursery. I knew He had been in the midst of it all. I wondered if perhaps His presence wasn't especially alive in nurseries everywhere, on this night, of all nights. And in that moment my heart was drawn to Christ in some deep and holy way I cannot explain.

I felt a tug at the back of my uniform, and turned around. "The baby's parents are here," said the ward clerk. "They saw what was going on through the viewing window before I could stop them. They are terribly frightened."

With the baby pink and kicking again, I slipped out and found his mama and daddy in the waiting room. They were holding hands.

"Your baby had a difficult time," I said, "but he is much better."

"He's alive?" asked the mother, her hands trembling at her cheeks.

"He's alive and holding his own."

Tears welled up in her eyes. The father's eyes, too, sparkled with the hint of tears. "Thank you," he struggled to say. "Thank you all."

"You've given us a wonderful Christmas present," said the mother. "Our baby's life."

I blinked back tears, unable to speak. I wanted to tell them that it was really *their* son who had given me a gift. He had touched my life with a special holiness. He had helped me find my way back to the Christ-Spirit that dwells deep in the heart of Christmas.

THE CALICO ANGEL

WAS HANGING the red-and-green calico angel from a pine beam in our den when my daughter asked, "Mama, have you ever seen a real angel?"

"Goodness, no," I said. I'd stitched the angel out of gingham and calico scraps long ago, and every year since, she'd looked down on our Bethlehem scene with a sort of Mona Lisa smile on her face. In the past I'd always wired a spray of holly on her outstretched hands, but this year I'd given the angel a sprig of mistletoe to hold.

My husband, Sandy, had come home with a bunch of it the day before. He held a twig over Ann's head and planted a kiss on her cheek. It was her first encounter with mistletoe, and she was enchanted by the idea that who-ever stood under it should be kissed. Sandy explained how over the years the gray-green leaves with their white luminescent berries had become a symbol of love.

I climbed down the ladder, thinking of the decorating, baking, and shopping still to be done. But Ann gazed at the ceiling, her mind lingering on real angels. "If nobody sees them, does God still *have* angels?"

"Well, I suppose so," I said. The truth was, I never thought much about angels. They seemed creatures of another time and place.

The next morning, as I plunged back into Christmas chores, Ann called to me in a bewildered voice. She was standing before the Nativity set. "Mama, come look at baby Jesus." At first glance I saw what appeared to be tiny pearls lying around the foot of the manger—as if someone had broken the string of a necklace. There was even one lying beside the Christ Child's cheek.

Then I looked up at the calico angel and noticed that the mistletoe was missing most of its berries. Ann followed my gaze. "Mama, Jesus is under the mistletoe!" she cried.

And so He was. I hadn't noticed when I'd hung up the angel. Ann and I stood there before the Nativity Child, both of us in awe as we looked from the mistletoe leaves to the "pearls" of love and adoration the angel had dropped. And suddenly Ann bent down and kissed the Christ Child's cheek. Before I knew it, I bent and kissed Him too. Above us, our calico angel looked down on us with her mysterious smile. In the gentlest way she had invited us to worship God's son.

And I remembered the Bible story. This was the same thing angels had done on that first star-bright night long ago. They had invited busy, ordinary people—shepherds tending their flocks—to come and adore the newborn Christ Child.

Ann's question glistened in my memory. *Have you ever seen a real angel?* Maybe I hadn't actually *seen* one, but . . .

CHAPTER FOUR

EYES TO SEE

THE BOY WITH
THE GOLDEN HAIR

I GROPED OUT OF BED at 11 o'clock that Thanksgiving morning without a thankful throb in my heart. Sunlight hung in the bedroom in shafts of cold yellow. I slumped against the window by the bed and frowned at a group of boys playing a noisy game of baseball in a vacant lot behind our apartment.

Sandy and I had just married that summer. He was a first-year graduate student in theology and I was a college junior. Our apartment was cramped, we didn't have the money to buy a turkey, and we were both bone-tired from heavy academic loads. I had never been apart from my family on Thanksgiving, but now I was 1000 miles away.

As I edged moodily around the bed, which occupied most of our cramped bedroom, I could see Sandy hunched over a table piled high with books. He gave me a smile and said, "Good morning," but before I could mutter my own, the phone rang. I sat on the bed and answered.

"Hello, honey. Happy Thanksgiving!" It was Mom. I blinked back tears.

"Oh, Mom, I miss you all so!"

When I hung up, tears were coursing down my cheeks. I sat unmoving on the bed as the memories flooded back. Mom would be bustling in her steamy kitchen, counting out gleaming pieces of silver, setting out the ancient pilgrim candles that presided over our table each year. How I yearned to lean against the pantry door and be a part of the celebration!

The kitchen by now would be filled with the sweet smells of all the good things to come. Daddy would be bent over a browned turkey, tucking cranberries and pickled peaches around it in an artful wreath. In between puffs on his spicy-smelling pipe, Granddaddy would be clucking at my teen-aged brothers wrestling on the rug. There would be the orange and brown quilt tucked around Grandma's knees, a serene smile lighting up her soft features. The long maple table would already be heavy with Mom's best floral pattern china.

But these scenes, instead of comforting me, were a torment. Sandy rustled papers in the next room. I forced myself off the unmade bed.

I wandered to the kitchen and randomly opened the cabinets to find a large can of spaghetti, half a jar of peanut butter, six stale marshmallows, a dwindling bottle of catsup and four old potatoes sprouting leaves. The refrigerator was worse. Day-old tea, three apples, and cheese with mold on one corner. Dismal!

"What's for dinner?" Sandy asked, when I appeared in the doorway.

"Maybe some kind soul will leave a Thanksgiving basket on our doorstep. Otherwise you're stuck with canned spaghetti and potatoes that look like potted plants," I said. Fleeing to the bedroom I left him staring after me with a bewildered face.

I dropped onto the bed, certain a soldier in a foreign foxhole at Christmas couldn't have been more heartsick. I felt like a Thanksgiving Scrooge, hoarding my troubles like gold bars. I muffled my face with a pillow and sobbed.

"Oh, God," I whispered, "I feel so awful. Can You help me?" But nothing happened. There was only the silence of the bedroom and the raucous baseball game in the vacant lot out back. Staring out the bedroom window, the sun seemed to throw my own reflection back into my face.

A small figure hobbled beyond the window, moving almost magically across my reflection. He created a strange double image, standing in my own mirrored reflection—a crippled boy, maybe nine or ten years old.

He stopped at the edge of the lot and seemed to contemplate how to maneuver his crutches across a shallow ditch. A flash of light boomeranged from the silvery braces around his legs. Sunlight and shadows played in his blond hair.

He glanced over his shoulder at the boys in the vacant lot. Red and blue caps dotted their heads and outsized mitts dangled from their hands. One tall boy balanced a bat over his shoulders like a barbell. They stood motionless, watching the crippled boy who turned and searched the tall grass.

I glimpsed the top of a baseball peeping through the weeds, just inches past the ditch, beyond his reach. He must have discovered it at the same instant. He slowly sank one crutch into the ditch and leaned forward, lifting the other crutch, his eyes fixed on the ball. He swung his lifeless legs. One landed with a thud against his crutch. Suddenly his right shoulder dropped. His crutches lunged forward and he sprawled across the ditch.

I gasped as he went down, seeing the embarrassed pain on his face. Lying on the ground, he looked backward once again at his friends, who waited patiently for him to bring the ball.

He had fallen almost on top of the baseball. With a smile, he wrapped his fingers around the ball and tucked it in his pocket.

Standing the crutches before him, he inched his body forward—up, up, ever so slowly, dragging his legs behind him. The struggle twisted his face until at last he stood erect.

He paused a moment to catch his breath, raising his shining head and gazing past the Texas pines—an exquisite sculpture against the pale blue sky. God's special joy seemed to leap from his face. His eyes sparkled with gratitude for his contribution to his friends' baseball game.

He turned and swept his legs through the crutches. Up, out, down—the steel cages on his calves seesawed across the lot. In those suspended moments, when my heart had reached out to him, I had ceased to see my own troubled

35

reflection. Now, as I watched him go, my eyes refocused on my own image in the glass.

With the sun's warmth whispering from the window and boyish shouts in the distance, I wondered. Did God nudge me to this spot to glimpse a small boy who was thankful for the chance to stumble after a baseball for his friends?

I turned abruptly and hurried to the kitchen where I climbed to the cabinet over the refrigerator. The silver wedding gifts, not yet used, hid under a cloud of dust. In a matter of minutes I had polished them to a sparkling sheen.

When I called Sandy to dinner, it was to a table glowing with silver, crystal and flickering candles. His eyes roved over the covered casserole dishes. I lifted the lids. Steaming spaghetti garnished with cheese, creamy mashed potatoes, and baked apples glistening under marshmallow topping. It looked delicious!

"Where did you get this feast?" he asked in amazement.

"It was here all the time," I said. "But it took a little gratitude to find it."

GOD'S
WINDOW BOXES

NE DAY WHEN THE WORLD was full of spring, my husband and I were traveling through the poorer section of a large city. Cracker-box houses were wedged among the tenements and billboards. There was little birdsong, few trees. Mostly it was a concrete world.

It seemed spring had forgotten to come here. I rode along with a strange restlessness beginning to stir in me, with a bit of sadness seeping into the car. Dogs without collars. Dirt without grass. Children without butterflies. It seemed a paradise lost.

At a stop sign, we paused before yet another dilapidated old house, scraped by the years of all its paint. But that's not what grasped my attention. There across the front of it was a window box with newborn red flowers peeping over the side. Tulips, I believe. An old woman was watering them from a tin can. She appeared to be unaware of all the concrete, of the sadness that seemed to be coming through its cracks.

Suddenly, as I watched her, she did something so lovely, so breathtaking, I can see it still. She reached down and patted the soil around her flowers as a mother pats a sleeping child. Then she bent her face close to them and rubbed a petal against her cheek. And for an instant I was sure I saw God in her face.

As we pulled away from the old woman watering red flowers on a gray street, I promised myself I would not forget her nor the truth she brought to me that day—that something deep in all of us yearns for God's beauty and we can find it no matter where we are.

Leaving the city behind us, I wondered if maybe I hadn't stumbled upon one of God's subtle challenges—that of searching for beauty in homely things, for spring in barrenness, and for a spark of happiness in sorrow. Maybe whenever a child picks a dandelion, or a person leans on his hospital window before a sunrise, or an old woman grows flowers in a slum, they are all meeting this challenge whether they realize it or not. For God has placed a fragile searching quality in each of us, a quality so easily lost.

I would like to go back and thank the old woman. Without knowing it, she told me that if I look for beauty in unexpected places, I shall surely find it. God's window boxes are everywhere.

CHAPTER FIVE

A PRESENT HELP

IN TIME OF TROUBLE

NOTHING, IT SEEMED, was as dark and forbidding as Africa at night. I sat on the porch steps, staring out at the heavy black curtain that had fallen around the house. Over my shoulder, a faint stream of light drifted from the bedroom window, where my husband Sandy and two-year-old son Bob prepared for bed. Yet, I'd slipped out to the disquieting darkness of the little porch. It fit my mood rather well.

A palm fluttered overhead, stirring the inky porch shadows. In the distance, the cry of an animal moaned from the dark outline of a hill. I drew up my knees and hugged them tightly, wondering if I would ever get used to this strange land with its malaria and cobras, food shortages and often unstable governments. It seemed so remote, so full of risks and uncertainties. Ever since we'd come to Africa several months before, I'd been uneasy.

❧

Nothing hand-wringing or consuming. Just a smoldering sort of anxiety that lingered inside me.

But tonight the uneasiness had flared up worse than usual. For tonight we weren't in our familiar house near modern Nairobi, Kenya, but were spending our first night in the neighboring country of Tanzania, in the tiny town of Kigoma. Kigoma rested on the shores of Lake Tanganyika, hedged in with jungle and cut off from Kenya by the awesome Serengeti Plains. Here we were more remote than ever.

We'd come to this unlikely back corner of the world as houseguests of an American doctor, to assist with his clinic work. I thought of our grueling two-day trip across the uncivilized wilderness of Serengeti and of all our grandiose safari precautions. There was the big, blue shoe box crammed with every imaginable first-aid supply, which had ridden faithfully on the floor in front; the extra tires and gasoline tied on the roof; food and water in the back; and compass, maps, knives, and flashlights in the glove compartment. And still, my uneasiness had managed to grow with every mile.

A warm wind hissed through the tall grass, and behind me down the slope, I could almost hear the lapping of the lake as it snaked 400 miles through the lonely darkness toward Zambia. I sighed nervously. Tomorrow Sandy would travel with the doctor and his team along those waters on an overnight medical trip—out of touch for two days. I pushed off the concrete steps and turned toward the bedroom, hoping my fearful mood would fade with the dark hours of the night.

❧

The next morning, there was lots of scurrying around, preparing for the trip. Alice, the doctor's wife, made sack lunches in the kitchen. And Sandy packed the last box of supplies in the doctor's study, while I watched from the doorway.

Suddenly Bob yanked on my skirt, "Mommy, where's Moppet?" he asked, his blue eyes frowning with concern.

Moppet was a stuffed yellow bunny, nappy, limp-eared, and missing his cottontail. Pathetic, but loved.

"Poor Moppet must still be in the land rover," I said, remembering we hadn't brought the rabbit inside yet. "We'll get him later."

Bob seemed satisfied, and I turned back to the little room where Sandy packed. There were very few medical supplies about. Just pills in small envelopes and large bottles.

"That's the last of it," Sandy said. Bob and I followed as he carried the carton down to the lake that shimmered against the backyard, then wound off through the jungle like an endless blue ribbon. A white motorboat rocked gently at the water's edge.

I caught Sandy's elbow. "I wish you weren't going," I whispered impulsively. "I feel so—so alone here."

He looked off for a long moment, as if he were recapturing some lost memory. Then he smiled. "Just remember what I wrote in the flyleaf of your Bible," he said. He gave me a hug and climbed in the boat.

"Bye-bye," called Bob, as the engine spurted to life.

I gazed at the plume of white water trailing after the boat, trying to remember what he'd written in my Bible. It had been four Christmases since he'd given me that Bible, and I'd long forgotten how he'd inscribed it. Besides, I generally used a more modern translation. This time I'd packed the one he had given me, and I ambled back to the house, making a mental note to check the flyleaf later on.

After lunch I settled on the sofa.

"My goodness, the children are quiet," Alice commented across the room. *Too quiet*, I thought. Bob had only been out of sight five minutes. Not a long time, but long enough for a two-year-old to get into most anything.

All of a sudden he toddled around the corner. I stared at his face, puzzled. His mouth and tongue were a peculiar bright red. "Candy," he mumbled, as if to explain.

"Now where did you get candy?" I asked, dropping down beside him. He held out a sticky hand harboring three or four red tarts. But as I stared into his small palm, my eyes widened with horror. Those were not candy tarts at all. They were pills!

Bob puckered up his mouth, as I shook the pills from his fist.

"What's the matter?" called Alice.

"Bob has swallowed some pills!" I cried, whisking him up in my arms. "Where could he have gotten them?"

I followed her down the hall to the little room where I'd watched Sandy pack only hours ago. An unmarked bottle lay open on the floor, containing the same red pills. I gasped. It was half empty! I picked it up, a blur of questions rushing at me. *What kind of pills were they? Had the bottle been full? How many did he swallow?* The uncertainties were horrifying. But the possibilities, disastrous.

🌱

My eyes swept to the isolated world beyond the window, as the other side of the nightmare emerged. There was no ambulance, no convenient hospital with a stomach pump, no poison control center, and no doctor. He had just left for two days.

"I've got to make Bob throw up those pills before they reach his bloodstream," I said, fear crowding my words. I checked my watch: 2:00 p.m.

"What can we do?" asked Alice.

I closed my eyes, trying to slow my whirling thoughts. The shoe box of first aid. Of course! There was a little bottle of ipecac in it, the antidote for noncorrosive poisonings just such as this. I'd brought it all the way from the States, along with the other first aid—quite certain I'd never need it.

"I believe I've got just what we need," I said with relief. The ipecac syrup would bring the pills up safely, quickly and effectively.

I ran to the guest bedroom, Bob bouncing in my arms. The shoe box was on the floor, beside my open suitcase. I pushed back the floppy, travel-worn lid and tore through the contents—bandages, snake-bite kit, malaria pills, aspirin, antibiotics—so many bottles. But the antidote wasn't there. I dumped the box upside down and plowed through its contents again. Slower this time. It *had* to be there! I'd packed it weeks ago in the blue box for this very trip . . . or had I? It had been so long, I wasn't sure. The truth was, it simply wasn't there.

I abandoned the box and hurried with Bob to the kitchen. Alice and I mixed up a baking-soda concoction,

❧

hoping it would bring up the pills. Bob swallowed a little and spewed it down his shirt. I tried gagging the poor fellow, only succeeding in making him writhe and fight back. I tried every way I could think of to get rid of those pills. Nothing worked.

I sank into a kitchen chair, frightened and baffled. My watch ticked 2:18. Bob's confused little face stared up at me, his skin flushed and wet, his eyes heavy-looking. Time was slipping away so quickly.

There is no help, I thought feebly. *Absolutely no help.* The dismal thought pounded and echoed like the relentless African drums I'd heard so often. Suspended in that moment of utter helplessness, I leaned over and clutched Bob to me. "If only Daddy were here . . ." I said. Suddenly Sandy's last words that morning trailed back to me . . . *Just remember what I wrote on the flyleaf of your Bible.*

I had to know. I returned to the bedroom, still holding Bob against me. I stepped over the jumble of useless first aid on the floor and dug my Bible out of the suitcase. Kneeling there beneath the window, I flipped it open to the flyleaf. Scrawled in slightly faded ink was "God is our refuge and strength, a very present help in trouble."

A very present help, I looked up, squinting through the gleaming spears of sunlight from the window. Was God actually present in this bleak situation with real help?

"Lord, please . . . be my present help," I said. "There is no other."

Bob whimpered against my shoulder. I stood up, groping for insight, not really knowing what to do next. Should I renew my futile efforts to make Bob throw up the pills? Or should we strike out for the nearest hospital, wherever it might be, and hope we weren't too late? Beyond the window, I noticed the land rover that had brought us to this piece of obscurity. Still streaked with dust from its trek across the plains, the vehicle rested under the trees like a tired, old lion.

"I want Moppet," Bob whined.

I pushed back the damp blond hair on his forehead. It seemed perfectly silly to waste precious moments getting that rabbit. I had to make a decision—and fast. But, oddly, Moppet suddenly seemed important. Strangely important.

"All right, Bob. Wait here, I'll get Moppet from the land rover."

I hurried outside, a strange insistence beneath my footsteps. I opened the door, my eyes roving the hot emptiness. One little yellow ear stuck out from under the front seat. I reached down beneath the seat. As I did, my hand struck something hard and smooth wedged in the darkness beside Moppet. Curious, I curled my fingers around the object and pulled it up. It was the little bottle of ipecac. The missing antidote. It had somehow jostled out of the shoe box on the Serengeti Plains. Unknown to everyone . . . but God.

I reached back for Moppet, my eyes filling with tears. I rushed inside and measured out half the syrup.

"Drink this," I said to Bob, tucking the bedraggled bunny in his arms. Slowly he took a sip, then another and another till it was gone.

Five minutes passed. Then up came the medicine he had swallowed. A large handful of discolored pills; pills that I later learned could have been permanently damaging, even lethal. I wrapped my arms around Bob and Moppet and held them tightly for a long time. "Thank You, God," was all I could manage to say.

As night fell, I wandered once again to the little porch steps. The constellations glistened above like tiny diamond bracelets strung on black satin. Inside, Bob slept safely, with beloved old Moppet snuggled under his chin.

We were still pretty remote. Beyond the hands of doctors, beyond modern hospitals . . . but never beyond God. And now I knew the antidote I'd really been missing all along, ever since I'd arrived in Africa, the antidote for fear and trouble and uncertainty. It didn't come in a little bottle. It came in a mighty promise: "God is . . . a very present help."

And so He is, I thought, smiling at the black and shiny night. So He is.

COMPASSION

OON AFTER MIDNIGHT I rose from the tiny, sleepless cot in my husband's hospital room. He lay terribly sick. Beyond the window no moon shone. Not even a street lamp pierced the darkness that churned against the pane. It seemed the night conspired with the darkness in my soul . . . with the churning anguish I felt over my husband's precarious condition.

As my fears blackened, I pulled on my shoes and fled out into the hospital corridor where dim artificial light laced the wall with shadows. Tears trembled on my face . . . a sob crowded my throat. A few feet away I saw the visitor's elevator, its doors open. I ducked inside and fumbled with the buttons. As it swept me up, my sobs gave way, echoing anonymously along the elevator's silent pathway. I do not know how many times I rode up and down while my despair poured out. But it was the middle of the night, and who would notice?

Suddenly I heard a soft ping. The elevator stopped. The doors opened. Inside stepped an elderly man with thinning white hair and eyes that searched the tears streaming down my face. He pushed a button, then dug into his pocket. As we lurched upward, he handed me a neatly folded handkerchief. I wiped my eyes, staring into his kind, steady gaze. And his compassion reached my heart like the first fingers of morning sun dispelling the night. God was strangely present in the little elevator, as if He were there in the old man's face.

The doors swished open. I thanked the stranger and handed back his handkerchief, damp and soiled with my anguish. Then he nodded me a gentle smile and slipped away.

As I returned to my husband's room, I was quite sure . . . God does not fail us in our distress. His compassion is everywhere. And the tenderest promise in the Bible is true—God shall wipe away every tear from their eyes.

And He shall . . . one way or another.

CHAPTER SIX

TIME'S PASSAGES

I Don't Want to Be a Mother Today

 TINY WAIL PIERCED the silence of the bedroom. I moved mechanically into the worn-out path from my bed to the nursery like a tired old soldier with battle fatigue. The numbers on the clock glowed green, iridescent, and grim. It was 4:02 a.m. ... Mother's Day.

The little cry flung itself furiously into the darkness. It was not her hungry-cry. That one had shattered the night at 2:50. This was the colic-cry ... the third one tonight. I lifted my three-month-old daughter from her crib and dropped wearily into the rocking chair, my eyelids sinking closed like iron anchors dropped to sea. She screamed into the crook of my elbow. I rocked back and forth, trying to weave time into something bearable. The creak in the chair groaned heavily. *The sound of motherhood*, I thought glumly. My arm began to throb beneath her as sleep crept slowly into her breathing. I dared not move. Just a few more minutes . . .

"MAMA! I'm thirsty," came a loud, invisible voice out of the night. I opened my eyes to an abrupt narrow slit. Three-year-old Bob stood in the doorway like a lost shadow. He stepped closer, clutching a stuffed dinosaur.

"Go to bed and I'll bring some water in a little while." My whisper had the ragged edge of desperation.

"But I want some water now!" he half-way yelled.

The baby jerked and cranked up her cry.

I could almost hear the last gasp down inside my heart. "Now look what you did! You woke the baby. Now go to bed!" I shouted. He didn't. He stood there and added his wail to the baby's. It was too much. My eyes turned away, falling on the green diaper pail. It was full again. I looked from it to the door. At the end of the dark hall, the den was littered with toys, pacifiers and broken cookies. And beyond that, short and tall baby bottles lined the kitchen counter like a miniature skyline. My small world.

And suddenly in that middle-of-the-night moment, something happened deep inside me. The flame of joy that burns so mysteriously inside each mother's heart simply went out. I sat in the nursery like a snuffed candle and drew the darkness around me. Actually my despondency had been gathering for weeks. It wasn't the kind of thing I liked to admit, but it was true. Something had gradually gone out of my mothering . . . the sparkle, the eagerness, the delight. It had all been swallowed up by an ocean of frustrations and demands. Oh, I loved my children. But, lately, caring for them had become a burden.

The cries raged. "Lord, I know it's Mother's Day," I whispered, near tears myself. "But I don't want to be a mother today. I'm sick of it."

The terrible honesty of my words startled me. How could I say that! How could I feel this way! I wondered if all mothers sometimes despaired of being mothers. Or was it only me?

My husband waded into the shrieking darkness, rubbing his eyes as if he'd wakened into a real live nightmare. "What's going on?" he said.

"I'm thirsty and she don't love me," cried Bob.

The baby squalled, her red face bobbing against my shoulder like a furious woodpecker.

"Here, give the children to me," he said, bravely. "You go to bed."

"They're all yours," I said, thrusting Ann into his arms.

I fell into bed, despising the way I felt. "Oh, Lord, help me," I prayed as I drifted over the edges of sleep. "Help me find some joy again."

I woke to the inevitable wail. My eyes focused on the window where the first sliver of daylight hemmed the curtain with a silver ribbon. The same sense of despondency filled my chest. I rose, dreading the day. I dreaded preparing the children for church ... the bathing, feeding, dressing, redressing. Every task was like a heavy gray bead on a chain around my neck.

On the drive home from church, Bob's voice floated over the front seat. "We talked about mothers in Sunday school."

"Oh, really," I muttered.

"My teacher said I made you a mother when I was borned."

"It's born. Not borned," I corrected.

"Tell me the story of when I was borned—I mean born."

I glanced around at him, getting a whiff of the carnations pinned at my shoulder. His face was poked out with curiosity.

"Not now," I said, looking away.

By mid-afternoon the sky was charcoal gray. A slow drizzle of rain washed the den windows. In a rare moment of quiet, I stood at the solemn panes, my depression deepening.

"Mama, *now* will you tell me the story of when I was born?" Bob stared at me.

I sighed and dropped onto the sofa. He climbed beside me, waiting.

"It was late one night," I began reluctantly. "Daddy and I had waited and waited for you. We thought you never would get here. But finally you decided to come. Daddy drove me to the hospital." I paused, my heart not in the telling.

"Then I was born?" he urged me on.

"Yes. The first time I saw you, you had all your fingers in your mouth making silly noises."

He giggled. "Like this?" He stuck four fingers in his mouth and snorted.

I managed a smile.

"Did you hold me?"

"Yes, we had a long visit that night," I said. "You were wrapped in a blanket, and your hair was combed up into a curl like the top of an ice cream cone."

I could almost see the hair, the small wrinkled face. It seemed like yesterday.

Outside, lightning splintered the grayness, and inside, Bob's eyes were wide and blue. I looked at the shifting streams on the window and wondered why motherhood could not have remained so fresh and golden as those first moments.

The story seemed ended. But suddenly, a small forgotten piece of it came back to me, almost as if someone had shone a light into a dark place in my memory. "I nearly forgot," I said. "There was a card tucked in your blanket that night. A card from the hospital."

"What did it say?" Bob asked, perched high on the sofa cushion. I squinted my eyes, unable to recall exactly. Suddenly I was searching our shelves, digging out his baby book. Dust sealed the pages with neglect. Bob hung over my shoulder, his eyes sparkling with mystery as I ruffled through the yellowed memories.

I found the card in the back of the book. Across the front it was personalized with a slightly faded, slightly smudged inkblot of his hand. Five newly born fingers and one incredibly tiny palm. My eyes drifted over the tender little image down to the inscription beneath it . . . a simple greeting card verse:

"Make the most of every day
For time does not stand still.
One day this hand will wave good-bye
While crossing life's brave hill."

The room grew quiet. Rain trickled on the panes. Bob took the card, his fingertips moving in silent wonder along the edge of the handprint. I watched, my throat feeling tight. How big his hands had become. And so quickly. His fingers were long and skinny next to the little image—his palm a baseball glove in comparison. And suddenly, his hand holding the tiny inkblot became a living picture of time moving, of life flowing swiftly and silently through its passages. It was a picture of how precious and fleeting each moment with my children really was.

As Bob clung to the little card, the words it bore touched me as if they had a secret magic all their own. There was a truth in them of immeasurable value, and I could not resist it. *Make the most of every day. Time does not stand still.*

It seemed strange how a few lines from an old verse had returned just when I needed them. Lines that had some-how made everything clear again and put my problems in their place. *Of course motherhood has frustrations and demands,* I thought. *Every worthwhile thing does. Why not accept them instead of dwelling on them? The important thing is to delight in my children now . . . now before these moments, too, became yellowed memories.*

With a suddenness that startled us both, I drew Bob to me and hugged him tightly, my heart catching as that fragile flame seemed to ignite inside me again.

"You're going to pop me, Mama," he said, laughing. But I held on. And with his warm, little body curved against mine, I looked down at the card, which had tumbled to the floor, and smiled. For I was quite sure this handprint, with its ancient wisdom for mothers printed beneath, was in truth a Mother's Day card . . . one sent specially by God, Himself.

Becoming Real

LAST YEAR I sat beneath a funeral awning in the warm Georgia sun and watched as my grandmother was buried. While the minister spoke, I remembered the last time I saw her. She held my seven-year-old daughter in her lap, and as Ann moved her finger along the folds of Grandma's face, Grandma said, "Those are my wrinkles. They mean I'm getting very old."

Later Ann asked me if wrinkles hurt. But it seemed to me she was really asking about what it meant to grow old. To answer her, I pulled Margery Williams's classic, *The Velveteen Rabbit*, from the shelf and read it to her.

It was the story of a new toy rabbit that came to live in a little boy's nursery. More than anything, the Rabbit yearned to know the secret of becoming "real." One day he asked the Skin Horse, who was so old his brown coat was

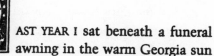

rubbing off, how to become real. "Real isn't how you're made," he told the Rabbit. "It's a thing that happens to you. When a child loves you for a long, long time . . . then you become Real." The Rabbit then asked, "Does it hurt?"

"Sometimes," he answered. "Generally by the time you are Real, most of your hair has been loved off, and your eyes drop out and you get loose in the joints and very shabby. But these things don't matter at all because once you are Real, you can't be ugly, except to people who don't understand."

When I finished reading I said, "You see, Ann, Grandma Monk is just getting 'real.' That's all." And there was a wonderful light in Ann's eyes. . . .

As the memory faded, I sat on the cemetery hill and thought about the children, grandchildren, and great-grandchildren who had sat on Grandma's lap, wearing it nearly away. I remembered all the joint-loosening miles I dragged her through the park . . . the afternoon I brought my baby chick into her lace-curtained parlor, poured oatmeal on the rug for him, and saw Grandma's eyes nearly drop out . . . the time I was learning to drive and carried her in a wild ride through the yard, narrowly missing a pine tree. More white hairs. Another wrinkle. The Skin Horse was right. It can be wearing to be loved by a child.

The service ended. Now I stood among the people beside her grave, thinking about birth and death and the journey in between. And I knew something clearly, more clearly than I'd known it before. We become authentic persons through our willingness to love and be loved—

even when it means becoming worn by sacrifice, even when the demands make our faces wrinkle and our joints grow loose.

Driving away, I caught the reflection of my face in the car window. It reminded me of the fine lines gathering around my own eyes and the hints of gray slipping into my hair. But I wouldn't think of these aging signs quite the same anymore. For growing old could be a wondrous passage. And the markings of it didn't matter, except to those who didn't understand. What mattered was becoming "real." What mattered was loving and being loved for a long, long time.

CHAPTER SEVEN

SEEK AND FIND

HIDDEN BLESSINGS

ESPITE THE TENSION of the last few months, we were going to have a quiet Thanksgiving day. We had found a little log cabin in the woods where we could hear pine branches brush the roof and wind sweep the mountains in the distance. It wasn't like us to be in a strange place on Thanksgiving. But somehow it had seemed important to come.

I put the turkey into the ancient-looking stove and turned to gaze at my family. My husband, Sandy, tended a fire in the fireplace, while our two children played before it on a braided rug. The scene looked so perfect . . . so content. Maybe today we could forget the problem that had consumed us for so many weeks.

"Daddy, sing Old Mac Farmer," cried five-year-old Bob. And suddenly the uneasiness was back.

A small shadow of pain moved over my husband's face.

How do you explain to a child that you can't sing with him . . . that you may never sing again because you've lost your voice? Old Mac Farmer, and more correctly, "Old MacDonald Had a Farm," was their special song. My husband and son sang it with great relish and mischief, including animals in the song that poor Old MacDonald would never have wanted. Dinosaurs, warthogs, skunks, and whales. I remembered the time Sandy sang, "On his farm he had a crab. Eee-i eee-i O. With a pinch, pinch here and a pinch, pinch there. Here a pinch. There a pinch . . ." Bob had dissolved into laughter as his daddy chased him through the house, pinching lightly.

"I can't sing," Sandy struggled to explain, pushing the words out with strain and effort. His voice was barely audible in the sudden stillness of the room. A raspy whisper. He sadly gathered Bob in his arms and gazed at the flames licking up the chimney.

I turned toward the window. Beyond, the brown and bony woods of autumn drew a curtain around our little cabin.

Sandy, a campus minister and college religion teacher, had lost his voice after chest surgery. Up till then he'd had a deep, slow Georgia drawl that was rich and charming. In fact, after hearing his voice on the phone for the first time—before I ever saw him in person—I turned to my college roommate and laughingly said, "I think I'm in love." He had that kind of voice. Standing there by the cabin window, I could hear his old, self-confident voice preaching from the pulpit at First Baptist Church in Augusta, Georgia, where he began his career as a young minister. I could see him shouting at football games and calling the children in for supper from the backyard. But now all of that was gone.

He had awakened after the surgery, whispering. At first we thought it was a terrible case of laryngitis. But weeks passed and we learned that the nerve to his vocal chord had been damaged ... paralyzed. Maybe it was temporary; perhaps it was permanent. No one seemed to know.

I could still see the look on his face the day the news came. He had clutched my hand tightly, as if he were losing his hold on everything he had worked for, everything he loved. On the campus where he ministered he had used his voice for everything: counseling, teaching, chapel services. He had worked with his voice the way a carpenter works with his hands.

"Could I be like this the rest of my life?" he whispered to the doctor. His face was incredulous.

"Wait four months and return. Then I can tell you something definite," the specialist replied.

The waiting had been worse than I'd thought. Memories drifted through my head of simple ordinary activities that had become impossible. Sandy could not be heard on the phone and had to whisper his words to me, which I relayed to the caller. He couldn't be heard by the bank teller or the gas-station attendant or the man who stopped him on the street for directions. Some people quit trying to converse with him at all; others talked to me as if he weren't even there. "Tell Sandy we hope his voice returns," a lady said while he stood right beside me.

He had managed to conduct his classes and chapel

services with a portable microphone, straining his throat so much he would spend our evenings in silence. How I had missed talking with him! And in a crowd, at a ball game or a church social, he had been lost. I watched him withdraw into a little box of silence. One day when I found him staring at a ringing telephone, I went to the bedroom and cried.

At last the waiting was almost over. Sandy's appointment was the week after Thanksgiving. I suppose that's why we'd come here to the little cabin . . . to find some reprieve from the tension, some vaguely sought help.

But here we were, doubt and gloom creeping over the old cedar walls. *Please God,* I thought, *help us cope.* For some reason I didn't ask God to restore Sandy's voice. That prayer was nearly worn out, tattered like a kite that has flown a storm. For the first time it seemed more important to cope with the moment than with what might come.

I closed my eyes against all the memories, then opened them again on the woods outside. My attention was drawn to one tree in the distance. A giant, golden tree visible above the others. Winter had been slow coming and strangely the tree had kept some of its leaves. In the sunlight it almost appeared to be on fire, each leaf burning like a little tongue of flame.

I looked around at Sandy holding Bob on his lap. "Let's go for a walk," I said abruptly. Sandy nodded and I bundled up the children.

The four of us started down a worn path at the edge of the woods. Soon we came to a small clearing and there in the middle of it was the tree I'd seen from the window. It was a grand tree. The kind with long serpentine branches that dipped close to earth. Sandy and I sat beneath it and watched the leaves flutter down, while Ann and Bob tossed them back up, making merry with autumn's confetti.

"Look, a spider web!" said Bob, who had come upon it while examining the underside of an old log. On the web was a spider. We squatted before it, watching it spin its exquisite silver house.

"I bet there're other treasures hidden here," I said. We began a kind of game. We found a blue bird feather in the leaves, which Ann stuck in her hair; a mysterious hole hidden by brush, which Bob assured us contained a rabbit. There was even a genuine arrowhead lying under a clump of rocks.

"Why, it's amazing how many little treasures are hidden right around this tree," whispered Sandy, who had been an arrowhead collector as a child.

All at once it occurred to me how happy and grateful we were all feeling. Suddenly I was seized by a peculiar idea. "Let's say our Thanksgiving blessing now. Right here under the tree," I said. Each Thanksgiving we went around the table as each of us pronounced something we were thankful for. We called it our Thanksgiving blessing. Funny, I'd almost forgotten about the blessing.

"Well, I'm thankful for finding this arrowhead," said Sandy, his voice quiet and fragile in the air.

"I'm thankful for spiders," said Bob. "And rabbits."

We turned to Ann. "My bird feather," she offered,

plucking it from her hair and lifting it up.

I looked toward the top of the tree. "Today I'm thankful for this tree," I said simply.

As we walked back to the cabin and as we ate our Thanksgiving feast the spell of joy lingered. For a few minutes we had searched beneath the tree for the richness and beauty buried there . . . the small camouflaged blessings that we were usually too busy, upset, or pre-occupied to notice.

But the holiday soon ended and when we returned home the golden tree and the thank-yous said beneath it faded behind us like an amber dream. The reality of Sandy's vocal paralysis rushed back . . .

The day of Sandy's appointment I stayed home with the children. Sandy drove alone to the nearby city. All after-noon I prayed the new prayer I'd found by the cabin window. "Lord, help us cope with whatever may come."

At dusk I heard Sandy's key turn in the door. He didn't have to say a word. It was there on his face. His voice loss was permanent and irrevocable. I folded my arms around him, the darkness of the thing finally swallowing me up.

"What are we going to do?" I said.

"When the doctor first told me, I was ready to fall apart," he said against my ear. "Then, driving home, I began to remember last week at the cabin when we took that walk and came upon the tree. It kept coming to me that we should try looking at this event the same way we looked for those small hidden blessings beneath the tree. We should try to find something to give thanks for."

Hidden blessings. Sandy wanted to search the underside

of this tragedy for something to give thanks for. I didn't think I could. But he was trying so hard.

So we sat on the sofa and began to look through the darkness of this experience, just as we searched through the shadows beneath the tree. And once more we found ourselves saying a Thanksgiving blessing.

"I'm thankful you're alive," I began a bit woodenly. "During your illness, we weren't sure you would make it."

He grinned, "And I'm thankful we have each other, the children . . . and God."

"I'm thankful that we've become closer through all of this," I added, realizing for the first time how much it had bonded us together.

"I'm thankful I can still minister on campus," he said. "I've become more of a listener, and I've found I can relate to others and understand them much better when I'm not talking so much."

My eyes widened. "It has helped *me* to listen better, too."

Sandy's green eyes beamed at me. "We can be thankful for medical science, too," he continued. "The doctor tells me there's a new surgical procedure which can help me regain some of my voice. It will always be raspy and hoarse, but I'll have more volume than I do now."

"Oh, that's wonderful!" I cried.

We fell silent as our tensions and anguish drained away. I was beginning to feel light and strong, just as I'd felt during those transforming moments beneath the tree when we simply gave thanks for what was simply there.

We were coping! Thanks to God, we were coping. The

Lord had revealed to us in the most delicate way that the secret to dealing with life's troubles is to look at them with grateful eyes. To search the underside for whatever blessings are hidden there. And then give thanks. That's when strength and joy flow in.

I leaned my head against Sandy's shoulder and heard a familiar tune float in the air between us. Whistling!

"I didn't know you could still whistle," I said.

"I didn't either," he replied, delighted at his discovery.

He ambled off toward Bob's room. He was whistling "Old MacDonald Had a Farm."

THE PERSEIDS

T IS AN AUGUST night, warm and quiet, the kind that's full of lightning bugs and cricket sounds. The children drag me across the grass in the backyard. They find a wide, open spot and stretch out on their little backs, staring up at the big black sky. I let out a resigned sigh and join them. Naturally the dog trots over and licks my face. I shoo him away and look at my watch. It is 9:30, time for the Perseid meteor shower, that annual event of shooting stars. The children have begged to stay up for it, and I have finally given in. Reluctantly, I might add. I have so many details to tend to before we leave on vacation tomorrow. I really don't have time for idleness. I rarely do.

No trace of a moon shows. The sky stretches over us like a dark, deserted stage. The crickets grow louder and the grass begins to itch. I drum my fingers on the ground, wishing I were inside doing something useful.

Then it happens—so quickly I catch my breath. One-two-three golden balls of fire streak across the darkness. "Oh, look, children . . . look!" I cry.

"Wow-w-w-w," says my son, his voice trailing after them.

One after another they come, blazing across the heaven like sparks tossed from a great boiling fire. And suddenly, without warning, a spell of reverence falls across the backyard.

"God made this," I whisper, almost without realizing it. The children nqd, their eyes open as wide as they will go. And we lie there in silence while the ground beneath us grows holy and God's presence burns—a flame across the sky, yet deep and luminous inside me, too. It is a rare moment. Not because the sight is so spectacular, but because I am aware of it. Because I have stepped across a threshold out of my familiar world into one of wonder and beauty . . . and discovered the Creator in the midst of it.

There in the fresh-cut grass beneath the darting splendor in the sky, it strikes me that every day has its wonders, more familiar than the meteor shower, but no less grand. Like the way the world turns pink when the sun comes up . . . the way the stars blink down upon my roof. Could it be that God filled the world with so many wonders to lift people like me away from our deadening obsession with details—to touch our lives, even for a moment, with a magnificent awareness of Himself?

As I amble toward the house with a child on each hand, I remember the Old Testament story of Jacob, who woke up from a sleep and said, "Surely the Lord is in this place and I knew it not." That August night the Lord was in my own backyard. He still is—if only I take time to know.

CHAPTER EIGHT

HEALING HURTS

IN NEED OF LOVE

THE HOSPITAL CORRIDOR stretched ahead of me, a long tunnel of green tiles. I was about to begin 8:00 a.m. nurse's rounds on the pediatric wing, when I noticed the ward clerk hang up the phone and nervously motion me back to the desk.

"There's a two-year-old child on the way up from Emergency with an arm fracture," she said. That sounded routine enough. But the clerk lowered her voice to a whisper: "It's child abuse. The mother brought him in and admitted the whole thing. The authorities have been notified."

A rush of dread hit my stomach like a lead fist. This was my first confrontation with child abuse. I'd been taught that an abusive parent is a victim in need of sympathetic help. But inside I shuddered with indignation. A two-year-old child hurt by his own mother. It was incomprehensible!

❦

The elevator doors banged open. Out rolled a stretcher and the outline of a small, sedated boy beneath the sheets. It was followed by two orderlies. But no mother.

"Tommy Miles from E.R.," said an orderly.

"He goes to 842B," I said.

I trailed along behind the rattling wheels, watching the intravenous bottle swing silently over the stretcher. I couldn't bring myself to look at the little face on the pillow.

We turned into the ward . . . into the heavy gloom of drawn curtains and morning shadows. I waited near the door as the orderlies lifted Tommy into the crib in the far corner, hung the IV bottle over the bed and left.

My nails clawed into the pockets of my uniform as I inched toward the crib and peered over the rail. A sleeping boy lay curled in the sheets, a black-stitched gash over one eye and new white plaster encasing his arm.

I gripped the rail and looked away. Deep inside, something cold and black and consuming spread through me. Part of it was outrage and revulsion, but mostly it was hate. Hate for the mother who had abused this fragile little fellow.

Across the dim ward, something caught my eye, something like a shimmer of light. I looked closer. On the windowsill, in a little picket of darkness, stood an ordinary greeting card. Yet, not ordinary at all. A slit of warm light had edged under the curtain, illuminating a stunning red word on the bottom of the card—LOVE. It glowed almost iridescent in the path of sunlight.

I turned back to Tommy's crib, haunted by the shining

word in the window. Love. All my life I'd accepted the principle of Jesus, to love not hate. But now, staring down into the innocence of Tommy's bruised face, loving Tommy's mother seemed impossible. Even ridiculous.

I forced myself to the business at hand. I looked at my watch and counted the drops from the IV bottle. Then I inspected the small blue clamp on the end of the IV tube, the shutoff valve. It was open just as it should be, allowing the fluid to flow from the bottle, down the plastic tube, into Tommy's small hand. *Such a skinny hand,* I thought. *Not chubby and dimpled like so many others.* I reached over and touched it.

His eyes flickered open, golden brown eyes, the color of amber and October leaves.

"Hello, Tommy," I said.

He looked past me, searching the ward, then withdrew to sleep again. *Poor little Tommy. What kind of mother do you have?*

Turning around, I saw a thin young woman in the doorway, her eyes as tired-looking as the brown dress she wore. She strained to see inside the crib, not daring to come closer. I knew immediately it must be she.

As I brushed past her, she spoke timidly. "Please, Nurse, is he all right?"

"He'll be all right," I said coldly. "Are you his mother?"

"Yes," she said. It was a whisper. An apology.

I squeezed my clipboard, filled with revulsion. How could she do such a thing? What kind of inner torment caused a mother to turn her rage on her own child? I couldn't imagine.

❧

"Can I use the phone in here?" she asked, leaning into the room.

"There is no phone in here," I snapped and hurried off, feeling her red-rimmed eyes follow me.

I checked another patient and headed for the nurses' station. As I passed the waiting room, I noticed Tommy's mother by the pay phone, fumbling through her purse.

"Excuse me, do you have a dime I can borrow?" she asked in a small, hesitant voice.

I shook my head. "No, I don't."

She shrank into the chair by the phone like a small, cornered animal, the most desperate-looking human I'd ever seen. Could one phone call be so important to her? In that one bleak moment the sun-shined word in the window seemed to whisper out to me. *Love. Love Tommy's mother.*

I backed off and escaped down the hall to Tommy's room, wanting to hide my turmoil. I slipped close to his crib. Tommy was so easy to love—a wounded little boy with black curls and amber eyes. But his mother. How could I love her? *How, Lord?* I thought.

Tommy moaned in his sleep, a tiny soft sound like the end of an echo. I looked down at the dark-fringed lids and puckered mouth. Then my gaze wandered up to the IV bottle suspended over his head. The fluid still dripped, as dependable and steady as a heartbeat. I watched it working, as I had so many times before—the healing contents in the bottle, the blue shutoff valve that controlled the flow. And unexpectedly, a gleaming window of insight began to open. I found myself wondering . . . could there be a reservoir of God's healing love inside me—like the healing fluid inside Tommy's IV bottle? If God was in my life, wasn't His love there too, just waiting to flow out? How had I missed that? I knew then that it wasn't a matter of how to conjure up love for Tommy's mother, but how to open the valve and start it flowing.

I reached over and cradled the little blue shutoff valve on Tommy's IV between my fingers. It had taken only one small act, one twist of my fingers to open it. What would it take to open my heart and start God's reservoir of love flowing?

I eased out of the ward and down the corridor, half hoping she had already gone. But as I neared the waiting room, I saw her slumped by the phone. I seemed to freeze. The hate had not left. *One small act of kindness*, I told myself. *Even if you don't feel like it, try.*

I cleared my throat. "Do you still need a dime?" I asked, reaching in my pocket.

Her head jerked up. I managed a smile and held the dime out to her.

"Thank you," she said.

As she reached out and took the dime, God worked a tiny miracle right there in the waiting room. The shutoff valve opened! God's warmth and caring flowed out from my heart to her like an unseen transfusion of love. I thought perhaps she sensed it too, or maybe she was only happy to find someone to be helpful, but all of a sudden her eyes glazed over with tears. Impulsively I reached for her hand and gave it a squeeze. She opened her hand and looked at the dime shining in her palm. "I just wanted to call a church and ask someone to pray for Tommy and me," she said.

I felt a twinge of guilt. All along she had been searching for love and help almost as hard as I'd been trying to withhold it.

She ran her finger down the list of churches in the Yellow Pages, clinked the dime in the phone and dialed. I nodded her a smile and returned to my rounds.

Minutes later Tommy's mother left the hospital with a social worker. Days later Tommy was discharged into temporary custody of a foster home. They were both gone from my life as abruptly as they'd entered it.

But I could not forget them. During the weeks that followed I wondered what had become of the amber-eyed boy and his mother. One morning that same social worker stopped by the pediatric floor on business. I took a chance. "How are Tommy Miles and his mother?" I asked.

The social worker broke into a grin. "There's still no father in that family, but those two are going to make it together just fine now," she said. "Tommy's mother is working through her problems with a counselor. And, you know, she's found a church that seems to help her a lot."

A church . . . I thought back to the slender, silver coin I'd almost refused Tommy's mother. It seemed God's love and that one thin dime had worked a miracle for both of us.

❧

BROKEN DOLL

WHEN MY DAUGHTER WAS SIX, her grandma made her a doll with a soft, cuddly body and a fragile china face. Ann loved her instantly and named her Amanda—Mandy for short.

"You'll need to be careful. She's breakable," I said.

Instead of taking Mandy to bed, a privilege reserved for her most beloved dolls, Ann placed her safely in the doll crib. I noticed, however, that she pulled the crib right up against her bed.

Gradually though, her caution wore off. One day Ann laced on her skates and took Mandy for a spin around the driveway. Ann took a tumble without a scratch. As for Mandy, well . . . her china face did not survive.

Ann threw herself into my arms, more shattered than the doll. I held her tightly and kissed the tears on her cheeks.

We called this "kissing away the hurt." The ritual had started the year before when Ann was accidentally hit by the backyard swing and got a whopper of a black eye. Distressed over the purple discoloration, she'd wanted to know how to make it go away. "Easy," I told her. "I'll kiss it away."

"Oh, *Mama*," she said with a giggle.

Ann knew, of course, that my kisses couldn't *really* make a black eye disappear, but like all children, she loved a bit of make-believe. I kissed her black eye every night, and in no time the bruise lightened and disappeared. Ann was duly impressed and we'd been vanishing hurts left and right ever since.

"You can glue Mandy back together, can't you, Mama?" she asked after her tears subsided.

I gathered up the fragments and went looking for the glue. When I finished, broken seams crisscrossed the doll's face and she was missing her nose.

After that Ann didn't put Mandy in the crib. Each night she took Mandy to bed and kissed the broken places on the doll's face just as I had kissed the black eye on hers. "I'm kissing away the hurt," Ann announced, trying out the make-believe for herself.

It so happened that when her grandma heard about all this, nothing would do except a new china face be ordered identical to the old one. In no time, I secretly tucked a new Mandy beside Ann's pillow while she slept.

When Ann awoke, she hurried to my bedside. "Mama," she said, "Mandy's face is all new!" And then she asked me with a sly grin, "Do you suppose it was my kisses that did it?"

I didn't really answer her. Both Ann and I knew that the new face hadn't come from kisses, but in a world like ours, where so many harsh realities exist, isn't the power of love even stronger than make-believe? After all, love really *can* heal our bruised hearts and broken places.

CHAPTER NINE

ONE BETHLEHEM NIGHT

THE BLESSING OF
THE CRÈCHE

NE CHRISTMAS I TRAVELED to Bethlehem. There is a little shop there that sits on a winding road, not far from the Nativity cave. As I stepped inside, a dark-eyed man with a wide, white smile appeared at my elbow. "May I help you, madam?" he said with a nicely polished Hebrew accent.

"I'm looking for a creche," I replied, "A Nativity set."

His eyes gleamed like two black pearls. He made a little bow to the rear of the store. I followed him along an aisle until suddenly he stepped aside, sweeping out his arm, and there in the middle of a table sat a creche. A creche so splendid it seemed to glow with the ancient holiness that inspired it. It had been carved from the olive trees that dotted the Judean hills like green umbrellas. The rich wood shone warm and golden in the dim light of the little shop. I touched each piece with reverence. Only moments before, I had stood in the heart of the holy cave where Jesus had been born, and my heart was still full.

The salesman stood nearby like a bird on a perch, his shoulders curved forward, his eyes darting. "You like, madam?" he asked, as my fingers touched the tiny tips of the star carved atop the stable.

He stepped closer. "It is the finest wood. And the workmanship is unmatched," he said. I nodded.

I walked around the table, trying to decide. "I'm not sure," I said.

"Ah, but, madam, you must have it!" he said. "A Bethlehem creche has secret blessings!"

In the end I purchased the creche, not for its alleged "secret blessings," but because of its irresistible beauty and because I was in Bethlehem and the long-ago miracle still lived in the air.

At home I stored it in a cardboard box in the attic. The next Christmas, I wanted to make the creche's first appearance beneath our tree special. I thought and wondered. How could it touch my family with the Bethlehem miracle? I found myself remembering the words of the salesman, "A Bethlehem creche has secret blessings." Perhaps he was right. Perhaps God *could* bless and inspire our lives through its presence, if only we let Him. And not just with a Bethlehem creche but *any* creche, even the tiny one my daughter had made from Popsicle sticks one Christmas past.

So I sat down and wrote a prayer. Then, filled with anticipation, I climbed to the attic and brought down the cardboard box. That night, with the tree lights shining in the darkness and dancing on the windows, my family gathered around the tree. An almost reverent silence settled about us as softly as a whisper in church. My husband opened the lid. The children took turns standing each item of the creche beneath the tree as I read my prayer aloud:

"It is time, Lord. Time to take the holy drama from this cardboard box and set it beneath the tree. As I blow away the dust, may this little creche come to life in our home and bestow its secret blessings.

"Bless this wooden stable, Lord. This lowly abode of cows and donkeys. May it keep me humble this Christmas.

"Bless this tiny star beaming at the top. May it light my eyes with the wonder of Your caring.

"Bless the little angel. May her song flow through our house and fill it with smiles.

"Bless this caring shepherd and the small lamb cradled in his arms. May it whisper of Your caring embrace on my life.

"Bless these Wise Men bearing splendid gifts. May they inspire me to lay my shining best at Your feet.

"Bless this earthly father in his simple robe. May he remind me of all You have entrusted to my care.

"Bless this Virgin Mother. May she teach me patience as I tend to my own little ones.

"And bless this Baby nestled in the hay. May the love He brought to earth that Bethlehem night so fill my heart with compassion and warmth that it becomes a

Christmas gift to those around me.

"Now the creche is here, Lord . . . and we are holy participants in Your miracle night."

I can't tell you *exactly* what happened to us that night, but I do know that I experienced a special holiness and a reverence for our family that stayed with me all through the Christmas season. That was my "secret blessing," and perhaps each of us shared the same "secret." For this little ritual has become the single most important Christmas preparation for our family.

THE SINGING
CHRISTMAS CARD

HE CHRISTMAS MY GRANDMA was 87, she fell and broke her hip. Confined to the hospital, she grew depressed about her health, but especially about missing Christmas with her great-grandchildren, who were not allowed on the ward. In the past she had taken pleasure in the little ones as they sang carols and listened to the Bethlehem story.

"I suppose this could be my last Christmas," she told me. This was not like Grandma. I kept wishing there was something I could do—something that would bounce her spirits out of the doldrums. But what?

At a loss, I gathered my two children together with paper and crayons. "Let's make Grandma Monk a Christmas card," I said.

Seven-year-old Bob danced up and down. "Yeah, let's make a *singing* Christmas card!" he exclaimed. Earlier that day while I was shopping, Bob discovered some new-fangled, musical cards that played "Jingle Bells" when you opened them up. He opened so many the store manager came to see what the ruckus was about.

I was about to tell him that we couldn't make a card like that at home, when I noticed the tape recorder on my desk.

My only part in the whole production was to turn on the recorder. The children began by singing "Jingle Bells," which went along in predictable fashion until the chorus. "Jingle bells, jingle bells, jingle all the way. Oh what fun it is to ride in Grandma's Chevrolet!" While the tape rolled they burst into uncontrollable giggles.

When order was finally restored, Bob nudged his four-year-old sister. "Ann's gonna tell the Christmas story," he announced into the microphone.

"A lady named Mary and a man named Joseph went to Bethlehem," she said, her little face full of earnestness. "They couldn't get any place to stay, so they went to a stable that had cows and horses, and Mary had a baby in a manger." She looked uncertainly at her brother. "The baby was crying and nobody could get any sleep," she went on. "His mommy rocked him till he got quiet. Then shepherds in a field came and woke him up."

"Oh, brother," muttered Bob.

"Next some wise men rode up on a camel," she said, beginning to enjoy her expanded version. "They came in and gave baby Jesus his Christmas presents. It was a busy night."

The day that tape aired in Grandma's hospital room, a

smile broke across her face so wide that it lingered well past Christmas. Her depression had lifted.

Today, as I think about Grandma and the children's Christmas card, I'm reminded once again: That's exactly what God did that "busy" Bethlehem night: He brought tidings of great joy into a dark corner of the world, and that good news of Christmas is meant for all people.

CHAPTER TEN

MAKING PEACE

How Do You Reach an Angry Little Boy?

N EXPLOSION of angry little voices burst from the back yard. I leaned over the kitchen sink and flung open the window. Beyond, in the simmering grasses of an August morning, my two children were at it again.

"I had this swing first!" yelled five-year-old Bob.

"I got it!" Ann shrieked, holding on with all the strength her two-year-old hands could muster.

"Let go!"

"No!"

They yanked the swing back and forth like a tug-of-war rope. My impulse was to stick my fingers in my ears and slink away. Lately every back-yard skirmish, every little problem, turned into a collision between me and my son. I had come to dread anything that called for one of our mother-son sessions.

❦

The volume under the swing set soared. Suddenly Bob had had enough of his sister's tenacity and gave her a shove, plopping her backwards in the grass. I ran outside, the referee in another back-yard battle. Only this time blood had been spilled. I could see it oozing from Ann's lip as I crossed the yard. I knelt beside her, ducking the swing that ricocheted around in the air. Her red face puckered up at me with two trickles of blood and tears intersecting her chin.

Bob gaped at her in horror. He turned, sprinting for the house like a shot arrow. Dabbing at Ann's lip with my apron, I discovered a practically microscopic cut. I kissed the tiny hurt and left her smiling, the sole owner of one battered swing. Then I trudged inside to face Bob.

As I stepped through the door, I winced at how this day was shaping up. The dishes were stacked in the sink like the great pyramid, the beds were unmade, the laundry unsorted. And . . . *a promise was broken*, I thought, noticing my Bible shoved behind a cereal box on the kitchen table. I had promised myself I would read one Psalm every morning before breakfast.

With a sigh of regret, I plodded down the hall to Bob's room. He sat on the floor in a puddle of sunshine, staring into the small island of shadow that fell around him. I stood like a tower over his curving back and short legs drawn up under his chin.

"Bob, you know you shouldn't push your sister," I said, forcing calmness into my voice. "And how many times have we talked about sharing?"

His mouth twisted down. "I don't like you!" he shouted,

as the tears streamed. "Not you, not anybody!"

I rocked back against the wall, bristling at his words. He had never hurled such stinging words at me before. How could he say that! My composure shredded.

"That's an awful thing to say to your mother!" I lashed back and stomped to the kitchen, leaving him sagging in the carpet . . . a million miles away from me.

I grabbed the detergent and filled the sink with hot sudsy water. Tears slid off my face and disappeared into the billows of soap. I'd done it again. A head-on collision. I couldn't understand my son at all! He was only five. What would it be like when he was 15?

"Lord, please, show me what's wrong," I pleaded, turning from the sink. Immediately my eyes fell on the corner of my Bible. The promise to read a Psalm a day formed in my mind. *Not now*, I thought. I was in no mood. *Do it*, something inside me urged.

I sank reluctantly into a chair at the kitchen table and flipped the Bible open to the book marker, Psalm 115, and scanned the first five verses. Just another Psalm. So many of them sounded alike to me. But as I began to read verse six, a strangely expectant feeling stirred through me. I fastened my eyes onto the words before me. "They have ears, but do not hear." (RSV) I looked up into the morning stillness, sensing that God had just laid a little package of truth at my feet, containing some quiet secret that I had never discovered. "Ears, but do not hear," I whispered to myself. Was that what was wrong? But my ears had heard my son's outburst just fine, I reasoned—every provoking word of it. Yet . . . maybe there had been more to hear than just words. Gradually the truth unraveled into one simple moment of awareness. My ears had only skimmed the surface. *I had not listened deep enough.*

I walked to the kitchen sink where golden light spilled in and the first breeze of the day rustled the curtain. And I prayed. "Lord, You always listen deeply, beyond the wall of words I erect, to the feelings that hide silently within me. And You always understand. Help me to hear my son like that."

Leaning against the sink, I tried to hear Bob all over again, just as he had been in that one painful moment on the floor of his room. But this time with God's special kind of penetrating ear.

As I focused my mind and heart and ears upon my son, I began to hear what I had not heard before. All the small hurting echoes inside his heart. Silent echoes of remorse and fear, self-anger and doubt. For the first time I understood what Bob had *really* been saying. Not I don't like you, but rather, I don't like *myself.* I don't like myself for pushing my sister and making her bleed, for not sharing and getting everybody mad at me.

The Bible was right, as always. I had ears, but I had not heard. I had not listened deep enough. What a difference it would have made if I had.

I turned to see a dejected little figure edge up behind me. He stared up at me with watery blue eyes and dripping lashes.

"I'm sorry I pushed Ann down," Bob said, his lip quivering.

"All forgiven," I said.

He sniffed loudly and his shoulders drooped as if some terrible big burden were still sitting on them. His eyes wandered around my shoulder to the sink that floated with bubbles. "Mommy, I'll wash those dishes," he said.

And for just an instant, for the instant it takes five words to flash along the pathways of sound . . . God sent me down into the crevices of my son's heart, where feelings so often seemed to get stuck. Strangely enough, I heard his words not as a request to help with a chore. No, I heard—"I really *do* like you, Mommy. Let me show you."

I grinned down at him and dropped a soggy dish rag in his hands. "I like you, too," I said. He flashed me a smile as big and dazzling as the August sun and zoomed a chair to the sink to stand on.

As I watched his eager hands scramble into the water, I caught a glimpse of the swing in a corner of the window. In no time at all Bob would move out of that little back yard into places with far more complicated matters than swing sets and little sisters. He would grow up and the need to understand would grow with him. But there in the yellow warmth by the kitchen sink, I smiled . . . as the possessor of a wonderful new secret might smile. For I knew that one day, when my son no longer needed a chair to reach the sink, God would help him fine-tune his ears to listen deep . . . and understand.

CATS AND DOGS

T THE HEIGHT of holiday shopping, in the middle of a bustling mall store, my children began to squabble. All day we'd been impatient with each other. "You two are fighting like cats and dogs," I said to Bob and Ann, trying not to remember that I was feeling as angry and sullen as they were. In my view fighting like cats and dogs was about as bad as things could get.

You see, when I was a little girl I found a stray cat that I persuaded my mother to keep. I named her Pretty, even though her fur was falling out. Ginger, our old spaniel, growled at her at their first meeting and Pretty stretched out her claws and hissed back. From then on they fought constantly. Pretty spent her days on the roof, glaring down at Ginger, who sat below, daring her to come down.

The memory of Ginger and Pretty flickered through my

❧

thoughts as I pulled the children out of the store. We walked along, each locked in stony silence. The mall was decorated with golden angels wherever we looked. One held a banner that said, PEACE ON EARTH, GOOD WILL AMONG MEN. *Ha!* I nearly blurted.

"Mama, let's go in the pet store," said Bob, breaking the silence. "No!" I answered. *"Please,"* they whined simultaneously.

"No, we're going straight home." I wanted to shut myself in the bedroom.

"It's all your fault," cried Bob to his sister. "You started the fighting!" . . . "I did not!" . . . "Did, too!"

Here we go again, I thought. Cats and dogs. Maybe it was too much to expect siblings to get along . . . Or nations to live at peace. Fighting was just part of the natural order of things.

Then, abruptly, as we arrived at the mall exit, it started to rain. A downpour. Without an umbrella, I decided to wait for it to slacken. That's when the thought came to me—*go back to the pet store.* I shook it away. I'd already said no. *Go to the pet store!* said the voice in my thoughts. So we walked back.

There in the window of the store, nestled together in a pile of shredded newspaper, were a puppy and a kitten. They were asleep, curled around each other like two spoons in a drawer. A cat and a dog!

An odd, tender feeling swept over me, as if God had drawn all three of us there to see them, to learn from them.

"They get along good," said Ann, her little face pressed

against the window. Bob, too, seemed entranced by the sight. In that moment the Christmas puppy and kitten became a quiet small symbol of reconciliation and peace. They reminded me that peace between mothers and children, even among people across the world, comes only when we are willing to come together despite our differences and work through our conflicts. It comes when we are willing to say, *You* are more important than what separates us.

"I'm sorry about all the fighting," I said. "Me, too," each replied. I wrapped my arms around them, and felt their embrace in return. And there was peace . . . good will among us all.

CHAPTER ELEVEN

LETTING GO

THE BALLOON THAT
LET THE CHILD GO

 WAITED OUTSIDE THE SCHOOL to pick up my third-grade son. A yellow bus filled the school drive. A crossing guard led a parade of children across an intersection. Above, an Indian-summer sun tinted the world red and gold. It was that time of year . . . school bells, lunch boxes, and, sometimes, for mothers like me, a secret pang or two.

It tugged at me even now as Bob ambled along the sidewalk with an oversized book satchel on his back. At that moment I wished he could always be seven, walking eagerly toward me on a school yard.

"Hi," I said, as he climbed in the front seat of the car.

He grinned at me and waved at a friend pedaling by on a bicycle. Suddenly he whirled around to me. "Mama, can I ride my bike to school?"

I didn't answer immediately. Instead my mind tumbled

back to the day he'd climbed out of the car for his first day of school. It had been hard to let him go—so small and untouched—into the risks and hurts of the world. It had seemed he was stepping over an invisible line and nothing would ever be the same again. He'd walked into his room slowly, then turned and waved. I'd watched, feeling something tear inside me, feeling as if something was ending.

Now those same unsettling echoes of finality were rippling through me again. A seven-year-old going to school and back on his own. Pedaling by himself . . . without me.

"No, son," I replied.

"But it's not far."

"No."

"And I'll be eight soon." His face was crunched up with longing . . . so much hope and longing that I had to look away.

"Not yet," I said quietly.

He started to argue again, but thought better of it. We drove home in silence.

Each day it was the same tug-of-war. "Mama, what about today? Can I ride my bike today?"

We pulled the little piece of freedom back and forth. Maybe it was silly. The trip was only five blocks in a safe, small-town neighborhood. But I couldn't seem to help it. Surely I wasn't wrong to be so protecting, I told myself.

It was simply my nature. The first time I'd left Bob in the church nursery, I stood outside the door for five minutes, listening to him cry and wondering if I should rush back in and take him home. If my husband hadn't pulled me into church, I probably would have. I was the same way with my four-year-old daughter Ann. I couldn't bring myself to wean her until she was a year and a half. And I remembered the day—the very day—she got "too old" to hold my hand across the street. How I hated endings!

Sure, now and then I wondered if I was thwarting Bob's fragile sense of challenge by refusing to let him venture into the unknown on his bike. But I could not relent. Somehow it seemed to go deeper than a bike ride . . . as if it was really something else I was resisting.

One Friday night as I tucked Bob in bed, he looked at me with pleading eyes. "I'm not a baby anymore," he said.

"No, I suppose not." And suddenly, standing at the foot of his bed, I knew this couldn't go on.

"Dear Lord, show me what to do!" I muttered on my way out. It was more an exasperated plea than a prayer. But there was real asking in it too.

Saturday dawned the perfect autumn day, bright and cool with a breezy wind to blow the clouds high. On the spur of the moment I got an idea to take the children to the shopping mall. I didn't need to buy anything. But we needed an outing, so off we went.

As we walked along, peering in store windows, we noticed a man with a cluster of helium-filled balloons that looked like a great nest of Easter eggs. They were irresistible.

We bought two. One blue. One yellow. The man placed the strings in their hands and the children strolled away, pulling the balloons casually through the air.

❧

"Watch out," I said, pointing up to where half a dozen escaped balloons hung from the ceiling. That was all it took. They wound the strings around their wrists with hawkish glances upward.

Then as Ann climbed up to a water fountain, fumbling with her balloon, I reached out for it. "Here, let me hold it for you," I said.

But she shook her head. "I hold it the goodest," she told me.

Finally we emerged into the gilded afternoon. And, sure enough, in the parking lot, the inevitable happened. Bob stumbled on the curb, and as he reached out to catch himself, the string slipped away. His balloon sailed up over the cars, the little string waving behind it. He threw back his head and gaped at it with a sad, startled face.

The balloon floated high and free in the breeze, climbing, it seemed, for the farthest cloud. I braced for his protests. But as Bob watched, his face changed from sadness to surprise, even pride. "Look how far it's going!" he cried.

It really was a spectacle. Far more thrilling then the sight of it bobbing above his head.

Then in one spontaneous instant Ann opened her palm and let her balloon go too. It swept along the sky after the other one. The moment seemed almost magical as the two balloons soared to astonishing heights. Below in the parking lot we pointed at them and laughed and waited till they were nearly out of sight, for there was something joyous about the sight of those balloons journeying across the sky.

Bob and Ann rode home with no more or no less in their hands than when they'd arrived. And the little incident was quietly forgotten.

But the next day as I wandered outside, my eyes fell on Bob's bicycle parked in the middle of the carport. A bright blue bike. As blue as the balloon.

Out of nowhere the episode was tugging at me. The memory of the balloon chasing the clouds. It came to me with the most amazing clarity. I was holding on too tightly, holding my son back from the horizons in his world. He was a balloon tied to my wrist. And I knew if I kept him there he would indeed be safe and sheltered. But he would not soar. There in the carport it seemed God was saying something to me—something I had never been able to hear before. That parenthood is really the process of disconnecting the strings that tie my children to me, preparing them for a life of their own. It means letting them go from the womb, the breast, the lap, the hand and, finally, from one's eyes . . . turning them loose to journey through life's passages and become fully born.

But why couldn't I cut them loose when the right moment came? I asked, half to God, half to myself. Why did I always cling to the people and moments dear to me like a child with a cherished balloon? Could it be that the answer had come to me back at the water fountain in the mall, I wondered. I could hear Ann's earnest little voice, "I hold it the goodest." Wasn't I really afraid no one could care for my loved ones as well as I? No one. Not even God.

I walked toward the bike and laid my hands on the handlebars. It was true, the bike was only a symbol of

🌱

deeper doubts. All that mother-hen fussing, the over-protecting and holding on, the fear of my children coming to the end of any of life's passages, surfaced from a lack of trust. Down deep, hidden away inside me was the question: Would God *really* love my family and take care of them as well as I could? Could I trust Him to do that?

The next morning the sky was inordinately bright and blue. Not a hint of the rain I almost wished would come and postpone this moment. I stood by as Bob climbed on his bicycle, trying to look grown up, to suppress his eagerness. I took a deep breath and made the tiny act of trust. "Lord, I'm letting him go. He's in Your hands now. I trust You completely to love him more than I ever can, to care for him better than I ever will."

It was a small thing, letting a little boy make his own way to school. It was another of life's little endings. But it occurred to me that in its own way this moment was as important as all the endings yet to come. As important as the day Bob becomes 16 and climbs behind the wheel of a car for the first time. Or the day he leaves home for college . . . or stands at the front of a church aisle waiting for his bride. For in each of those moments God calls me to do the same thing—trust Him and let go.

At the edge of the carport Bob stopped and cast a serious look over his shoulder. "Mama?"

"Yes, Bob?"

"Don't worry. I'll be fine. Okay?"

I smiled. "Okay." And I knew with a certainty I could not explain that he was right. He would be fine. Just fine. And I would be too. For I discovered a peace and freedom flowing to me that I'd never quite had before.

I watched him pedal down the street. Then he was gone, disappearing into the morning on a bright blue bike and a prayer.

CAPTAIN MARVEL

HEN OUR SON, Bob, was three he announced that he wanted a puppy. We found an eight-week-old brown-and-white springer spaniel for sale. "He's a good one," Bob decided. The puppy seemed grateful and licked his chin.

Bob named him Captain Marvel after his favorite cartoon character. He was a marvel all right. He gnawed a hole through the electric blanket and chewed the bows off my bedroom slippers.

Captain pranced behind Bob like a little brown shadow. During cowboy games, Bob stuck an Indian feather in Captain's blue collar and taught him to "pretend dead" when he fired his cap gun. Even if Captain was simply afraid of the popping gun, the stunt never ceased to amaze us onlookers. But it was routine stuff for Bob and Captain. They had an understanding about things.

When our daughter was born, Captain slept under her crib at night and came to my bed when she woke up, just in case I was too sleepy to hear her whining to be fed. By the time Ann was toddling in the backyard, she and Bob had learned how to tie a rope from Captain's collar to their red wagon and take wild rides through the grass. I noticed, though, that Captain slowed down for big bumps. He and I had an understanding about things too.

I gave Captain a sound spanking one day for lying on my newly planted marigolds, but he took it much better than the children did. While Ann cried, Bob let me know that dogs couldn't tell the difference between flowers and grass. I apologized to the dog and gave him hamburger for supper.

The years passed. Captain grew too old to pull wagons. But his devotion never wavered. When Bob was 12 and got the flu, Captain mopped his face with his tongue and refused to leave his side. And I'll always be grateful that he had the stamina to sit beside Ann, wagging his tail as she practiced the piano.

When Captain turned 12 he spent most of his time on his quilt by the fireplace. One morning he could hardly get up. I rubbed his fine old head and we carried him to the vet. "He's suffering," the vet explained. "He won't be getting any better. It's his heart." We knew the time had come.

Bob was 15 now. He bent beside his dog and held him. I remembered how Captain had stayed at Bob's side when he was sick, and I was glad Bob could do the same for him. "You've been a good dog," Bob told him.

My husband stayed while the vet put Captain to sleep. It happened gently. "He let out a breath and his head relaxed into my hands," he told us. The little dog with a feather in his collar was gone. And this time it was not "pretend."

That night we hung his blue collar in the garage and talked through tears about how much we'd loved him and how much it hurt. The pain of loss was great, yet how much worse it would have been not to have loved at all. That's one of the bittersweet things about grief.

You *were* a good one, Captain Marvel. You were the best.

CHAPTER TWELVE

EASTERTIDE

A BROKEN STAR

O N SATURDAY MORNING I stood on the gloomy porch of the little seaside cottage, gazing at the sky, trying to forget the reasons that had prompted my husband Sandy and me to come to the beach for the Easter weekend. The past months had been fatiguing and painful, with a death in the family and financial setbacks and a number of difficult problems to solve. Hope and perspective had worn thin, and so we'd come here to the cottage overlooking sand dunes and sea oats. As I listened to the waves roar, I wondered if our lives would ever be smooth again.

"How about a walk on the beach," Sandy said. "Maybe you can find a few good shells." Sandy knew well that I'd been a novice collector since I was a child. I loved ocean treasures, and I loved the lure of finding them even more.

I grabbed a bucket; we rolled up our pant legs and

headed into a stiff breeze. I walked almost relentlessly down the sandy corridor, as if to walk away my vague traces of despair. The ocean danced, waves slapping the strand, churning a silver froth. The sun poured a glittering dial of light across the surface that seemed to point us on and on. We hiked a long way, searching the edges of the sea as we went. A few cockles, some periwinkles and a jackknife clam rattled in the bottom of the bucket.

Then, at the rim of a little tidal pool, I spotted a strange silhouette beneath the water. I dipped in my hand and came up with a starfish.

"Look," I cried. "It has only two arms!"

I turned it over, countless white "feet" moved underneath. "It lost three arms and it's still alive," I said with surprise. It gave me a peculiar feeling, like some vaguely remembered dream.

I turned to Sandy. "What do you suppose happened to it?"

"Some predator or maybe a storm," he mused.

My first thought was to throw it back. This was not the sort of specimen you kept for a collection. But something stopped me. Instead, I placed it gently into the bucket, wishing I'd happened on a perfect starfish with five arms, but too attracted to the mutilated little star to put it back. The "star of the sea," as it is sometimes called, had always held a fascination for me. I remembered the old seaman's tale that said starfish were the remains of stars that fell from the sky. I peered into the pail. Broken and wounded, the creature did indeed bring to mind a fallen star.

"Why don't you toss it back?" asked Sandy, noticing my preoccupation.

I shrugged. "I think I'll keep it." It sounded too crazy to mention that I felt a sudden kinship with the star, which had experienced its own loss, too.

Back at the cottage I placed it in a cooler lined with sand and salt water, intended for the crabs we'd failed to net.

Easter Sunday dawned, a pink light streaming in the window. I plugged in the coffee, thinking that we would go home today. Back home to the same circle of problems. Suddenly I felt very tired. I wandered onto the porch and looked in on the starfish. As I stared down into the cooler, looking at the scars where the other three arms had been, I was surprised at the relief I felt that the creature was still alive.

Sandy and I dressed and drove into the little seaside community, searching for a church where we could attend Easter services.

"Let's stop here," I said, as we came upon a small church beside the road. My eyes locked on the sign in front. It said "Star of the Sea Chapel."

We were early. Only a few parishioners had arrived. An usher milled about in the vestibule as we came through the front door.

"Welcome. You folks visiting?" he said.

I nodded. "We're here for the weekend."

There was a natural friendliness to the man. He stood against the door with an easy smile, as though we were neighbors instead of strangers. "Enjoying your stay?"

"It has been very nice," replied Sandy. "Nice and quiet. Mostly we've been walking and picking up shells."

His face lit up, and I suspected he was a collector, too. "It's a good time of year for collecting," he said. "Finding much?"

"Not much. The best we could do was a starfish missing three arms," I said with a little laugh that sounded more glum than gleeful.

"Of course they grow back," he said offhandedly.

I fell silent. They grow . . . What did he say?

The usher read my confused look. "The arm of a starfish—it grows back, you know. Some of them can make a brand-new body from a single arm."

"That's amazing," said Sandy.

"They've got an amazing power of restoration, all right," he said.

The conversation turned to other small talk. More worshipers arrived at the door and our new friend turned to greet them. "Welcome. You folks visiting?" I heard him say to others as we stepped into the sanctuary.

Several times in the Star of the Sea Chapel my mind wandered back to the starfish I'd plucked from the tidal pool. A new starfish from a single arm? The thought of it touched me with awe. What a fine mystery I'd been missing all my life . . . bits and pieces of starfish growing into new animals.

When we returned to the beach house I took the porch steps two at a time and bent over the cooler. The starfish was there, same as ever. Two arms. Three scars . . . broken and humble as before. I turned it over and miraculously the tiny white feet moved.

I changed clothes, transferred the star to the bucket,

and marched over the dunes, down to the scalloped edge of the sea.

I crouched beside the lacy ruffle of a wave and lifted the star from the bucket. And all at once I remembered it was Easter. Easter! I looked at the broken star as if I were seeing it for the first time. As I held it in my hand the little star spoke to me the message of Easter. It said: When you are broken, wounded, scarred, and tired ... when you have lost just a little, or so much there is hardly anything left, take heart. That is when God does His most beautiful work.

I felt a new beginning surge in me like the clean sweep of a wave. I knew I could bounce back from my little troubles ... from every loss that came my way. For there was a new life to be had if I would renew myself in quietness and hope. Like the arm of a starfish.

I laid the broken star on the wet sand. Water tumbled gently over it and when the foam and sizzle cleared away, the star was gone. Vanished, it seemed, into the mystery of Easter.

THE SEVEN
LAST WORDS

T HE VOICE CAME in the still hours of the night. "Mama, I'm thirsty." I straggled into my son's room and touched his cheek. He was burning with fever. I went to get water and a cool cloth. Wouldn't you know, three days before Easter and Bob gets sick. No doubt it had something to do with his stomping in yesterday's rain puddles in bare feet—after I told him not to!

He gulped the water. I pulled a chair alongside his bed and stroked his hot little face. "Don't go, Mama," he begged. "I'm not going anywhere," I told him, feeling the uneasiness that always comes when one's child is sick.

As Bob fell into an uneven sleep, I thought about the Good Friday service I would have to miss the next day. It featured the last seven phrases uttered by Christ on the cross. While I bathed Bob's face, I tried to recall the things

Christ said. "Father, forgive them," came to mind first. Pondering those words, I felt overwhelmed by Christ's mercy. I found myself thinking of things I needed to forgive. "Lord, help me to forgive this little boy for wading in the puddles barefoot," I prayed. "He knew not what he was doing."

Slowly another saying came to me. "Today shalt thou be with me in paradise." As I remembered Jesus' promise to the thief on the cross, I recognized it as a promise to me, too. "This day with its thermometers, medicine, and cool cloths, I shall be with you." Paradise is here and now, too . . . wherever Christ's presence is.

Bob wakes momentarily to make sure I am there. I gaze at him as a third saying of Christ's returns to me. "Woman, behold thy son!" The words remind me how precious this little one is to me. They remind me to behold the relationships in my life more often and give them tender care.

Next I remembered the tormenting plea, "My God, my God, why hast thou forsaken me?" I think of it as an intense identification with us humans . . . with every sort of circumstance. People with disappointments, pain, problems, sick children. I felt comfort knowing Christ understood what I felt.

Looking down at Bob's fever-dried lips, I remember that Christ also said, "I thirst." I imagined how it must have been for Mary, standing nearby, unable to give Him water. It came to me how Jesus once said that if we give someone a cup of water, we are giving it to Him. That made stumbling after water in the dark for a thirsty child a way of quenching Christ's thirst, too.

Bob moaned softly. I tucked the sheet around him, thinking of another of Christ's sayings from the cross. "Father, into thy hands I commend my spirit." I smoothed Bob's hair and prayed, "Father, into Your hands I place my son . . ." I leaned my head on the bed. There was one more saying, but I was too sleepy.

I awoke around dawn and touched Bob's sleeping face. The fever had broken. I trudged back to bed, the haunting words of Christ from the cross still lingering in my mind. "It's finished," I sighed.

CHAPTER THIRTEEN

THE BOND
BETWEEN US

CRUMBLING
SANDCASTLES

NE MILD SUMMER day beside the
sea, my husband and I were lying
on our beach towels, reading, each locked in our own
separate worlds. It had been like that a lot lately. We'd
been busy, preoccupied, going in different directions. I'd
hoped the leisure of vacation would be different, but so far
we'd spent most of it marooned in silence.

I looked up from my book at the ceaseless roll of the
waves, feeling restless. I ran my fingers through the sand.
"Wanna make a sandcastle?" I asked my husband.

He didn't really, but he humored me. Once we got
started, though, he became surprisingly absorbed in the
project. We both did. In fact, after a while we were
working over that heap of beach sand like it was about to
be photographed for *Sandcastle Digest*. Sandy made
bridges across the moat, while I crowned the top of the

🌿

castle with spires. We made balconies and arched windows lined with tiny angel-wing shells. It looked like Camelot.

Neither of us noticed when the tide changed. We never saw the waves slipping up until the first swish of water gnawed a little piece of our castle away. Indignant, we shored it up with sand and patted it down. But as the waves returned with monotonous regularity, our hands grew still and our eyes drifted off toward the horizon. Sandy got on his beach towel. I got on mine. We went back to our silence.

The next time I looked around, the sandcastle we'd labored over was awash in the shifting tide. The bridges were washing away and the spires were starting to lean.

I gave it a soulful look, an inexplicable sadness coming over me. And suddenly in the midst of that ordinary summer, I had a moment of pure, unbidden revelation. *There sits my marriage,* I thought.

I looked at my husband. The soundlessness between us seemed to reach clear to the sky. It was the hollow silence of a midlife marriage, a marriage in which the ceaseless noise of everyday living threatens to drown out the music of intimacy.

Dear God, when had the tide shifted? When had mortgages and laundry and orthodontist appointments become more important than those unspeakably long looks we used to exchange? How long since we'd shared our hidden pain or stumbled together upon a joy that was round with wonder and laughter? How had it happened that two people who loved each other could allow such distance to creep in?

I thought of the attentiveness we'd lavished upon our relationship in the beginning, and how, eventually, the endless demands and routines of running a household, raising two children, and juggling two careers had stilled our hands and averted our eyes.

That night, after the children were asleep, my husband found me standing in the shadows on the porch, staring at the night. "You've hardly said two words all evening."

"Sorry," I muttered. "I've just got something on my mind."

"You want to tell me what it is?" he asked.

I turned around and looked at him. I took a deep breath. "I'm thinking of us," I said. "I'm thinking that our relationship is being drowned out by the demands of day-to-day living. We've taken our marriage for granted."

"What are you talking about? We have a very committed marriage!" He was indignant.

"Of course we have a committed marriage," I told him. "But sometimes it seems commitment is all we've got. Sometimes we are two strangers existing under one roof, each going separate ways."

He didn't say a word. *Now I've done it,* I thought. *I've rocked the boat to the point of tipping over. I've told my husband our marriage is bordering on empty commitment. Good grief!* We stared at each other. It was like we were stuck inside some big, dark bubble of pain that wouldn't pop. Tears welled up in my eyes and started down my face. To my amazement, tears slid down his face, too.

And suddenly, in what is surely the most endearing moment of my marriage, Sandy took his finger and traced the path of tears on my cheeks, then touched his own wet face, blending our tears together.

Strange how such things can begin to re-create the mystery of relatedness between two people. Sandy and I walked down the porch steps onto the beach under the blazing stars. Slowy we started to talk. We talked a long time. About the small agonies of being married, about the struggle of it all. We talked about the gnawed and fraying places in our marriage and how they'd happened. We spoke aching words about the unmet needs between us.

We were whirling the darkness that had settled in our relationship. And yes, it was uncomfortable and scary, like bobbing around in the ocean without a boat. But trading chaos and braving pain is often the only way to come upon a new shoreline. For God is in dark water, too.

Finally with the hour late and a sense of deepening and newness growing between us, I said rather dreamily, "It might be nice someday to say our wedding vows to each other again."

"What's wrong with right now?" my husband said. I swallowed. Was there no end to the surprises this man would spring on me tonight?

"B-But what would we say? I mean, I can't remember the vows exactly."

"Why don't we simply say what's in our hearts?"

So out there beneath the light of the stars, with the crash of waves filling the night, we took each other's hand and tried to put words to the music we had begun to recapture between us.

"I promise to listen to you," he said. "To make time for genuine sharing . . ."

"And I promise to be honest, to work at creating more togetherness between us," I began.

I don't remember all the words; mostly I remember the feelings behind them, the way my voice quivered and his hand tightened over mine. Mostly I thought that what we were doing was rebuilding the castle, restoring the bridges, raising the spires.

The next morning we left the children stationed in front of the television with their breakfast cereal and went walking along the ocean edge. The sun poured a golden dial of light across the water that seemed to point us on and on. We talked as we went, a little awed by the events of the night before—knowing in the harsh light of day that saying words is one thing, but living them is another. We couldn't leave our newly spoken vows back there dripping in the moonlight. We had to take them home to the frantic schedules and the broken dryer and the Dorito crumbs under my son's bed.

Miles down the beach we waded knee-high into the surf and stood soaking up the turquoise sky and jade water. We were about to turn back to the condo when it happened. A huge, bottle-nosed dolphin came splashing out of the water a mere twenty yards away, startling us so badly we fell backward into the surf.

Sitting in the water fully clothed . . . a dolphin diving and surfacing before us in a spinning silver dance, was such an unexpected and exhilarating wonder, the two of

❧

130

us laughed until our insides hurt. I cannot remember a joy ever so plump and full.

At last we picked our delirious selves up and walked in our soggy shorts back up the beach where a few crumbling sandcastles dotted the shore. I took note of each one of them.

And I began to hear a voice deep inside me whispering: "When tomorrow comes and life beats upon your castle walls, remember the power of honest pain and blended tears. Remember the healing of laughter deeply shared. Remember what's important. Hold onto it always."

THE MARRIAGE LESSON

OU CAN LEARN lessons about marriage in the most unlikely places. Nowadays I smile when I think about the one I learned in a baseball park. It happened one summer night in Atlanta.

"Let's take in a Braves game," my husband said. I looked at Sandy with dismay. I hated baseball. I mean, really *hated* it. He, on the other hand, loved it.

"How about a dinner theater?" I said quickly.

We couldn't agree, so finally we flipped a coin.

"Why didn't I say heads instead of tails?" I muttered, tagging behind Sandy through the stadium gate. We trudged up and up and up through the smell of hot dogs to a hard narrow bleacher bench littered with peanut hulls. I sat in disgust, frowning through the glaring lights at the field where a grown man was trying to hit a little white ball with a stick.

"Want a hot dog?" asked Sandy.

"No!" I snapped. He looked hurt, and I felt miserable.

A man behind us kept yelling, "Go home, Ump!" I wished somebody would tell me that.

"How many more innings before it's over?" I asked.

"Eight," said Sandy.

Before too long I noticed all the players run off the field. "How many now?" I asked again.

Sandy sighed, "If you really want to leave," he said with a mixture of sacrifice and exasperation, "we will."

Suddenly I felt terribly ashamed. If I'd won the toss of the coin, he probably would have tried hard to enjoy the theater. The truth was all too clear. I was placing all the emphasis on being loved, rather than on loving . . . on taking, rather than on giving. There in the noisy bleachers, I had once again arrived at one of the hardest moments in marriage. The moment when you bend your own desires and needs for the sake of the other—simply because you love him. And do it without resentment, without keeping score.

So we stayed, and ate hot dogs, and cheered, and discussed all the hidden merits of the game. I suppose it was a small event in a marriage. But sometimes that's where marriages are made or broken . . . in those small, everyday events of "give or take." And as usual, the Bible has the best advice for those moments. "Love does not insist on its own way; it is not irritable or resentful" (I Corinthians 13:5, RSV).

And sometimes, a nice, if not mysterious, surprise emerges from a small moment of giving in a marriage. You

❧

see, to my husband's surprise, and my own, I've become a genuine baseball fan. I quote batting averages and RBIs and get real goose bumps from the crack of the bat. Now, when it comes to "give or take" over baseball, it's over who gets the sports page first.

CHAPTER FOURTEEN

THE POWER OF
BELIEVING

FIVE
SMOOTH STONES

HE BACK DOOR CLOSED with a slow, heavy thud. "Is that you, Bob?" I called from my study. No answer. Just two small feet shuffling down the hall. I peered around the door in time to see him duck into his room like a rejected little puppy. Bob, my bright and sensitive second-grader was home, and this was not his usual "Hey-Mama-I'm-home-where's-the-cookies?" greeting.

I glanced over at my desk strewn with travel brochures. I'd been sitting there going over the details of my upcoming trip to the Holy Land. A trip I'd dreamed of for years. Reluctantly, I shoved my happy plans aside and ambled down the hall to Bob's room.

I found him slumped on his bed, his face a picture of some secret misery. I tilted his chin up to mine. "What's the matter?" I asked.

His mouth curled down into a quivering little crescent. Tears sprang to his eyes. "At re—recess I was the last one picked for the kick-ball team," he said, trying hard—so hard—to dam up the sobs crowding into his voice. "Then I kicked at the ball and missed it. And they la—laughed."

Suddenly the dam broke and hurt, scalding tears poured down his cheeks. "Oh, Mama," he cried, "the *last* one!"

As I held him to me, I felt my own eyes sting with tears. He clung to me as if the world had stopped spinning.

"I'm never going to play again!" he said.

At that moment his self-worth wouldn't have filled a thimble.

"I think you're a fine ballplayer," I said. "Why, I've seen you kick your soccer ball . . ." His look cut me short. It seemed to suggest that mothers' opinions don't count.

"Just remember," I babbled, not thinking, "the YMCA soccer season begins before long, and then you'll really show them."

His eyes widened with fresh horror. He had already signed up to be part of the "Y" team. It was all he'd talked about.

"I can't play on the team now," he cried. "I just can't!" He fell back against the bed, shrinking in the shadow of this new fear.

I stared helplessly at the back of his head buried in the pillow. I'd only made it worse. Why couldn't I ever seem to help him overcome the childish fears that crept into his world? I remembered the endless weeks he'd refused to let go of my hand at the kindergarten door, while I'd stood there helplessly, and the months he'd insisted on sleeping with all the lights blazing in his room. I hadn't helped much those times either. Now we faced another irrational fear, and I felt more helpless than ever.

That evening after dinner, the children and I piled on the sofa for the nightly ritual. Story time. Last month we'd read our way through Kipling's Mowgli stories. This month we were reading those marvelous adventures of the Old Testament. I opened the Bible story book to the place we'd left off. My daughter squirmed on the cushion with anticipation. But Bob sat quietly, his heart obviously lingering on the crushing events of his day.

Suddenly, on impulse, I flipped the pages over to another story. "Once long ago," I began, in a dramatic whisper, "there lived a great Philistine giant named Goliath. Goliath was the biggest giant that ever lived. His arms were strong as iron, and he was almost as tall as a tree!" Ann squealed appropriately. Not a sound from Bob.

"Nobody would fight this giant. They all ran away. But there was a boy named David, just a small shepherd boy, who said, 'I'll fight that giant.' And do you know what David did?"

"What?" said Bob, becoming caught up in the story.

"David bent down over a brook and chose five smooth stones from the bottom. He took his sling and marched right up to that giant."

Bob's eyes were round with intrigue. The story always captured him with its irresistible miracle—the underdog beating the mighty giant.

"Who won?" Ann asked impatiently.

"Well, David shouted to this giant, 'I fight in the name

of the Lord. God will deliver you into my hand.' And then David hurled a stone from his sling and it hit Goliath. *Wham!* It got him right between the eyes."

A smile played across Bob's lips.

"And David won?" asked Ann.

"He sure did. With a small stone and a big belief in God. Now, off to bed."

I watched Bob plod down the hall. *My little underdog,* I thought. *Just like David.* And in those moments, I began to compare Bob with the shepherd boy David, intertwining their circumstances in my mind. Two little boys facing giants. Of course, David's was a flesh-and-blood giant. But giants come in all shapes and varieties. And Bob's was simply the overwhelming specter of playing on the soccer team and risking more ridicule and pain. I wondered if Bob, like David, would find the courage to go out on the field and face the fear head on. And I wondered if I would ever be able to give him the confidence to do what he seemed so afraid of doing.

As the days wore on, Bob dragged around, avoiding his soccer ball. He seemed different somehow, as if some small light had been extinguished inside him. A friend of his hinted Bob was inventing excuses not to play with the other boys at recess. I grew worried. I began almost reluctantly to prepare for my trip to the Holy Land, now only days away. I hated to leave him floundering miserably in his fear.

The night before I was to leave, I tucked Bob in bed. In the corner sat the neglected soccer ball. I eyed it with dismay, knowing he loved it.

🌿

"Won't you change your mind about playing with the soccer team?" I asked—for the hundredth time.

Fear flickered across his eyes. "I can't, Mama."

The giant was only growing taller, and Bob's self-esteem, shrinking. As he closed his eyes, I felt my helplessness give way to a kind of despair. As usual, I had solved nothing, and I was feeling pretty inadequate as a mother.

Oh, Lord, I thought, *I don't know how to help him. Let him find the courage he needs to face this giant.*

The next day I climbed on a 747 jet. Soon I found myself jostling along in a tour bus through the rocky hills of Judea. The sky billowed over us like an old gray tent staked to the hills.

The bus groaned up a steep hill as rain broke through the grayness. We started down into a vast valley. "We are entering a special place," said the tour guide. "You are now in the valley where David slew Goliath."

My head snapped up. David and Goliath? My heart was pounding. The bus pulled to a stop alongside the road.

"The Philistines camped over on that hill and the Israelites over here," pointed out the guide. "And if you want to get out, you'll find a brook still running between the two hills. Many speculate that it is the very brook where David plucked the stone that killed the giant."

The rain drummed on the roof. As I sat there staring through the murky wetness at the valley of David and Goliath, all I could see was Bob's face. All I could hear was his sad little refrain. "I can't play ever again."

I flipped up the hood on my raincoat and walked off the

bus, out into the place where David had found his courage. Twenty yards away I saw the tiny brook, an ancient ribbon of trickling crystal water. I went and stood with my toes at its edge, listening to the rain being softly enveloped into the stream like scurrying whispers. The bottom was lined with small stones, glistening silver, black and brownish-red. I knelt down and plucked out five smooth stones and dropped them, cold and wet, into my handbag. God had planted an idea in my mind.

I arrived home weary and excited . . . with a purse full of rocks.

A few weeks later, on the afternoon of the soccer game, I pulled out Bob's yellow jersey and blue gym shorts.

"What's that for?" asked Bob, striding into his room. "I can't . . ."

"Hold on," I interrupted. From behind my back I whisked a handful of stones—five smooth stones.

"What's that for?" he asked again.

"Do you remember when I told you about walking in the valley where David slew Goliath?" I said.

He nodded.

"And do you remember how I picked these stones from the brook where David might have picked his? Well, I brought them all the way back just to remind you of a promise.

"You see, Bob, you're a lot like David," I explained. "You've got a giant, too—that soccer game with your friends. I thought you might want to face it like David did. With a promise."

"What's the promise?" he asked, his eyes beginning to

sparkle with a mixture of understanding and excitement.

"The promise is the same as David's—God is with me and I can do it."

I placed the stones in his hand and left . . . hoping.

He emerged wearing the yellow jersey and blue shorts. The shorts had a curious bulge in the back pocket. As he ran over and gave me a hug, a *clack-clack-clack* rustled from his shorts. I smiled. David was ready for battle.

The soccer field was nestled between two small hills, looking for the world like a big green valley. Bob lined up for the kickoff. I could only imagine how his heart thumped. I saw him look over to the bench where he'd left his stones for safekeeping. Five small reminders of a powerful promise.

The whistle blew. His teammates carried the ball down the field. All of a sudden the black-and-white ball was hurtling at Bob. He hung back for a moment. Then he plowed his foot into the ball with more confidence than I would have believed. It took off like a bullet . . . like a stone being flung from a twirling sling. And it landed right in front of the goal. Bob's teammate kicked it through for the score. The fellows jumped up and down. "Way to go, Bob!" one of them called.

Bob whirled around to me with a face so full of joy, I'm sure I'll never forget it. It was the moment when a defeated little boy, whom nobody wanted on the school-yard team, slew his fear of failure and humiliation. He'd done it with a promise. One so simple a child could understand it, yet so awesome no power on earth could defeat it—*God is with me and I can do it.*

🌿

FIRST DATE

IT'S FATHER'S DAY, Daddy, and here I sit wrapping your gift, filled with memories about growing up as your daughter. For instance, do you remember that time long ago when I went on my first dinner date? I was pretty young and shy, and still liked horses better than boys. But you encouraged me to go out. You knew I'd have a fine time.

A corsage came that afternoon. I will never forget the way my heart turned over when I lifted it out of the box. You said I must be very special to get flowers. Me— special? I couldn't stop looking at them. I studied myself in the mirror wishing I were prettier. I had an awful scratch on my nose. But when it was time for me to go, you said I looked beautiful. Those were your very words.

"Don't stay out too late," Mama said, laughing. You smiled too, and tapped your watch. I was so nervous I slammed the car door on the hem of my dress.

At the restaurant I was sure everybody was staring at me. Hadn't they ever seen two people on a date? Or was it my nose everyone was gazing at? I felt awkward—you know how unsure of myself I was in those days.

The table was just for two with a candle glowing on it. Conversation was easier than I'd expected. Now that I think about it, it was I who did all the talking.

I kept talking right through dessert, about how I wished I could grow up to be a nurse or a writer and travel to Africa to take care of starving children. I was full of dreams back then. They seemed pretty unlikely to me, but that night I talked about them, and somehow started to believe I could do some of those things.

Then when I came back home, I was kissed on the cheek. I wanted to say in return, "Thanks for the corsage and the dinner and for making an uncertain girl feel so special." But none of that came out. All I could say to my date was, "You're too much!" I said it over and over. In the language of a 12-year-old that meant someone was too wonderful for words.

Well, Daddy, I'm almost finished wrapping your gift now. But suddenly it doesn't seem like very much. A shirt. Did I give you a shirt last year too? Why do my gifts at Father's Day always seem so inadequate? Is it because I know deep inside that no matter what I give, you have given me still more?

You gave me confidence in myself 25 years ago. How was it you put it? "You can be anything you want to be. Just believe in yourself." That's what you said the night we dined in that restaurant on our one and only "date." And even today, when words don't come, I still say, "You're too much, Daddy!" You really are.

CHAPTER FIFTEEN

NEW LIFE

A MOMENT OF GENESIS

"MAMA, IT'S GENESIS! Come quick." Eight-year-old Ann's voice came faintly from the backyard.

Barely perceiving her words, I went right on working, a scenario that was typical of late. I'd been sitting at my desk for hours glued to a project I'd been working on for months—writing my first book. The night before, my husband had jokingly referred to it as the "Pac Man" project after the infamous yellow video game creature that gobbled up everything in its path. It's true I'd been at it day and night—too busy, overextended. And today, I was feeling lifeless and glum, as if I'd crawled under a blanket and couldn't find the exit.

"Mama, hurry. It's Genesis!" Ann's voice intruded again, louder this time. Genesis? I thought that's what she'd said. Reluctantly I shoved back my chair, feeling a peculiar twinge of pain in my right side. The pains had been coming and going for several days and I kept thinking I would see about them as soon as I caught up on things. Which would be never with all these interruptions.

What on earth was Ann talking about anyway? The only Genesis I knew was the first book of the Bible and . . .

Suddenly I stopped in mid-step as something faint and half-remembered focused in my mind. Surely she didn't mean Genesis the butterfly.

I plodded outside under a shiny March sun, shielding my eyes from the brilliance as though I were coming out of hibernation. I looked across the yard for Ann and I was surprised to see the forsythia bush already blooming. Ann popped from behind it waving one of its yellow-gold branches like a baton and dancing after a pair of orange-and-black butterfly wings that dipped and weaved in the air. My mind tumbled back a whole year, to the spring before . . .

I had come home one day with something called a "butterfly garden." It was made up of a big green box with oval cellophane windows and a jar of caterpillar larvae—three brown squiggles no bigger than the shavings off a newly sharpened pencil.

Ann placed the jar on her bedside table. I often joined her there, watching as the squiggles grew into fuzzy caterpillars. One was larger and livelier than the others, and he quickly became Ann's favorite.

"What can I name him, Mama?"

Just then I caught sight of her Bible sitting on a shelf, and a name popped out. "Call him Genesis," I said.

Ann wrinkled her face. "But that's a Bible book."

I wondered myself what had possessed me to blurt out such a name. "Well . . . Genesis is about new beginnings and . . . the gift of life," I said. "And that's what butterflies symbolize."

From then on, he was Genesis.

One morning we found him hanging from the lid of the jar like an upside-down question mark. Gradually he formed a hard chrysalis around himself. The other two followed, and we carefully unscrewed the lid and attached the cocoons inside the green box to wait for the butterflies' emergence.

Genesis was first, naturally. The day it happened I heard Ann shouting from her room. When I arrived the cocoon was wiggling, just a ripple, then violently. "What's happening?" Ann cried.

"Maybe he's coming out," I said.

We fell silent as an orange-and-black creature wriggled out and unfurled its wings, expelling the extra orange color on the floor of the box. For a few minutes he didn't move. Then, like a tiny sunburst, the butterfly flashed around the box in a gleaming dance that seemed to celebrate the joy of simply being alive.

"Look at Genesis," Ann cried. And all at once the name came alive. We were actually seeing a "genesis," a moment of a new beginning. A surge of new life.

Each day Ann dipped forsythia limbs in a sugar solution and held them through an opening in the box while the butterflies fed. They grew, as did her friendship with Genesis. She was certain she could tell him from the others. But the day arrived, as we knew it would, for setting her friend free. Exodus did, after all, follow Genesis, I explained. So she opened the box and sadly watched him fly away on a breeze. Genesis was gone.

The next day, though, she noticed an orange-and-black butterfly near the patio door. "Genesis!" she cried. We raced outside. Familiar, yes . . . but Genesis? The instructions said something about sighting the butterflies in the vicinity for a while.

Ann pulled a limb off the forsythia and lifted it high, standing motionless on the grass, looking rather like the Statue of Liberty holding her torch. The butterfly circled her head, drawing closer. I held my breath. In one majestic sweep, it lit on the tip of the limb just as it had done so often inside the box. It was like some golden moment out of a fairy tale. Frankly, I would never have believed it if I hadn't seen it clear as day.

Soon Genesis glided away. "He'll come back again," Ann said, watching him go. "I know he will."

"Maybe," I'd conceded, wrapped in the enchantment of the whole thing . . .

Genesis never returned, even though Ann repeatedly searched for him. For a while it got to be a real thing—Ann in search of Genesis. But now Ann raced up to me, breathless and excited. "He came back! Did you see him?"

I looked back toward the house where my half-finished project waited, along with unanswered letters, a few bills, and dinner preparations. "It looked like Genesis, but it wasn't he," I said.

The radiance drained from her face. "Oh," she said in a

voice so low I could barely hear it.

Before I could try to soften my answer, the strange pain that I'd been feeling lately caught in my side again. I braced myself against the elm tree while it subsided. Then I trudged toward the door, determined to get busy before this virus, or whatever it was, put me in bed.

The discomfort plagued me all evening and most of the night. The next morning I went to the doctor. An hour later I was in the hospital about to have surgery for a ruptured appendix.

I awoke from the operation thankful that things went well, but pretty soon I began thinking of the children, my husband and, yes, the work. The hospitalization had happened so quickly, without an ounce of preparation. I'd left the house with a half-made casserole in the kitchen and a letter that stopped mid-sentence in my typewriter.

I sat in my hospital bed early one morning, wondering about all the things I'd left undone—the promise to speak at a banquet, writing deadlines. My mind swirled with a hundred details and demands, just as it had before the operation; only now it was worse.

"How long before I'm able to resume my normal schedule?" I asked when the surgeon made his rounds.

"Six weeks," he answered without a blink. "And I want you doing nothing for at least four." As he left, I stared at the back of the door in dismay. I would never, I mean never, catch up on everything now. I looked at the thick bandage across my abdomen and sank back on my pillow, feeling utterly dismal. "Please, Lord, help me," I prayed.

I must have fallen asleep, for the next thing I knew I

awoke abruptly. No one was in the room. Feeling compelled to get out of bed, I maneuvered to a chair by the window. I was starting at the floor when out of the corner of my eye I glimpsed a tiny yellow butterfly hovering in the air beyond the pane.

His wings were so sheer that when he turned, it seemed I saw the sun shine through and change them into thin blades of light. Then he broke into a joyous little pattern of flight—*just as Genesis had done that day he'd wriggled out of his cocoon and soared exuberantly about the box.* And the same reaction I'd had then—the spark of joy and new life I'd felt over Genesis—came back to me now, full and fresh. For the first time in weeks I saw how easy it was to become mired in the details and demands of life and take for granted the simple joy of being alive.

It seemed God had used the tiny creature on my hospital sill to teach me something I'd been too blind and distracted to see before. That when life becomes so busy it's more burdensome than joyous, that's the time to search for a moment of "genesis"—to pause and catch life's spark again. For that's what Jesus wished for us. Not life overworked, but life abundant.

I looked at the bright morning. I couldn't wait to go home, to walk in the grass, to pick forsythia and follow the flight of new wings. But I wouldn't wait till then. From this moment I would take time for the precious gift of being alive in God's world.

I picked up the phone and called my daughter. "Guess what?" I told her. "Genesis came back after all."

And laughter, like music, danced right out of the phone.

THE REDWOOD BURL

ODAY AS I PEER at the tiny crystals of ice on my kitchen window, I find myself thinking of my friend Mary. Diagnosed with cancer, she seems to have lost all hope. Her words to me were wintered and gray: "I don't want to give in to despair, but I have nothing inside to fight with."

A bitter wind gusts at the window, drawing my attention to the small green plant silhouetted against the pane. In spite of my preoccupation, I smile at it. This is no ordinary houseplant. This is my very own redwood tree.

I pour a bit of water into the bowl where it grows, remembering how I brought this little "experiment" home from my visit to Muir Woods, that magnificent grove of redwood trees along California's Pacific coast. Walking among the cool, misty trails of the forest, I'd arched my neck trying to take in their breathtaking size. The largest rose 253 feet into the sky, a monument of strength and durability. Touched with awe, I sat down on a bench nearby. How had this forest of ancient, towering trees survived the onslaughts of centuries? Fire, lightning, blight, earthquakes . . .

And then a park service guide ambled along the trail in my direction, and answered my questions. She mentioned how the bark was resistant to fire, decay and insects. Then she pointed up to a large knotty lump several feet in diameter that was growing on the trunk of a tree. "Another secret lies in that burl," she said. "Hidden inside it are thousands of dormant buds. If the tree is traumatized, the burl is activated and sprouts new life. It's nature's way of insuring the redwood's continual recreation."

Before leaving the forest I stopped to browse in the gift shop. That's where I came upon some tiny living burls for sale, complete with instructions on how to grow redwood sprouts. On impulse, I bought one and brought it home.

I placed the small piece of wood in a bowl of water and waited. Soon green bumps appeared on the burl, gradually unfurling into feathery shoots. Through the winter I watched it grow on my kitchen sill.

But now, suddenly, I look at it with the same sweep of awe I had in the redwood forest. I feel as if I am seeing one of God's loveliest truths spelled out. When life's traumas come—and they always do—there is tucked within us all a burl of buds, a hidden potential that enables us to fight back and grow again. For if God designed so beautiful a capacity in the redwood, how much more would he fashion within his children?

I gaze at the little redwood. I will take this burl to Mary, I think. Maybe it will whisper its truth to her as well: that in every crisis is an inner strength and hope just waiting to be tapped. Spring is on its way now. It can come again to the heart as well.

❧

CHAPTER SIXTEEN

YOU'RE NEVER ALONE

THE FALLEN
BIRD'S NEST

IT WAS SCARCELY midafternoon, yet the doctor's waiting room was dark. Outside, enormous black clouds roiled and rolled. A storm was on the way. From my green chair in the corner, I felt strangely part of it—the peculiar darkness, the impending storm, clouds rumbling like a rockslide. In more ways than one, it seemed things were about to topple.

I'd come here because of a lump in my breast. I'd discovered it myself and naturally I'd gone to the family doctor hoping he would pat my hand and say, "Nothing to it." Instead, he'd sent me here, to a surgeon.

Lump. I turned the word over in my mind. It always rang the same ominous note . . . striking a particular chord buried years before when I'd worked as a nurse. It was a memory I never tampered with. Now it was all coming back with the swiftness of a dream.

But Mrs. Holly was no dream. She was literally the first patient I ever had. She'd had a lump, one that began her long battle with cancer. I cared for her for months. In all that time she never had a visitor. One morning as I brought her breakfast tray, I found her leaning at the window. Against the breaking light her frail little silhouette reminded me of the dark contours of pain and longing that seemed to shape so much of her life.

"Where is God?" she asked, gazing far into the distance as if she might catch His presence vanishing over the horizon.

"Why, He's right here with us," I replied, serving up the answer almost as easily as her meal.

She turned and looked at me intently. "I wonder..." she whispered. And at that moment I felt nearly as lost and unconvinced as she did. We never spoke of it again, but the episode always hung unfinished between us, like a puzzle you can't solve or a book you never complete.

I sat by her bed as she died. There were just the two of us. I kept thinking about the question she'd asked that day. Maybe it was my imagination, but I felt as if she was thinking of it too. She was too weak to talk, but near the end she gave me the faintest little smile. Then she closed her eyes and died. All alone, it seemed.

I felt unsettled for weeks afterward. Sometimes my eyes mysteriously filled with tears when I passed her room. "I know she was your first patient," a colleague said. "But you can't get emotionally involved like this." I took her advice. I packed up the hurt and unanswered questions and buried them. All that remained of the experience was a queer little dread that twisted in the pit of my stomach at every mention of the word *lump* . . .

The nurse's words cut through my thoughts. "Mrs. Kidd, the doctor will see you." I marched after her, trying to shake the old, disquieting memory.

After the exam the surgeon cleared his throat. "We need to take out the lump and get a biopsy," he said.

"Do you think it could be . . . malignant?" I asked.

He smiled gently. "Now, Sue, most lumps turn out to be benign, and I think it's entirely probable yours will be also. But you know I can't make absolute promises."

Surgery was set. I would check into the hospital in a few days.

An odd stillness squeezed the air as I scuffed my shoes across the parking lot. There wasn't a breath of wind. I told myself I had every reason to be hopeful, that Mrs. Holly was just one person, that thousands go through this and come out fine. I told myself all the reasonable things. But it was not a reasonable moment. Alone in the car, the little dread turned into a fear that overwhelmed all the logic in the world.

As I pulled into the driveway at home, the first drops broke from the swollen skies. I spotted my son in the backyard pulling his bicycle out of the rain. "Hurry, it's already coming down!" I yelled.

Bob bumped his wheels over the roots of the oak tree, scaring up a chipmunk that lived in the woodpile. "Will the storm hurt the chipmunks?" he called.

"They'll be okay."

"How about *them*?" He was gazing into the crook of an oak limb, at a bird's nest he'd discovered the week before.

Dear God, life was collapsing on my head and my son was standing in the rain worrying about birds and chipmunks. "Yes, the entire animal kingdom will be fine!" I practically shouted. "Now come on!"

The incongruity continued on all evening—small inconsequential details going right on as though no threat existed.

Finally, with everyone asleep, I tossed on my pillow, listening to the rain crash on the roof. Raveled in my thoughts and fears were old haunting images of Mrs. Holly and traces of the unsettled feeling I'd had after she died. That unfinished business . . . it made no sense.

Not wanting to wake my husband, I wandered to the den, where I sank into a chair. Lightning irradiated the panes with light, illuminating the backyard. For an instant I glimpsed the oak pitching and swaying in the night. *Nothing is really certain in this world*, I thought. I drew my knees beneath my chin as the wind whirred and slapped like helicopter blades in the blackness. And suddenly Mrs. Holly's question blew out of the storm. "Where is God?" Only this time it was no longer an echo lost in the years between us. It was my very own question.

"Where *are* You?" I cried, startled to hear the words, coming from my lips. Even more startled to realize how abandoned I'd felt since discovering the lump. It wasn't just facing life's uncertainties that seemed so fearful. It was facing them alone, without God.

Now a door was opening inside me and before I could

stop it, the rest spilled out too. The part I'd never been able to put into words. "And where were You back then when Mrs. Holly looked for You?" I whispered. "If You weren't there for *her*, how do I know You'll be here for *me?*" The awful doubt I'd carried inside for so long trailed off in the shadows.

I felt terrible saying it, almost disloyal. In all my life I'd never blurted out a doubt to God. But there was relief in it too. I went back to bed much lighter, as if a clean new space had been created inside me.

The next morning a bit of sunshine dribbled over a cloud. The children scurried out to play. It wasn't long before I heard shouts erupting from the backyard. "Mama! Come quick!"

I leaped a row of brown puddles. And there beneath the oak, at the tips of the children's tennis shoes, lay the bird's nest. Sprawled beside it were two newborn birds. They groped in the grass, looking helpless and wet. I looked at them in dismay. Just what I needed.

"They fell from the tree!" cried Bob. "And you said they'd be okay. You said . . ."

"I know," I interrupted, remembering the branches lashing in the wind.

There was nothing else to do. I knelt down, scooped the hatchlings into my hands and placed them in the nest. But as I knelt over that little scene, it came to me. One small fragment of an old familiar verse. "One of them shall not fall on the ground without your Father" (Matthew 10:29). For a moment I didn't move, as I held the words in my mind and felt them descend slowly into my heart—

into a clean, new space, which before had been a closet for my doubt. I could hear God answering the doubts and questions deep inside, answering them in the gentlest sort of way. "I'm here . . . I've been here all along."

I tucked the nest into the ivy that draped the brick fence, while the children agonized over whether their mother would find it. But the next day she appeared on the fence with a beakful of food. The birds were fine.

And I was, too. Just as the doctor predicted, the lump was benign. But just as important, the episode helped me understand something. If God seems far away in the midst of a dark moment, it's not He who's missing, but my ability to perceive Him. And sometimes the way is cleared simply by offering God one's doubts with a gentle honesty.

Somehow I think that's how it happened for Mrs. Holly. For, as that old memory began to heal inside me, I grew sure she'd found the assurance of God's presence. In fact, I wonder if that faint smile she gave me before she died was meant to tell me so.

Yes, I think she knew, just as I do now. No one is alone.

BLOOD BROTHERS

N A HOT AND HAZY summer day, under the canopy of an oak tree, my son Bob and his buddy Michael, both nine, are swinging on the ropes that dangle from the limbs. Swinging through the sun-flecked shade in a dreamy, timeless way. Today these two little boys are a picture of opposites. Michael, fair-skinned and freckled, has a cowboy hat pulled low over his blond hair. Bob, on the other hand, with brown hair and a face as tan as the prairie, is wearing a red Indian feather. They've spent part of the afternoon watching the Lone Ranger and Tonto on television. Now they ride the old rope swings ... a cowboy and an Indian brave, shouting, "Hi-yo, Silver, away!" It's all wonderful magic that rolls like a tumbleweed out of their imagination.

But as I watch from the kitchen window, the magic is

broken. Suddenly Michael slips from the swing and lands on a tree root. He picks himself up, staring at his palm and a slight trickle of blood winding onto his wrist. I shake my head at all the cuts and scratches of summer. Already that morning Bob had cut his thumb on a tin can buried in the alley and I had treated and bandaged it up. Band-Aids, of course, are good for making helpless mothers feel useful.

Beyond the window, Michael holds back the tears by biting his lip. Bob stops swinging and stares at him with a trace of sympathetic pain stealing into his face. I reach for the trusty box of Band-Aids and make my way outside. But as I approach the oak, I notice the two of them locked together in whispers. Next my son peels off his bandage and lifts his tin-can cut toward Michael. Then in a secret moment under the tree, the magic that had been inter-rupted suddenly resumes. For these little fellows stand beneath a golden sun and touch their wounds together just as Tonto and the Lone Ranger had done . . . solemnly becoming "blood brothers." And when they are finished, the pain in Michael's face has vanished.

I approach quietly, treat the wound, and slip away, thinking how easily the imagination of children can turn an ordinary event into dramatic action. But I'm also sure that something very special has happened across the landscape of this summer day.

You see, that small event reminded me what it really means to be a Christian brother or sister . . . even to someone "opposite" or different from myself.

"Love one another with brotherly affection," the Bible says (Romans 12:10, RSV). Perhaps we do that best of all when we open ourselves to the pain of another, when we identify with his wounds and become a source of compassion and comfort. And when you think about it like that, I guess you could say we all have at least one "blood brother." After all, isn't that what Jesus does for each of us?

CHAPTER SEVENTEEN

A LITTLE CHILD
SHALL LEAD

PUTTING MOTHER IN THE PICTURE

"A-A-A-MA! COME LOOK!" Ten-year-old Ann is shouting at the back door.

Now what? I am huddled in my favorite chair, enjoying a small oasis of quiet in what has been a frustrating day with my two children.

It is a week since school ended, and suddenly the kids are home behaving like two wild ponies let out of a corral. They jump on the beds; chase the dog through the house, turning over a trash can; spill soft drinks; grumble over who gets the remote to the television, and whine that there's nothing to do—the perennial woes of summer vacation.

This morning, while watering my marigolds, they drenched each other with the garden hose. Soggy tennis shoes, dripping clothes—it was too much. "Go to your rooms!" I yelled.

And that's how it's been all day—all week. My face has taken on a certain grimace. Several times a day I stand the children before me and give a lecture about their behavior, but nothing gets through.

"Mama, come see!" Once again Ann's voice cuts into the quietness. She glides to a halt beside my chair, breathless. "There's a chipmunk outside."

I look at her. A chipmunk? "I'm reading," I explain.

"But Mama—"

"Not now." I try to think of something to occupy her. Then I remember. "Why don't you do your Sunday school assignment?" I ask. She had come home last week with an assignment to make a little booklet illustrating four ways to love someone: a teacher, parent, neighbor, friend—anyone she wanted to choose.

"All right," she says, but her voice is so quiet I barely hear her.

In the late afternoon I go looking for her. I peer into Ann's room. She says she has just finished her assignment. "Can I see?" She twirls a lock of brown hair around her finger. "Come on," I prod. More hesitation. Then she relents, dropping the booklet into my hands.

Four Ways to Love a Child by Ann Kidd. I read the title twice. At once I see. The booklet is meant for me. I start to tell her the idea was for her to show ways *she* could love someone, not ways *I* could love someone. But I keep quiet. Is she feeling so in need of love? I manage a feeble smile and turn to page one. I have the funniest feeling about this.

🌿

"Go see chipmunks and stuff like that with your kids," it says. Beneath is a picture of a smiling mom and a little girl peeking around a tree at a chipmunk. I gaze at it, aware for the first time since summer vacation began that I've treated the children more like interruptions than family members whose lives I want to share and enjoy. Her picture of togetherness rearranges something inside me. I look up for Ann, but she has slipped from the room.

I turn to page two. "When kids mess up, give them some hugs." I smile at her sketch of a mother and child reaching to embrace each other. Hugs had been rare this week, especially when the kids "messed up." I recall the angry banishment to their rooms earlier in the day, and I think—maybe the moments they mess up are the very times I should embrace them with the assurance they are loved.

"Give kids a chance to talk" is scrawled on page three. I look over her crayon drawing, thinking of the lectures I've delivered all week and of my tendency to run on about some grievance while the children stand there unable to squeeze in a single word. And I ask myself, shouldn't my children have the right to invoke silence from their parents long enough to get their own thoughts and feelings across?

There is one more page. "Laugh alot," it says. I wonder if Ann is referring to the water follies she and her brother had with the garden hose this morning. Could laughter have unwound the tension and shifted things into perspective, helping me to see that it was, after all, only water?

I close her little booklet. Yes, the children have been difficult this week. But so have I—hoarding time without sharing it, disciplining without loving, lecturing without listening, even forgetting my sense of humor! I sense God telling me that it isn't just the children's behavior I should be trying to change, but my own. In that moment, I know that the love I show in the small, nitty-gritty moments of whines and water fights, grumbles and interruptions, may be the most elusive love of all—and the most important.

Ann saunters back into the room, chewing her lip. She gazes at the booklet still in my hand. I give her a hug and a wink.

The next day I am puttering in the kitchen when through the window I spot Ann's chipmunk beneath the oak in the backyard. I dash for her room where she's dipping a brush into red tempera paint. "Come quick!" I cry. "The chipmunk's back."

She whirls around so fast that she tips over the paint. As it runs across her desk, she reaches for the jar and drags the sleeve of her blouse through the red puddle.

For a split second I forget the chipmunk. I am about to give in to one of those small wear-and-tear frustrations of raising children. But just in time I remember Ann's *Four Ways to Love a Child* and I laugh instead. It is, after all, only paint, and outside there is a fleeting moment for us to capture and tuck away in a little girl's heart.

BECOME AS
LITTLE CHILDREN

WARM SUN, soft breeze, hazy sky—
it's that kind of day along the
Carolina coast. My family bounces along, part of a happy
group in a chartered tour boat, speeding through dark
green backwater on our way around the peninsula. A salty
wind blows across the deck, disappearing into the roar of
the engine.

Soon we are climbing waves, sliding over bulges, the
marshes far behind us. Then the engines are cut off, the
drone dies away. We rock on the silent surface of the sea.
The Captain points to the jetty. I lift binoculars to my
eyes. There on the rocks, lined up like a chorus line
waiting in the wings, are hundreds of pelicans. Hundreds!

Bags of popcorn are passed through the crowd on board.
One by one they are emptied over the side until popcorn
bobs everywhere on the water. It's part of the tour, of

course, feeding the birds. Now everyone falls quiet, expectant.

Suddenly the air becomes a profusion of feathers . . . a whirling explosion of dance. Pelicans surge toward us, filling the sky. Hundreds of them spin round the boat like a carousel, scooping popcorn from the sea. There is grace and rhythm to their exuberance. The birds glide and pirouette, rising and falling with the sea. We have the feeling they are not doing this for the popcorn at all, but for the sheer joy of flying over our boat.

Like the other youngsters aboard, my children begin to skip around the deck, reaching their arms to the birds. They dance along with the pelicans. It is an irresistible urge. I too feel the joy of this moment; but I suppress the urge to skip. After all, I am a grownup. Grownups don't skip.

Then suddenly I remember. That was very nearly what I had told myself last year at the aquarium's porpoise pool. Everyone had been invited to pet a porpoise. But it was the children who surrounded the pool. And there was something wondrous about it—the way the smiling fish lifted their noses for a human touch, the awe in the faces of the children as they stretched out their fingers. I too longed to touch a porpoise. Just once. But, like the other adults, I hung back on the outskirts, self-conscious, inhibited, and hurried. I had regretted it since, that I didn't find the courage to become a child for just a moment and join the celebration around the pool. . . .

The children dancing on deck draws me back to the present. *Dear Jesus, I remember what you said about our becoming as little children. You want us to see the world with their innocent eyes, to take pleasure in Your creation, to laugh, even to skip!*

The pelicans sweep up and down the sky like jubilant chords of music. My children skip by. One of them reaches out a hand. And I grab on. I am skipping, too. And I have no regrets.

CHAPTER EIGHTEEN

THE LEAST OF
THESE

JAMES LENDS
A HAND

HE SATURDAY BEFORE Thanks-giving, I stood on the front steps of a shelter for the homeless in Atlanta, staring miserably at the door. My husband, Sandy, and I had come from our home in South Carolina as weekend volunteers, but I was giving up the time grudgingly. I'd planned a big Thanksgiving dinner and wondered how I'd get everything ready.

It was the first time I would host the dinner at my house, and I kept thinking of my mother's resplendent Thanksgiving table. I had no idea how I would live up to her sweet-potato souffle and fresh-baked pies. Not with my schedule.

I guess that's why I'd latched on to "The Busy Woman's Thanksgiving Checklist" that I found in a magazine and stuck on the refrigerator. It was so sensible, parceling out chores over a whole week. Make menu. Shop for turkey.

Plan centerpiece (there were instructions for making your very own cornucopia). *Et cetera, et cetera.* The list, as long as my arm, programmed your life for a week, till the moment you sat down to dinner, basking in praise. My dream, exactly. Yet I'd barely begun checking off items before we departed for the shelter.

I plodded up the steps as a gust of wind seemed to whisk the last bit of light from the sky. The resident manager ushered us into a large room lined with rows of cots. I couldn't help but notice a young man in a tattered green suit and canary-yellow tie. His face was rosy and twinkle-eyed with a gap-toothed smile. He darted from cot to cot clutching a wide blue book. "Wanna see my book?" he asked hopefully. No one wanted to see it.

"That's James," the resident manager said. "A simple-hearted fellow. Can't read or write. But he's one of a kind."

Moments later I caught the sound of whistling drifting from the adjacent dining room. It was such an unexpected sound, I peeped around the door. There was James, whistling as he set the table.

After dinner Sandy and I wandered into the lobby. I noticed James in his sunny yellow tie, sitting by himself, absorbed in his book. I tried to slip by into the office where Sandy and I had set up our cots. Still preoccupied by Thanksgiving, I was going to scour a recipe book for cornbread dressing. But James was motioning to me. "Wanna see my book?"

Reluctantly I joined him on an old vinyl sofa. He slid over so I did not have to sit on a gaping tear. I gazed at his eager, childlike expression, swallowed hard, and opened

❧

the book he reverently handed me. Inside was a curious collection: a paper napkin from a fast-food restaurant, a bluebird's feather, a church bulletin, a faded birthday card, a pocket calendar . . .

James told me about each—how he'd eaten the most delicious meal ever in the restaurant, how he'd found the feather in Piedmont Park where he shared his afternoons with the birds. The church bulletin came from a tiny mission where he'd been welcomed. The card was on his cot on his birthday. The calendar was last year's Christmas "gift" from a store clerk. James treasured them all.

Some pages were inscribed with autographs. "They are my friends," he said proudly. One was a man who'd helped him find clothes; another, a lady who brought meals—people who'd done kindnesses large and small.

"I would sure like to have a home and family," he said, staring down at the worn pages between us. "But still, you can see I got me a lot to be thankful for." And all at once I understood. This book represented James's humble list of *blessings*. Blessings he checked off every day.

James's life was filled with lacks, but what he had he cherished. He'd discovered how to focus upon the simple gifts in his life, not upon his problems. A piece of Scripture echoed in my mind. "Walk . . . abounding . . . with thanksgiving" (Colossians 2:6-7). Was that the secret behind this whistling man's simple joy?

He reached into the front pocket of his suit and pulled out a stubby pencil. "Would you sign my book?" he asked.

I smiled, feeling the back of my throat tighten. "To my new friend," I wrote, then signed my name and read the words back to him. His gesture in response was so soft I almost missed it. He brushed a finger across my words, as if caressing the thought. Then he stood up, tucked his "blessing checklist" under his arm and said good-night.

As he sauntered away, I thought of "The Busy Woman's Thanksgiving Checklist" and knew in the deepest part of my heart that I'd been following the wrong list. Thanksgiving means checking off blessings, not chores.

Right there on the torn sofa, with James's snaggled smile in my memory, I asked God to forgive me for concentrating more on my petty problems than on my blessings. And I promised to be more receptive to the delicate, everyday joys He'd woven into life, like James, who really *was* "one of a kind."

You probably guessed, I never did cross off all those items on the "The Busy Woman's Thanksgiving Checklist." I posted a new list instead: "The Grateful Woman's Thanksgiving Checklist." It was much longer than the busy woman's version, it was *longer* than my arm.

And you know what? When Thursday rolled around, my table *was* a bounty, not because I was slave to its tasks, but because counting my blessings had filled me with enthusiasm and energy. Just before dinner I was doing some last-minute fussing in the kitchen. Sandy called in, "Hey, who's that I hear whistling?"

I stopped and called back, "Just a little something I learned from James."

CIGAR STORE INDIAN

E STANDS ON THE SIDEWALK beside the front door of the department store like an old cigar-store Indian . . . a tall, motionless man wearing no expression on his face, only sunglasses. He clutches a cigar box, which he thrusts out in a gesture of greeting and hope when footsteps come his way. The box rattles, the feet hurry by, and his arm sinks back against his seemingly wooden body.

As my seven-year-old daughter and I approach the door, I notice her steps slowing. She has caught sight of him. I've seen him on the streets before. But this is her first encounter with a beggar. She seems transfixed by the sight.

"What's he doing?" she asks too loudly.

"He's asking for money," I whisper.

Then comes the eternal question. "Why?"

"Because he's poor and he needs help," I say, hoping that satisfies her.

As we draw beside him, the cigar box is thrust in our direction. Ann stops and peeps inside it. I grab her hand and pull her through the door.

As I'm browsing in the store, Ann wanders off. I quickly follow her to the front door where she's peering through the glass at the beggar.

"Mama, can we give him some money?" she asks, her eyes reflecting both sadness and hope.

"Well . . . sure we can." I snap open my purse. She peeps inside it just as she did with the cigar box. All I have is a dollar bill and two quarters.

I hand her the quarters. She stares at the two coins for a moment as if there is something big and important going on inside her. Then she blurts out, "Mama, give him the dollar, too, and I'll pay you back from my allowance."

Her words cut through all my distraction and un-concern, and they touch me deeply. There is a ring to them, a resonance that is unmistakable and piercing. I hand her the dollar. I watch her walk over to the beggar and gaze up into his blind face before she lays the money in his box.

I know it's one of those moments that will stay long in my memory . . . Ann and the cigar-box beggar. I suspect God is hidden in the little episode. I think it is His voice I heard sounding through my daughter . . . God's voice saying, "Give him the dollar, give him all you have, and I'll pay you back in joy and growth." And that is a lesson I needed to hear just then—to help me grow more sensitive

🌿

to the needs of those who wait expectantly on the edges of my world . . . to be less preoccupied and more responsive. More generous.

But the incident taught me more than that. It reminded me that we should always pay attention to the casual events that cross our days, and listen well to the words in the air about us. For God's voice can come in small and commonplace ways we're apt to miss. It can come in the language of a little girl and a beggar.

❧

CHAPTER NINETEEN

MENDING WHAT MATTERS

THE TEENS—
A WHOLE NEW
BALL GAME

 S I WALKED to the mailbox that Monday, the sun was not shining. The clouds were the color of nickel, round and silver and rumbling just a little, like the rattle of a piggy bank. I glanced at the sky as two or three drops of rain splashed on top of me. I was not surprised. It seemed like it had been raining on me since I got out of bed.

The storm started when my 13-year-old son, Bob, and I had an argument earlier that morning. It was over something small and ridiculous. He wanted to wear an old, faded sweatshirt with cutoff sleeves to school, if you can imagine that. I insisted on the nice, new shirt his grandmother had given him for Christmas, the kind with the button-down collar and little blue monogram on the pocket. I pointed to the letters. "It's not everybody that has his initials right on his shirt," I said reasonably.

He rolled his eyes to the kitchen ceiling like something funny was written up there. "Nobody wears initials on their shirts, Mama. *Nobody!*"

Well, soon we were shouting, I mean, *really* shouting. He said terrible things. I said terrible things. Finally he yanked on the grandmother shirt. As he picked up his books, I reached over to give him a hug. Never before had he gone without a hug. But this time Bob stiffened and drew back. Then he was gone.

I hunched in my chair, stirring my coffee over and over. Dear God, had that really been the two of us going at each other like that? I felt drained. Like someone had opened the soles of my feet and emptied everything out.

The truth was, I wasn't sure how to deal with Bob anymore. Not since he'd entered the world of adolescence. He'd scarcely arrived in it, and already we were skidding into little puddles of rebellion that left me feeling exasperated and hopeless about the rest of the journey. Bob was a fine boy, a good boy, but suddenly there were days he questioned everything I said. Days he seemed to test me deliberately. There'd been so much conflict and quarreling between us lately that I was ready to throw up my hands and quit. How in the world would I get through the teenage years still ahead?

Shaking away the morning's events, I sighed and walked on, a kind of parental battle fatigue washing over me. Just ahead, the mailbox looked as defeated as I felt. Ever since a car plowed into the side of it, the pole had been bent and the door hung ajar.

Reaching inside, my hand brushed against a stack of

envelopes—then something peculiar, like broom bristles. I bent down and peered inside. The day's mail sat on top of a small collection of weeds and pine straw. Odd . . . how did this get in the mailbox? Somebody's idea of a prank, I decided. I brushed out the debris, remembering the day long ago when Bob had loaded the mailbox with a water balloon, which popped, drenching the mail. I pushed the lid as closed as it would go, wishing for half a second I could have that little fellow back. The boy who liked to play pranks with water balloons—and who wore the clothes I laid out for him every single morning.

A drop of rain splatted on my nose. I shuffled toward the house, not bothering to hurry. Suddenly parenthood felt very heavy.

That afternoon Bob breezed in from school and disappeared into his room. "How was your day?" I said, tagging behind him, trying to ignore the growing rift between us.

"Okay," he said, pulling off his shirt. He tossed the monogrammed thing on the floor at my feet. I glared at it, like he'd thrown down a gauntlet. He rummaged through his drawer for the inevitable sweatshirt with cutoff sleeves. I wheeled around to leave, then turned back. "Did you put pine straw in the mailbox?" I demanded.

He gave me a confused look, as if all his suspicions about me were now confirmed. "Never mind," I said.

But the next day when I opened the mailbox, there it was again! A smattering of pine straw, some twigs and two dead dandelions lying in the box. Once again I raked them out, blowing the dust off the mail. There was something very strange going on here.

The mystery continued all week. Each day I found a bouquet of weeds in the mailbox. And every day I whisked it out. Was it the neighborhood children up to some mischief? Or Bob? Perhaps, but I didn't bring up the subject again. As a matter of fact, I quit discussing *anything* with Bob. Every time a conflict arose I simply flexed my authority, then left the room or changed the subject. It was just easier that way.

On Saturday Bob wandered into the den where I was reading the newspaper. "Mama, can I go to the movies?" he asked. I flipped the newspaper to the theater section. The movie he was asking about was rated PG-13. The number 13 indicated an extra note of caution to parents. I looked at my *13-year-old* son. The irony was not lost on me.

"No, not this movie," I answered.

"Can't we even talk about it?" he pleaded.

"There's nothing to talk about," I said, walling myself behind the paper. It would only end up in shouting again.

"Mother, you don't understand," he cried, tearing from the room. "You don't even try!"

I sat there in the hot echo of his words, desperation rippling through me. "Oh, God, is this how it's going to be for the next few years?" I prayed. "Please, Lord, show me what to do."

When mail time came again, I walked out as usual, and there, as usual, was the same maddening bundle of twigs and straw. When would this stop? I reached in to pull out the latest deposit, and I caught flash of something buried inside it. It was small and round, the color of hyacinths and May sky and summer twilight. It was a tiny blue egg. *A bird's egg.*

Chirping burst from a nearby limb. There sat a bird, a piece of pine straw dangling from its beak. I gently pushed the ragged mound back inside as the truth opened to me like the unfurling of a wing. Why hadn't it occurred to me before? Had I been too preoccupied to see that the debris I'd yanked from the box all week had been the early meshing and intertwinings of a nest? I was amazed at the mother bird's tenacity. She had found our broken mailbox, and every day she had started a nest inside it. And when she returned to find it torn apart, she had tried again. Over and over again.

Suddenly I felt like God was whispering inside me. About mothering and nest-building and love that keeps on. I thought about the delicate meshing and intertwining of relationships in my home—that fragile nest of intimacy where we lived our days. How easily it unraveled! How quickly it became frayed and torn apart by the ordinary wear and tear of living. I could hear Bob's voice pleading with me: "You don't even *try.*" Was he right? Had I been so afraid of the trials of adolescence that I had retreated from the demands and quit trying? Had I somehow given up on our relationship the moment things got difficult?

I lifted my eyes to the branches above, then beyond to the curve of the sky. *With every new season of family life, new strains come,* I thought. *That's normal. Why not meet them head-on with new commitment instead of despair! The important thing is relationships—and rebuilding them as often as it takes.*

Inside, Bob sat beside his desk thumbing his globe around. "Hi," I said. He looked up at me and stared. For an instant I could see the vulnerable little boy I'd once known. But a boy growing up too, needing new independence as well as limits. "Wanna talk?" I asked. "I promise to listen."

So I sat there and listened and listened. And it was nearly the hardest work I'd ever done, but it seemed to soak up the pain and resentments between us and give us a new beginning.

Afterward we printed a small sign. "Dear Mailman," we wrote. "A mother bird has built her nest inside the mailbox. Would you deliver our mail to the door temporarily until her eggs hatch and the birds fly away?"

As we taped it to the mailbox, Bob reworded the mailman's motto: "Nothing can stop the mail from getting through. Not rain nor sleet nor snow . . . nor birds' nests," he said.

I grinned at him. Then I threw my arms around him. This time he didn't pull back. He stood right there beside the street and the battered mailbox and hugged me back. I mean *really* hugged me. And we twined our arms together like a nest that is freshly woven, and walked inside.

Before you knew it, we had three baby birds in our mailbox. Every day the mother perched atop it and filled the air with song. I always stopped to listen. For it was the song that would get me through all the teenage years and beyond—the sweet, stubborn sound of love that never quits. At all.

THE SOUND OF
FORGIVENESS

LL DAY THE SUN hibernated in the gray clouds like an old golden bear hiding in a dark cave. In its absence a winter wind had woven the corners of the kitchen window with tiny patterns of ice. Four small frosty spider webs. I stared at them, suddenly feeling the deep chill that had lodged within me all day. The words my husband and I had exchanged before breakfast were still frozen inside me. It hadn't been a big argument. Just silly, angry words. But they'd hurt. A stew simmered and I turned to give it a stir, remembering his last slightly cutting remark before he'd left for work. Even now something ugly inside me wanted to retaliate . . . insult for insult. *No sir*, I thought, tapping the wooden spoon decisively on the pot. *It's not over yet!*

Twilight spread like a deep purple bruise across the sky and the angry hurt I felt deepened with it. The window rattled. Frost crept farther across the pane. Then by chance, or perhaps not by chance at all, my son sat down on the kitchen floor where I paced about. He was writing on something. The sound of soft scratchings floated in the air. *Scribble. Scribble . . . swish.* I stepped around him, busy with dinner, busy nursing my grudge. *Scribble. Scribble . . . swish.* I found my attention focusing on the peculiar pattern of sound. Finally I paused in my anger and looked down at him.

My child, who is often my teacher, cuddled a blackboard slate in his lap. His hand clutched a stubby piece of chalk and scribbled on the slate. Then in one quick, clean movement he swished the eraser across it. The ugly marks disappeared. Vanished. His eyes gleamed with the magic he had made.

I watched for a while, and as I stood by his blue-jeaned legs, I found a hidden lesson. It was all there in my son's lap, whispering from the blackboard. Husbands and wives are human. They have moments of failure, scribbling on one another's lives, leaving dark, ugly words—angry graffiti that mar and wound. The work of forgiveness is to make the scribble vanish . . . to erase the wrong and remember it no more.

"Lord," I prayed, "I've been so wrong to cling to this small scribbled slate of wrongs done to me. I erase it now with Your help, wiping away every mark placed there. It is forgiven." *Swish.* The sound of forgiveness seemed to echo inside me. I felt new and light and warm . . . like a thawed window with sun polishing away the webs of frost. Forgiveness was indeed love's best magic. It was a vanishing act.

And it was done without a moment to spare. My husband breezed through the door on a wave of frigid air. His look was more uncertain than angry. "About this morning," he began, looking first at the floor, then up at me, "I'm sor—"

"Oh, I'm sorry, too!" I cried, my eyes suddenly stinging. And as we clung together in the kitchen, all was silent except for a faint and magical *swish* somewhere in the room.

CHAPTER TWENTY

ENDINGS AND BEGINNINGS

BIRTHDAY BLUES

AST AUGUST as I drove my 12-year-old daughter to her first horse-riding lesson, I found myself thinking of the birthday card I'd received that morning from a teasing friend. It pictured three buzzards circling a birthday cake. The caption read, "Forty—the beginning of the end."

It was still a week till my birthday, but already the age jokes had started. I'd tossed the card onto my dresser with a chuckle. But there was just enough truth in it to leave me feeling vaguely troubled. Somehow I'd never thought much about aging, or about how time sweeps so swiftly through its passages. During my 30s, I'd managed to keep alive an illusion that I would be young forever: There would always be time to do everything I wanted. But that wonderful decade—when my children were small and hopes and dreams were young, when everything seemed like a beginning and opportunities stretched forever—was ending.

Maybe it was me, or maybe it was just the fallout of turning 40, but suddenly, bumping along that old country road, I felt an unexpected pang of loss, a sense of ending. It was as if I was standing in the last golden moments of summer just before autumn browned the earth for good.

I let out a huge sigh. It was so big that Ann whirled toward me on the front seat. "What's wrong Mama?"

"Oh, I don't know. Maybe I should be like Jack Benny and refuse to go beyond thirty-nine," I muttered.

"Who's he?" she wanted to know. I looked at her and felt even older.

As we drove onto the horse farm, I took note of the sign: OMEGA FARM. *Omega* means "ending." It seemed to be the word of the day.

I gazed through the car window at the red-roofed stables and neatly fenced slopes of countryside. Ann studied them too, moving to the edge of her seat as three young horses came into view. They tossed their chestnut manes in a glaze of sunlight and broke into a gallop. We watched till they were out of sight.

"Mama, where's the plaster horse I painted last year?" Ann asked.

I gave her a curious squint. "It's in that bag of keepsakes in the closet," I answered. She knew the one. It contained all the tender, ragged stuff mothers can never throw away.

"I think I'll hang that horse in my room," she explained. I smiled. Maybe she was getting into the equestrian spirit after all. Back when I'd first suggested horse-riding lessons,

🌿

she wasn't enthusiastic. "Try it, Ann. I know you'll love it," I'd coaxed.

"How do you know? Did you ride *way back* when you were a kid?"

"No, but I always wanted to," I said, remembering. When I was 12, my room was filled with shelves of glass horses, books about horses, sketches of horses. Once, in school, I had to write "I will not draw horses in class" 100 times, but it didn't much cure me. One of my cherished memories is the time my grandmother took me to a horseshow and I saw those magnificent creatures up close. I watched their exquisite high steps and canters and promised myself I would ride with the same dash and dazzle. But it never happened.

Now, with a daughter of 12 myself, that unhatched dream was just another reminder of how old I'd gotten.

At the stable the riding instructor, Barb, was all ready with a stable horse named Whisper. I watched from the shade of a pine tree as Ann climbed into the saddle and floated through the amber dust of that late sumer afternoon. I noticed the way her eyes widened and her hair bounced back and forth, following her rhythm in the saddle.

As I'd predicted, Ann was delighted with the whole experience, but by the time we arrived home, the delicate melancholy I was feeling had escalated into downright glumness.

That evening, as I sat on the edge of the bed, my eyes fell upon the birthday card that had started the whole thing. It was still on the dresser besides a half-burned candle we'd used a few nights before during a power outage.

I could almost feel time melting away. My shoulders slumped. That's how my husband, Sandy, found me. He sized up the situation immediately. "The birthday buzzards getting to you?" he asked.

"It's embarrassing to respond to a birthday like this!" I answered. "But I feel like something important is ending."

He wrapped an arm around me. "Everybody goes through some reflection when they move into another decade of life. It's natural." Outside, thunder snapped and splinters of light reflected on the panes as if to emphasize his words.

It rained all night. I lay awake, my sudden attack of mid-life misery growing darker as the night aged. Oddly, that feeling of misery was laced with images of red-roofed stables and my daughter swaying on the back of Whisper, the horse.

Finally, tired of the whole dreary thing, I began to pray. I told God I was ashamed to be so depressed, but I was really having trouble handling this "beginning of the end" thing. Last of all I mumbled a plea. "Please, God, could You help me?"

The next morning, as I climbed out of bed, for the first time in my life I actually felt old. My back hurt and there were blue shadows under my eyes.

As I trudged into the den I noticed Ann plundering through the bag of keepsakes from the closet. Kindergarten pictures and old letters to Santa were strewn everywhere. She'd found the plaster horse to hang in her room and was now engrossed in the rest of the bag's contents.

"Look, Mama! It's the *Me Book* I made in third grade."

She handed me an assortment of pages tied together with yellow yarn. On each page was glued a photograph of herself, one for each year of her life.

I thumbed through the short chronology, my eyes wandering over pictures of her as a baby, at one, two, three, all the way up to eight. It was a tiny marching picture of time itself. Soon—too soon, I thought—she will have 40 pages also.

Just then my eyes caught sight of two words at the bottom of the last page. Right where you would expect to see "The End," the teacher had had the students close their books by writing, "The Beginning."

I stared at the words as if they had some holy twist, as if they were God's answer to my prayer for help the night before. This was not the beginning of the end, He seemed to say, but the beginning *at* the end.

At the window, little pearls of rain still clung to the glass. But inside me things were shifting. Aging, this inevitable, collection of pages in my *Me Book*, could become a journey of diminishing joy unless I remembered that the final words on every page of life were always "The Beginning."

Why, who knows what wondrous new beginnning might commence in my 40s, I thought. *Or my 50s, or 60s, or 80s?*

When I took Ann to her next horse-riding lesson, I casually said to Barb, "I don't suppose you have any forty-year-olds taking lessons, do you?"

She saw straight through me. "No, but there's always a first time. Why don't I sign you up?"

My first time upon Whisper, there was such a disparity between my uncorked delight and my antiquated muscles that I literally bounced out of the saddle and onto the ground. Sitting in the dust, I was tempted to wonder if I was kidding myself. I looked up and nothing was circling overhead but God's clean blue sky; the birthday buzzards were gone. I climbed back on the horse and rode till the sun smeared the sky red and dropped behind the trees.

Riding, after all those years, meant a lot more than fulfilling a lost dream. It was my way of living out the truth God taught me. Whether you're ending a year, a decade, a project or a job—whatever it might be—the truth holds. The end is where you start from.

GROWING UP

ODAY I NOTICED *Alice's Adventures in Wonderland* on your desk. It was open to the page where Alice suddenly grows nine feet tall. Her reaction was, "Dear, dear! How queer everything is to-day! And yesterday things went on just as usual. I wonder if I've changed in the night?"[1] When I read that, I sat down on your bed and thought about you . . . how you turn fourteen years old this month.

It seems like only yesterday (parents are always saying that, aren't we?) that I was waiting for you to be born. You were due on Valentine's Day. I embroidered a pink heart on your gown and we hung valentines across your crib. Of course you were born 11 days late, but I still called you "little Valentine."

Your first night home from the hospital I crept into your nursery in the middle of the night and watched you sleep. You made this funny sucking motion with your mouth. And even though everyone knows you never wake a sleeping baby, I picked you up. You opened your eyes and looked at me. We sat in the rocking chair and I told you how beautiful you were, how much I loved you. I told you all things we were going to do together. Play patty cake, read books, shop for ballet shoes, throw tea parties in the garden, catch fireflies in the dusk, and have long mother-daughter talks while french-braiding your hair.

Now it's slumber parties and curling irons and boys and telephones and loud music and "Hey Mama, can I borrow your blue sweater?" Who would think a 6 pound baby girl could grow up to wear *my* sweater? I know, there I go again. It's part of the parental condition to be shocked when your child grows up. We know intellectually that babies become toddlers and toddlers become kids and kids become (gulp!) teenagers and teenagers become adults. But when you see it happen . . . when it's *your* child, there's this strange disbelief about it. An apprehension of sorts. Maybe we're uneasy about losing something precious—a closeness that we fear may not be recovered. I'm glad you're becoming a young lady, but sometimes I have an urge to keep you small enough to hold on my lap. Be patient with me. It can be hard coming to grips with the truth that life flows on through its passages, that nothing stays the same. Especially you.

Today I look back and know there are times I wasn't there for you, times I didn't listen or understand. But did you know that sometimes I still slip into your room and gaze at you while you sleep? And I still think how beautiful you are and how much I love you . . . I just remembered. We never did have that mother-daughter talk while french-braiding your hair. But when it comes to mothers and daughters or fathers and sons or *any* relationship for that matter, it's never too late to weave closeness, no matter how much we've changed.

So . . . how about tonight? French-braids?

Your Mother.

1. Lewis Carroll, *Alice's Adventures in Wonderland* (New York: Random House, 1946), p. 17.

LOOK OUT FEAR, HERE COMES FAITH!

Look Out Fear, Here Comes Faith!

Marion Bond West

Guideposts®
Carmel, New York 10512

Copyright © 1991 Marion Bond West for compilation, arrangement, Introduction, and the articles entitled, "The Genuine Birthday Present," "A Touch of Forgiveness," "Learning to Laugh Again," and "Rescue on the Cimarron Turnpike."

All rights reserved.

Material from *Guideposts* magazine and *Daily Guideposts* is used with permission. Copyright © 1972, 1975, 1977, 1979, 1980, 1981, 1982, 1983, 1985, 1986, 1987, 1988, 1989, 1990, 1991 by Guideposts Associates, Inc., Carmel, New York 10512.

Material from *No Turning Back* by Marion Bond West, copyright © 1977 by Broadman Press. Used by permission of author.

Material from *The Nevertheless Principle* (recently reissued under the title, *Overwhelmed*) by Marion Bond West. Published by Chosen Books Publishing Co., Ltd. Copyright © 1986. Used by permission of the author.

Material from *Two of Everything But Me* by Marion Bond West, copyright © 1978 by Broadman Press. Used by permission of the author.

"The Hardest Battle" by Julie West Garmon, copyright © 1991. Used by permission of the writer.

This Guideposts edition published by special arrangement with Servant Publications.

91 92 93 94 95   10 9 8 7 6 5 4 3 2 1

Printed in the United States of America
ISBN 0-89283-740-3

Library of Congress Cataloging-in-Publication Data

West, Marion B.
    Look out fear, here comes faith! : one simple word from God can change your life forever / Marion Bond West.
        p.   cm.
    Includes bibliographical references.
    ISBN 0-89283-740-3
    1. Christian life—1960-   2. West, Marion B.   I. Title.
BV4501.2.W4346   1991
248.8—dc20   91-21848
                                                                          CIP

Also by Marion Bond West

Out of My Bondage
No Turning Back
Two of Everything But Me
Learning to Lean
Overwhelmed (formerly titled
The Nevertheless Principle)

*To Gene—my knight in a white station wagon
who drove all the way from Oklahoma to
Georgia (never having met me) and rescued me
from the loneliness of widowhood by making
me Mrs. Gene Acuff.*

CONTENTS

INTRODUCTION

*E*ver since I wrote my last book, friends have asked me, "When's your next book?" I always feel like responding with the quip, "When's your next baby?" For the two experiences are a great deal alike for me. Both require unbelievable amounts of time and energy. I can't simply put down a manuscript (or a baby) and walk away when I'm tired, hungry, or sleepy. Either can require my constant attention—ten, even twelve hours a day. And sometimes I lie awake at night, dreaming of the book- (or baby-) to-be.

Writing a book is the hardest thing I've ever done, except for being a mother. Writing articles, I can handle. But I had about decided—no more books. Not for a long time, anyway. Recently married and learning to be a minister's wife in my fifties, I didn't have the time or energy to even think about another book.

But after Gene and I married, he became obsessed with the idea of publishing my pieces from *Guideposts* in a book. He talked about it as though production was under way. I listened to him, gazing steadily at his face, mostly concentrating on his dimple rather than the book he so enthusiastically spoke of.

Then one day, I received a phone call telling me that a book publisher was interested in my work from *Guideposts*. When I told Gene, he got that unmistakable, jubilant expression of a man whose wife tells him, "I'm pregnant, dear."

The book Gene had believed for since we'd been married was on its way.

A few months later, a letter came from an editor at Servant.

Since Gene is always interested in prepublication details, I read the letter aloud to him as he made a salad. Suddenly, I came to the words, "For the title of your book, we've decided... " I stopped in the middle of the sentence, my eyes already having seen the title. I couldn't continue. Tears plopped onto the neatly typed letter.

"What is it?" Gene asked, his salad forgotten. He was at my side instantly. I couldn't believe I was crying! I'd about lost the ability to shed tears when my first husband, Jerry, was dying. Only rarely now did I cry and it always surprised me. Gene finished the sentence aloud, " ...we've decided on *Look Out Fear, Here Comes Faith!*"

Gene held me and cried too. That's one of the things I adore about Gene. He cries—and he doesn't run away when he cries or pretend he's taken a cold. We've had some fine times crying together.

When I could speak again, I said, "You know Jerry never did exactly encourage my writing." No one else's wife back then was writing about every detail of her family's life. Most of the women he knew were planning dinner parties, driving carpools, playing tennis, molding ceramics—he never understood why I *had* to write. He tried, he really tried.

But after we knew something was wrong with him in 1982 (we didn't know just how wrong; he had a brain tumor), I wrote a story about how terrified I had been when he underwent all the tests in the hospital. I knew I couldn't live without him. Jerry had really encouraged me with this one story—even helped me with the spelling. One night as we settled down to sleep, I asked him, "What do you think I should call the story?"

If he hadn't answered, it wouldn't have surprised me. Jerry was an engineer and engineers don't spend a lot of time thinking about titles or words. They're logical and unemotional; they think about numbers.

I waited in the darkness, thinking of titles—unable not to think about titles. I adore titles. Then he spoke, "What would you think about... 'Look Out Fear, Here Comes Faith?' I sat up in bed, nearly hysterical, screaming, laughing, bouncing around...

And now, almost a decade later, this unexpected book has been titled by Jerry!

Gene tightened his hold on me. "It's going to be a good book."

Since then, for several ten or twelve-hour days, I've been arranging the material in this book. That has entailed reading stories and devotionals I've written over the past nineteen years.

In rereading them, I've become a busy, often frustrated mother of four young children again. It's been a remarkable experience, since all my children are now grown and I live in a new, spacious house with Gene. There are no little fingerprints, no crumbs or spilled, sticky drinks on the floor. I have leisure time. Energy!

During the time I worked on this book, no one wailed, "Maaaama!" There were no fights to settle. No washing or ironing had to be done. Gene took the phone calls. I didn't have to take anyone to basketball practice or piano lessons.

I sat very still at my desk and recalled that first acceptance letter from *Guideposts*. I'd stood in the front yard in Athens, Georgia and screamed, then cried and spit on the signature to see if a real, live person had signed it. The year was 1972, and I'd had a spiritual experience with a broken dishwasher. How elated I'd been to discover that God cared about the everyday things in life.

Little did I know that that was just the beginning in my new life with Him. It's taken me nearly a lifetime to realize that God doesn't help those who help themselves. He never has. He stands ready to help the helpless. For so many years I had it all wrong. I tried to be strong, to be independent, and to "help myself." That's what the world teaches. Slowly, I began to discover that that's not at all what the Word teaches. Even knowing that powerful truth, I still today have to fight the urge to "do it myself." After all, I have such marvelous ideas!

Oswald Chambers wrote in *My Utmost for His Highest*, "Faith must be tested, because it can be turned into a personal possession only through conflict."

I didn't know that principle during all those years I prayed, "Lord, give me faith." God gave me simple tests at first, even though they seemed overwhelming at the time: unrequited love in high school, frustrations in learning to be a wife and mother, years of rejection slips from publishers, minor surgery, broken friendships, a move to a new town.... Then came the harder ones... the death of a beloved collie, desperately sick children, a ten-month battle against fear and cancer, and finally the departure from this life of my husband of twenty-five years. (And most recently the loss of a grandson.)

I didn't know that the Christian life requires one to be broken. I learned it painfully. I thought I'd die from my first, real agony. And I didn't care much if I did. Mature Christians calmly explained to me that I had simply experienced "brokenness." "It's a requirement," they assured me, all smiles, "for the Christian life." I discovered that there are many experiences of brokenness—not just one. Each one amazingly conforms us to the likeness of Christ—if our response is proper. We are reduced to a state of humility and need, whereby we want Him more than anything in our lives.

So life isn't like my first grade reader, where Mother, Father, Dick, and Jane laughed and played together in golden sunlight, and all their words to one another were of encouragement and love. (Even Spot and Puff were obedient and healthy.) But maybe Mother and Father and Dick and Jane never had the opportunity of having their faith tested and turned into a personal possession through conflict.

This is a hard lesson to learn. But if I had to choose all over again, between the life of conflict and a life without the assurance that faith is my personal possession, I would choose the life of conflict. Whatever you are struggling with today, when you feel so tired and helpless and perplexed that you're ready to give up, remember, God has an answer for you. And it is there that you will find a faith that belongs to you alone.

As I finished compiling and editing the material for this book, I was dead tired—but very happy and excited. I felt as though I'd delivered an unexpected, but very precious, much-wanted child. My love for this "child" is instant, spontaneous, intense.

My prayer is that God will have the freedom to teach you, love you, comfort you, and speak to you in whatever way He chooses through this book. He knows your needs, fears, inadequacies, and struggles. He is absolutely more than able to meet you where you most need Him.

There is a war going on—an old one—every one of us must take part in it whether we want to or not. This war is a very real part of our daily lives. But more than ever in my life, I am now reminded:

"For God has not given us a spirit of fear, but of power and love and of a sound mind" (1 Timothy 1:7).
"And without faith it is impossible to please God..." (Hebrews 11:6).

Yes, even in these times, our battle cry can be: "Look Out Fear, Here Comes Faith!"

Marion Bond West
Watkinsville, Georgia
March, 1991

CHAPTER ONE

THANK YOU, EVEN FOR THE HARD TIMES

THANK YOU, LORD, FOR MY BROKEN DISHWASHER

hen I opened the dishwasher and saw it full of water, my heart sank. We couldn't afford the repair bill, and already I knew it was probably food from a carelessly scraped dish that was stuck in the drain. That such breakdowns could usually be avoided, if I would be more careful, was something I had heard quite often from my husband Jerry. I dreaded telling him.

I was physically tired and nearly in tears. Then I remembered a book I had been reading early that morning before the children were up. I had read that God wants us to thank Him even for the bad things that happen to us. Heaven knows, I often forget to thank Him for the good things. My home, my husband, four children, the love in our home, our church, our faith....

I prayed, "Thank You, Lord, for this broken dishwasher. And thank You that I have a dishwasher and someone to wash dishes for. Thank You for letting me read that book this morning and thank You that I'm not upset by this broken dishwasher. If you want it fixed, Lord, show me how."

I'm so unmechanical I have trouble screwing in a light bulb, so I was astonished at the last part of my prayer.

I reached down in the drain and felt—nothing. I did everything I knew to do; still the machine remained silent and full of water. "Well, Lord, I tried."

Later in the day I noticed a flow of water coming from under the kitchen sink. I opened the cabinet and looked in horror as water poured from a small hole in the pipe. "Thank You, Lord, that the hole isn't so big." I had memories of the kitchen flooding ankle deep instantly when a hose on the washing machine broke. Still I had to do something right away about this present leak. I called my husband but was told he was out.

Suddenly, I remembered what to do. I ran outside to a pipe. Jerry had told me if the kitchen ever flooded again to turn this little handle. I turned and ran back to see if the water was stopping. It was! I had done something mechanical.

I sat on the kitchen floor and pondered the hole. It was suddenly obvious, even to me, that a new pipe had to be put in. We were going out that night and Jerry already had a broken dishwasher to face—no water and a broken sink would be just too much.

A neighbor said she was going out and would bring the piece of pipe so at least Jerry would have it when he came in.

When she gave me the pipe, I held it up to the old pipe to be sure it was the right size. It suddenly occurred to me that I might be able to replace it. The children were amazed and urged me to wait for daddy. I didn't really know what tools to use, but finally got the old pipe off and the new one went on like clockwork. Three dinner knives that had been missing for years were in the trap.

I turned the water back on and to my utter amazement the dishwasher drained. "Oh, thank You, Lord, thank You so much. You worked it out for me. And the hole was so little and came at just the right time."

When Jerry came in, he couldn't believe I had fixed the sink and the dishwasher. The children screamed, "She did, Daddy! Mama was just like a plumber."

I shared with them what had really happened, and that I had said, "Thank You, Lord," when the dishwasher refused to empty.

And I thought, if God cares about a broken dishwasher and I can turn it over to Him, why, I can turn anything over to Him, good or bad.

❦

A MOMENT OF JOY

Sitting in front of a shopping center waiting for a friend the other day, I was feeling impatient and fretful because she was late. The passing parade wasn't helping much. Whining children tugged at their mothers' coats. Some were even screaming. The mothers wore grim expressions that seemed to match my mood.

Then a mother and her child came out of a store, and I shall never forget them. Never. She was the happiest-looking mother I'd ever seen. Her son was wondrously contented. They weren't aware of other people at all.

The young mother was in a wheelchair and held the little boy on her lap. She managed the chair herself. They appeared to be alone. She rolled them out of the store and, once on the sidewalk, she did a little fancy spin. Round and round they went as the little boy laughed out loud. She did, too. I could almost hear the child think, *Look at my mama. Isn't she something!* Then they disappeared into the crowd. When my friend came, I was still smiling, and I uttered a silent prayer: *Father, teach me again that joy never depends on circumstances. Amen.*

CHAPTER TWO

CHILDREN ARE A GIFT FROM GOD

JON'S WINNINGEST GAME

"**M**ama," my ten-year-old son, Jon, called from down in the den. "Do you think we could pray about the game tonight?"

I was surprised. I'm usually the one who suggests to my twin sons that we pray about little things—like ball games.

I put down the tomato I was slicing and went into the den. "Sure, Jon. I'd love to pray with you." I'd already been praying on my own about the game. Jon played shortstop and was good at this position. But tonight he had to pitch. It was only his second time to pitch and his team—the Yankees—were playing some really tough opponents.

We'd just discovered that Jon needed new baseball shoes. My husband had said before he left for work, "Be sure and get Jon new cleats before the game tonight." So as soon as Jon and Jeremy had come in from school, I said, "Let's go get the new cleats, Jon."

In the sporting goods store, Jon remained unusually quiet. After he had tried the shoes on, he asked, "How much are they?" When the clerk told us, he looked quickly at me. I smiled reassuringly. Jon whispered to me, reminding me to ask for the ten-percent discount that was allowed players on local teams. When we got home, he laid the shoes out on his bed with his uniform. Then he told me, "They really feel good, Mama, and they're good looking, too."

Back at home, sitting on the den steps, we got ready to pray. "Why don't we claim some Scripture?" I suggested. Jon understood what I meant. We'd done this before.

"What Scripture?" he asked.

I guess the Scripture about hinds' feet came instantly to my mind, because of Jon's new shoes. I answered, "I love the one in Habakkuk 3:19. It's about hinds' feet."

"What kind of feet?" Jon sounded astonished.

I explained that hinds were deer that had unusual feet and they could walk where other animals or even men couldn't walk. I told Jon, "When I have to do something really hard, something that could scare me, I remember this Scripture and believe that God can give me hinds' feet. That means I can walk in places that would be impossible without God's help. If we ask Him, He'll give you hinds' feet, too."

He grinned and looked down at his feet as I read from the Bible. "'The Lord God is my strength, and He will make my feet like hinds' feet, and He will make me to walk upon mine high places.'"

"The pitcher's mound is a pretty high place," I added, hoping he understood.

"Yeah," he agreed, and we held hands to pray. Jon held mine so tightly that I almost drew it back. After I prayed, Jon prayed, "God, thank You for my new cleats. Help me do good tonight. Help Tim and Billy and the other boys. And... make my feet like... hinds' feet tonight."

From the beginning, the other team looked great, especially their pitcher. Our fielding was way off. There were several doubtful calls from the umpires, and Jon walked quite a few players. Remembering how much the game meant to him, I kept praying, "Lord, give him those hinds' feet."

Even though Jon's team was losing, I'd never been more proud of him. He stood erect, did his best, accepted the bad calls from the umpires. Several times when he pitched to a friend on the other team, he smiled, just as if he were pitching a no-hit game. I could tell from his enthusiasm that he never gave up hope of winning. When people shouted to him, telling him what he was doing wrong, he didn't get angry or frustrated. He kept his mind and heart on the game. I knew when he dropped his head before a pitch that he was praying.

Jon's team lost sixteen to six.

After it was over, he shook hands with the players on the other team and said, "Good game." He didn't complain or blame anyone. He walked away from the field without murmuring. His new cleats were now coated in red dust and I knew his heart was coated in disappointment.

Watching Jon walk toward the car, I thought about the years to come. The new cleats would soon be outgrown. But he had countless other shoes to walk in, through many difficult situations. Soon he'd fill the shoes of a teenager, then a husband, a father.

"Will he remember back to the night that God gave him hinds' feet in baseball cleats?" I wondered. "Will he remember that God can do it in any situation in life?"

I like to think that he will, and someday I hope Jon will tell *his* son about that night the Yankees lost their ball game, and how he pitched wearing new cleats. I hope he'll tell his little boy how God gave him hinds' feet to walk calmly and surely, right through the midst of defeat.

"BEE" YE KIND

I was disturbed several years ago because one of my then seventeen-year-old twin sons and I weren't getting along. Jon meant the world to me, but it seemed all we did was snap at each other.

One morning as he left for school I followed him to the door, nagging about yet another thing. "Just leave me alone," he mumbled. I watched him go down the front steps. He didn't know I was watching. He stopped at our picture window and appeared to be examining the bricks on the window ledge. He hurried to his truck and came back with a towel and placed it on the bricks. *What an odd thing to do*, I thought. I stepped outside and asked sharply, "Jon, what are you doing?"

"Look, Mom," he answered in a voice so soft it startled me. "See, bees can't stand the cold. He's almost dead. He's only a baby... shouldn't have to die." As I watched, Jon gently tucked the towel around the bee.

All morning I checked on the bee. Finally about noon I checked again and the bee was gone. When Jon came in from school we actually had a pleasant conversation about bees.

"You really went out and checked on him?" my son asked, still using his gentle voice.

"Oh, yes," I answered, using an even softer voice.

"A lot of mothers wouldn't have cared about a bee," Jon said.

"Neither would a lot of teenage boys," I said.

We were both smiling.

CHAPTER THREE

WHOEVER SAID
MOTHERHOOD WAS EASY?

"ARE THE COPS COMING, MAMA?"

My twin sons came bursting through the back door. "Mama, Mr. Deal is gonna call the police on us. We hit the ball over in his yard again and, boy, is he mad! And the dog barked at him again and he doesn't like that. Are the cops coming, Mama?"

Mr. Deal had been our neighbor for nine years. There had been other ball incidents during those nine years. Each time I had smiled and always corrected my boys sternly. For nine years my husband had smiled and refused to cross Mr. Deal in any way. We always agreed to whatever he asked, even if we sometimes felt it was unreasonable.

Mr. Deal was retired. His yard was always immaculate. Ours always had six or eight boys playing ball in it, an assortment of dogs and bicycles. His grass was a manicured thing of beauty. Ours often needed cutting. His car shone like polished glass (except for several times when our cat walked across it). We never seemed to get around to washing our car.

I thought about my son's statement. "The dog barked at

him." Our collie knew instinctively that Mr. Deal didn't like her. All of a sudden I felt like barking at Mr. Deal, too. After nine years of smiling, I just couldn't muster up another smile. I didn't even feel like correcting my boys this time, even though I knew I had to.

There was a loud knock on the front door. Before I answered it, I knew it would be our neighbor. When I opened the door he seemed to glare at me, eyes narrowed. "Your boys keep knocking that ball over in my yard. I've asked them over and over to stop. They won't! Why don't they go to the park to play?"

I couldn't believe what happened next. I screamed in an ugly, sarcastic voice, "I'm sorry! I'm very sorry about your precious yard. Everything my boys do upsets you." He responded in an angry voice and I screamed back at him. Never had I done such a thing—screaming at a neighbor! I still couldn't believe it was happening. I'd always been a soft-spoken person, able to control my emotions.

Bam! I slammed the door in his face as hard as I could. Then I stormed back into the kitchen to glare out the window as if that could somehow help my anger. How could I have let this happen? I was a committed Christian, a Sunday-school teacher....

My children were unusually quiet. They'd never seen Mama behave like this. I didn't *allow* temper tantrums at our house. Usually I had an appropriate Scripture for any situation that arose. Now, as I looked out the window at the bright April sun, one came to me. *Don't let the sun go down with you still angry* (Ephesians 4:26). I tried to push that particular Scripture out of my mind. Surely there was another.

I told Jon and Jeremy not to go back over the fence, ever. When my husband Jerry came home from work, I told him what had happened. Gently he said, "It was bound to happen sometime. I'm sorry it had to be you. I wish I'd been home to handle it."

"Me too," I said as we ate in silence. It was then that one of the boys explained that Mr. Deal had just planted his garden and the ball kept going into the garden. Somehow I hadn't realized that. Then I did remember that he'd said something about a garden when he came over. "He's just planted his seeds, Mama," Jeremy explained. I thought grimly: *He didn't want them to get their balls even when he didn't have a garden.* But somehow that rationalization didn't make me feel any better. The anger remained stubbornly in my heart, and it hurt.

After supper, I said, "You all know what I have to do as a Christian." All eyes were on me. "I have to go and apologize." Jerry nodded.

"Are you scared, Mama?" Jeremy asked.

"Why can't *he* apologize?" Jon asked.

"I'm not responsible for anyone's behavior but my own, and the Bible says not to let the sun go down on your anger." As I spoke, rays of the late afternoon sun crept in through the window.

"Can't you forget about it, Mama?" Jon suggested. That was what I wanted to do. Oh, how I wanted to forget it.

"You don't have to do it," my husband said, "but if you go, I'll go along."

Standing at the kitchen sink, clearing away the dishes, I looked out at the sunset. It seemed to be lingering a little longer today—just for me.

"Let's go," I said to Jerry. He nodded, and we went out the front door together. I didn't even change the bedroom shoes I was wearing.

As we rang the Deals' bell no one came to the door. "Guess he's not going to answer," Jerry said. "Let's just wait and see him in the yard sometime."

Relief flooded through me. We started back home. The setting sun was casting long shadows on our lawn, and I knew it was also going down on my anger. "I have to go back." I said. We turned around without saying anything else and headed back for the Deals'. This time my husband knocked rather loudly. We heard Mr. Deal coming to the door. He opened the door quickly and said in what I thought was a gruff voice, "Come in."

We went inside, and he asked us to sit in the den. He explained that they couldn't hear the doorbell. His wife was reading from an old, worn Bible. We all made small talk while I admired their unbelievably orderly, clean home. The apology couldn't seem to get past my throat. Finally I said quickly, "Mr. Deal, I came to apologize for losing my temper. I'm sorry. I want you to forgive me. The boys won't come into your yard or garden again, I promise." Only getting started was hard. The rest felt natural.

Immediately he responded, "I didn't mean to make you mad. I... love your boys. I'd do anything for them. I even want to take them fishing, but I'm afraid something might happen to them. I never had a son, and I... "

Jerry interrupted. "I'll go with you. We can take them together."

Mr. Deal smiled slightly. "I'd like that." Then he looked at me as we got up to leave. "We're neighbors and I want us to get along. I don't intend to be a mean old man. I've worked hard for everything I have, and I... "

"It's all right now," I smiled. My icy anger had vanished completely. He and Jerry shook hands. Mr. Deal and I just stood there looking at each other. Just for an instant, a split second, I saw beneath his harshness. Deep down there was a gentle, but unsure man. To my amazement, I reached over and gave him a big hug. He hugged me back, hard. Then I hugged Mrs. Deal and she too returned my impromptu embrace. There were tears in her eyes. There might have been some in Mr. Deal's, too. I couldn't see very well because my own vision was blurring.

After Jerry and I were outside and headed home, I cried, making sobbing sounds like a child. My husband put his arm around me and gave me his handkerchief. He didn't ask why I was crying and I was grateful for that. I wasn't sure myself. I think it had something to do with the darkness of the night. The sun had gone down and the stars were coming out. But the sun had not gone down on my anger.

God had somehow replaced my brittle anger with His marvelous love. I wasn't sure exactly how He did it, but it appeared certain that the miracle had to do with two very small words: I'm sorry. Hugs help a lot, too.

꡴

ACCIDENTS HAPPEN

*P*erhaps my greatest moment as a mother centers around a bucket of antique-white paint. My fourteen-year-old son decided to paint his room. He bought the paint himself and assembled all the needed materials. I had told him earlier that I would help him the next day. But Jeremy is like me. Impatient. Once an idea takes hold of him, he must take action.

Just as I reached the top of the stairs with an armful of laundry, I saw him. The open bucket of paint was turning upside down, seemingly in slow motion. For a brief instant our eyes met in horror. Then the paint flew everywhere—over my son, the hall carpet, the wallpaper. The only place it missed was the wall of Jeremy's room.

I didn't speak. I couldn't seem to form any words. I ran for wet towels. Jeremy did too. We started mopping up paint and flooding the carpet with water. Fortunately it was water-based paint.

Jeremy's eyes met mine frequently. At first his expression seemed to be: *Can you possibly consider forgiving me?* Then: *Is there a chance that just this once you are going to understand that this was a horrible accident?* And as we got the last of the paint up, our eyes met once again and his clearly said: *You are the most wonderful mother in the world. I'll never forget this!*

I felt so good about having held my tongue and my temper. How I wish I had known how to react over spills when I was a younger mother.

꡴

A RAINY DAY PRAYER

*D*ear Lord,

I heard the rain beating on the roof even before
I opened my
Eyes this morning.
It's the fourth day this week it's rained.
Lord, I'm so tired of rain and of trying to entertain my
Children.
I'm tired of wiping their little noses and reading stories,
I'm tired of making jelly and peanut butter sandwiches...
And of eating them.
I'm tired of mopping up spilled milk.
I'm so tired of answering questions
And picking up toys
And looking at the clock
And listening to the rain.
I don't want to get up and do it all over again today, Lord.
I'm not sure I can.
I want to go somewhere with my friends
Under a blue sky
And talk about adult things
Maybe eat lunch out
And window-shop.
But I can't.
I must stay here inside and listen to the rain and care
For my children.
They're tired of rain too, Lord... and I guess of me.
Please dear Lord, come in
And be our sunshine today.

CHAPTER FOUR

HAND IN HAND

"Please Hold My Hand"

"Mother, ask them to let you come to the operating room with me and hold my hand. That's all I need... just till I go to sleep."

"I don't think they'll let me, Julie," I said sadly. "Rules are rules."

I knew, from the two previous minor surgeries Julie had experienced during the past several years, that she would put on a brave front, smile and go to surgery without any complaints. But down in the operating room, as she waited to be put to sleep (there was always the wait), she'd shake. Not tremble mildly, but shake so violently that she'd be sore from the shaking.

This operation to remove wisdom teeth was not serious, but Julie had a horror of this trembling that was beyond her control. "Mother, I dread the shaking more than the surgery or the pain. I'm eighteen-years-old, engaged to be married, and I shake so hard I rattle the bars on the bed. I'm shaking already!" And she was.

"I have an idea," I told her. From my purse I pulled out a small card. The day before, when I'd been searching through my desk drawer for a stamp, the smiling face of a little girl on the card had seemed to look up right at me. She had red hair like Julie and was saying, "Hi, I just wanted to tell you that... " The rest of her message had been on the inside of the greeting card. I cut off the printed message and added my own so that the adorable little girl seemed to be whispering, "I need someone to hold my hand while I'm waiting to be put to sleep. I won't shake if you'll hold my hand. Thanks. Julie."

I read the note to her and added, "If you'll let me, I'll tape this note to your sheet. Someone in the operating room will see it. I even remembered tape."

"They'll think I'm a baby," Julie said softly.

Just then an attendant came to take Julie to surgery. I helped her tuck Julie's long hair under the small green cap, and watched forlornly as she was placed on the wheeled cart. At the door I read Julie's lips, "I love you." I kissed her on the forehead and waved good-bye.

Twenty-five minutes later the doctor phoned me to say that Julie was in recovery and would be back in the room in a short while. He said surgery had gone beautifully.

When they brought Julie back, her eyes were open and she was smiling as best she could with the gauze pads sticking out of her mouth and the ice pack tied around her head. She winked and made an "okay sign" by putting her thumb and forefinger together in a circle.

Then she began waving her hand around to get my attention. She couldn't talk and wanted to write. I handed her a pad and a pen. Still groggy, she scribbled, "I have to see the nice black lady who came to get me. She kept me from shaking. Even wrapped me in warm sheets. Please find her."

When I promised I would, Julie immediately went to sleep.

Later in the day, I asked one of the aides if the woman from the operating room could stop by Julie's room.

"Oh, that's Ernestine. I'll ask her to stop by."

Ernestine came in flashing a warm smile. I showed her the note from Julie. Even with the gauze pads in her mouth, Julie managed to say, "Thank you." Ernestine brushed off my attempts at gratitude and talked instead about Julie's pretty red hair.

When the doctor came by that evening, he asked right away, "Did you put that note on Julie?"

Not sure of what he was going to say, I admitted that I had.

His stern face broke into an enormous grin. "Well, that was about the neatest thing we've seen in the operating room. We want to help people. Often we just don't know what their fear is. Ernestine stayed right with Julie. I wish more people would tell us about their fear, so we'd know how to help them. Thanks for the note."

After the doctor left I sat down and looked out the window. I could see people moving in the busy street below, some walking, going into shops, riding in cars. I wondered how many of those people harbored unspoken fears. And pondered how much better it would be for all of us to admit our weaknesses, ask for help, confess when we're afraid.

Watching Julie sleep, my heart was filled with gratitude. She'd had the courage to admit to strangers her desperate need... *please hold my hand*... and the Lord had provided Ernestine.

THE JOY OF HOLDING HANDS

I missed my family when I remarried and moved to Oklahoma. It was always a joy to return to Georgia, which my husband and I did often. One day, while back in Georgia, my daughter Julie asked me to pick up her four-year-old Katie at kindergarten. Sitting in the long line of cars waiting for my turn to drive by the school door, I recalled the countless times I had done the same thing for my four children.

Katie bounded out to the car, delighted to see me, and we drove off. I had to stop by the drugstore, and as Katie and I got out of the car, she immediately put her hand into mine. She seemed to do it without thinking or making a big deal of it. I'd forgotten what a wondrous thing it is to have a small, trusting hand thrust into your own. As we left the drugstore, once again her hand found mine. No words. Not even a glance. Just her hand securely nestled in mine.

Driving home I thought about the incident. *Why, God must feel exactly as I had!* What joy he must experience when with complete trust and without fanfare we simply slip our hand into His and walk alongside Him quietly and with absolute faith. It's a joy I want to extend this very day.

CHAPTER FIVE

GIVING FROM THE HEART

YES, MY JULIE

My friend Carolyn stood in my kitchen looking tense and ill-at-ease. "Marion," she said, "there's something I have to tell you, and I might as well not beat around the bush."

I stared at her. A hint of what I thought she was about to say had already touched my pounding heart. My mouth became strangely dry.

She continued in a soft, gentle voice. "Do you know that Ricky is giving Julie a ring for Christmas... an engagement ring?"

Ricky was her eighteen-year-old son. Julie, our seventeen-year-old daughter.

"No," I said, trying to appear calm while my heart hammered loudly and I felt sick to my stomach.

"I didn't think you suspected. I went with Ricky to pick it out. Julie doesn't know she's getting it. She can't seem to... talk to you about... their plans. I just had to come and tell you. It wasn't easy."

"Thank you for coming, Carolyn." *Hold yourself together. See her to the door. Smile.* I walked to the door with Carolyn, but the smile wouldn't come. My heart felt like the meat hammer was tearing away at it. As I watched her driving off, a silent scream was within me. *No, my Julie! Engaged at seventeen... married at eighteen. No!*

I couldn't give her up. Not yet. Ricky was a perfect choice for Julie. I loved him. They'd been sweethearts since she was fourteen, he fifteen. But, surely they were too young for marriage.

We'd assumed Julie would go to college for four years and have a career before marriage. She was an A student. I quickly thought back to a recent conversation that Julie and I had as we were looking at college brochures. Panic had seemed to fill her usually happy face, and her voice trembled, "Mother, I just want one thing... to be a Christian wife and mother. I don't want a career. I want to stay home and bake cookies and play with my children and cook for my husband. That's all I want."

"That will come," I had said, laughing, and handed her another college brochure. "Look at this one. Pretty nice, huh? And this is where they're offering you a partial scholarship."

She looked at it politely. It seemed tears brimmed her eyes for a moment, but I thought maybe it was my imagination. I rattled on about college life. Julie had never done one thing to displease us.

Funny I should remember that now. As I prepared supper, I knew I had to tell my husband Jerry about the ring. Christmas was only three days away. The house was filled with the smells, sounds and excitement of the holiday. I moved about in the midst of the festivity like a robot, feeling nothing except a deep, hollow ache. One sentence stayed in my mind. *No, my Julie.*

After supper, Jerry and I were alone for a moment and I told him. He remained quiet as I spoke. Then a look crossed his face. He seemed to stare beyond me. He seemed to struggle inwardly before he nodded his head. I knew what the nod indicated. He hurt too, but we would give Julie and Ricky our blessings. I knew Jerry approved of Ricky. We just felt they were too young, and I knew how much Julie's going to college meant to Jerry.

Knowing we were going to say yes verbally still presented a problem for me. I had to say yes within my heart.

Christmas Eve Julie and Ricky stood in the kitchen waiting for us to come see her ring and give our approval. I noticed they were standing in the exact spot they'd stood in when she first brought him over for me to meet. I think I knew then they would be married someday. But it shouldn't be someday... not yet.

Julie held out her hand and we all gathered around. There it was. A lovely diamond on her finger. Tears blurred my vision and I saw instead a little hand making mud pies, tiny fingers cutting out paper dolls, a small hand reaching for mine as we crossed the street....

I blinked the tears away and said, "It's beautiful." Then we all hugged one another. They wanted to be married in a year, on December 9. Julie wanted to attend a local junior college for a year studying to be a medical office assistant. She would continue working for two doctors at a veterinary clinic. It would be a tough twelve-hour-a-day schedule. Ricky's schedule would be difficult too. He was already attending the college Julie planned to enroll in. He worked with his father, too.

As they left to spend part of Christmas Eve with Ricky's family, I watched them drive away. I determined to let go of Julie and make wedding plans happily. I could do it if I really made up my mind.

And so for months I smiled and said all the right things. Julie and I began making wedding plans. I stayed very busy. I'm going to be fine, I told myself... grimly. And then one Sunday as I sat in the kitchen all ready for church, I felt tears and hurt rising up inside me. I couldn't stop the pain or the tears. In front of my family I began to cry, making terrible noises in my throat. I was humiliated before them. I couldn't believe it was happening. One by one they moved to another part of the house. The thought *No, my Julie* plowed through my mind. I knew; I couldn't let go of her in my heart. *Oh, God, I can't do it. I'm helpless. Please help me. Let me know, somehow, that You see me, hear me, will help me.*

Right then I felt a small, sturdy hand patting my back.

Someone had come to give me comfort. I looked into the face of Jon, one of our ten-year-old twins. "You're going to be all right, Mama. You'll see. You're gonna stop crying too." Never mind that his face was dirty and his sneakers untied. I leaned on him and listened to his simple words. I knew they were more than words from a child. Somehow God was speaking to me, giving healing.

My tears, even the unshed ones, dried up. The ache began to vanish. Jon turned and walked away. What had happened? Things were different now!

Helplessness. All I'd done was to admit I was helpless. I couldn't do it on my own, and God had responded quickly and powerfully. Now there was something I longed to say to myself and to God. The time would come when I could say it to Julie. I whispered sitting alone in the kitchen. "Yes, my Julie." It felt good. I said it again.

The rest of the year passed with incredible speed. All the wedding plans were complete. Julie's wedding date, December 9, 1978, dawned cloudy. A drizzle fell. Julie came into my room early that morning in her old pink robe with the torn pocket. Her hair was in large pink curlers. "How soon do you think the rain will stop?" she asked, looking out the window.

"In time. We won't worry."

"Okay," she smiled.

I felt happy. Then I remembered the terrible stories I'd heard about mothers of the bride who had fallen apart on the day of the wedding. A pesky silent voice gave me more negative thoughts. *Now you'll fall apart. Julie's leaving for good. She's only eighteen. Don't you feel a little like crying?*

"Father, I can't handle these thoughts. I know they aren't from You." It seemed right then that Scriptures meant just for me came into my mind. I spoke them softly. "The Bible says not to be anxious about anything, but to pray about everything. Marriage is of God. The Holy Spirit will never leave me comfortless." I was feeling better with each word I spoke. For good measure I added, "I can do all things through Christ.... "

29

The enemy fled. My joy was back.

A while later Julie came back into my room and said, "Hey, Mama, it's stopped raining." She had on her wedding dress. Jennifer, her sixteen-year-old sister and maid of honor joined us. She was dressed, too. As we looked out the window at the sun, I remembered that only a few years ago they used to play wedding, dressing up in old curtains and pulling flowers from the yard. We weren't playing today. This was for real. And I was happy.

At a few minutes after two in the afternoon, Julie and Jerry stood in the doorway of our church as the music swelled. Julie's happy face seemed to light up the aisle as they started down it. When they passed by me, they stopped. *What's happening? Maybe Jerry's not going to give her away. They didn't do this at rehearsal.* Then I understood. Julie leaned over and kissed me. Her veil fell across her face and mine too, so that for a moment we were both inside it. "I love you. Thank you," she whispered, handing me a white rosebud. I took the rose and held Julie for a precious moment. Then I let go of her for a lifetime. As I released her, I said without reservation and with utter joy, "Yes, my Julie!"

Watching Julie become Ricky's wife, I remembered her words, "All I want is to be a Christian wife and mother." *All? All!* That was everything. I thought of the plaque they'd hung on the wall in their future home that said that Christ was the head of their house. I couldn't stop smiling. My joy overflowed. I knew that God had met my desperate need because of my helplessness. Surely, He knows all about letting go of children. He gave up His only Son with love and joy.

A JOYFUL GIVER

My mother recently shared a story with me about my grandmother. One day when my mother was a little girl in Elberton, Georgia, she walked down the dusty road that led to her home. A horse and buggy rumbled by and stopped. A lady asked, "Little girl, we've come for a picnic but forgot to bring something to spread our lunch on. Would you ask your mother if she has any newspaper we can borrow?"

My mother ran to the house while the lady waited. "Mama," she called, "there's a lady down the road. They're having a picnic and she forgot to bring something to spread their lunch on. She wants to know if you have any newspaper she can borrow."

My grandmother nodded, wiping her hands on a worn apron and going to a drawer. Carefully she pulled out her freshly starched and ironed linen tablecloth—her only tablecloth. "We don't have any newspaper, dear, but this will do nicely," my grandmother said, smiling.

When I think of that story now, I smile at my grandmother's grand gesture. How extravagant it was, lending her treasured tablecloth to a stranger—and for a picnic! But, of course, Jesus talked about grand gestures of giving: going the extra mile, giving up your cloak, turning the other cheek. It reminds me that when I give, I shouldn't just give the sweater I'm tired of, the money that's left over at month's end, the time that would be free anyway. Those things are worthy, but sometimes I should do what Grandma did; Give from the heart—freely and extravagantly!

CHAPTER SIX

FOR ANIMAL LOVERS ONLY

My Friend Mollie

$\mathcal{T}$he instant my husband walked toward me I knew something was terribly wrong. I'd been away all day at a seminar. It was now late afternoon.

"Mollie's hurt bad," Jerry said simply and quickly. I think I let out a low moan. Then I began asking questions. Early in the morning, just after I left, our beloved four-year-old collie had been hit by a car and seriously hurt.

In my mind I saw it happening. I didn't want to watch, but I couldn't stop the vivid pictures. Jerry had stayed home from work on a Friday to catch up on yard work and be with our thirteen-year-old twin sons while I was at the meeting. Thoughts of *if only I hadn't gone* began. I tried to force them away.

Mollie hurt. I couldn't yet believe it. Memories of the first time I saw her eased into my racing mind. It was sweet relief from the horrible pictures of her darting out in front of the car.

After our seventeen-year-old mutt, Muff, had to be put to sleep with disorders of old age, we didn't talk about dogs much, even though we are dog people. Then one fall, I mentioned to Jerry in a casual way that I'd been thinking about getting another dog. A collie. I suggested it almost hesitantly, knowing what loving another dog would involve. I almost hoped he'd say no. He beamed, "I've been thinking the same thing. A collie for Christmas." We searched the want ads that day and then drove out to see some collie pups. There were four left. Jerry picked up the best looking one. While he held it, a smaller and more timid puppy came up to him and laid her head on his foot. She didn't make a sound. He put down the frisky pup and picked up the shy one. She laid her head on his shoulder, glancing once at him briefly. "The other dog is finer," my husband announced weakly.

"I know," I stroked the long-nosed puppy, "but he's not for us, is he? This one is." When we learned the puppy's mother had Love as her middle name, we named our choice "For the Love of Mollie." The people we bought her from kept her until Christmas Eve so she could be a surprise for Jon and Jeremy and our teenage girls, Julie and Jennifer.

When I saw Mollie again it was Christmas Eve and Jerry was bringing her into the kitchen with a big bow around her neck. She seemed afraid and unsure of our love and acceptance, but uncomplaining—hopeful. I was afraid and unsure too that night. Our seventeen-year-old daughter Julie had just become engaged. I knew I had to give her up. Perhaps that's why I clung to Mollie with such deep needs. From the beginning I loved the dog far too much. Eventually our entire family did.

She grew into a majestic beauty, but even more beautiful was her spirit. Content in our large backyard, her world, she never wanted to venture out without permission. She fancied herself a guardian to those she loved. Often she tried to impress us and make us believe she'd chased off some terrible enemy. She barked at airplanes and turned around joyfully for our approval when she saw that she had "driven" the planes away. We always praised her. After a bath, she would run like a race dog around and around the yard, then tumble into one of us. During the hot Georgia summers, one of the boys filled up our yellow wheelbarrow with water, and Mollie immediately hopped in and dunked her head. She could hold her breath for a long time and would look up at us from beneath the water with a comical expression on her face.

Gentle beyond all comprehension, she romped with our cats and chased them, only to let them escape. One of her favorite sleeping spots was the back steps. When I opened the door to allow the cats to come in or out, they simply walked over Mollie as though she were a huge sable-and-white doormat. She would raise her head and look with approval. If one of the cats wanted in on cold nights, Mollie learned to throw herself against the door and open it, allowing the cat to enter. But she would not come in herself until someone said, "Okay." Then she would bound in and down into the den as though it had been months since she'd seen us. Before she went back out she usually ate the cats' food while the cats watched, seeming almost to approve.

We often took her on family walks through the woods. How she loved it, charging ahead of us, then circling back to check on us. I suppose my favorite times with her were early in the morning. I would go outside before seven and sit on the back step in my nightgown. She would come up and lay her head in my lap the way she did the first time she saw Jerry. The world smelled wonderful and new and moist. I would tell her, "I love you, Mollie Sunshine." She would look right into my eyes and wag her magnificent tail. I know she understood. And her love was always totally unconditional and never changing.

She had no fear of cars. She assumed that everything that moved loved her as we did. Her only fears seemed to be thunder and the garbage man. She barked at him each week, looking over her shoulder at me as if telling me that she would protect us.

It had happened so suddenly. Jerry had been cutting the front grass and had let her out to walk alongside him. He took his eyes off her for an instant, and she darted into the street. She'd done it before, but there was so little traffic on our street. This time, she picked the wrong minute to investigate something on the other side of the road. We were critical of people who let their animals roam. We rescued stray dogs from the highway. How could this have happened to our Mollie, right in front of our house?

My husband said she didn't cry out or struggle as he ran to

her. She appeared relaxed, almost apologetic as he took her to the vet, five minutes away. X-rays revealed a badly fractured hip and pelvis and a broken tail. Her tail would have to be removed during surgery. It was broken where it joined her body.

"Well, why aren't they operating now?" I questioned.

"We have to wait until Monday to see if her bowels and bladder are working. The vet said he has to know that before surgery can be done. He has an orthopedic vet ready to do the surgery Monday morning."

"When can I see her?"

"Tomorrow. They're closed now."

Thoughts of Mollie alone at the clinic tormented me. I phoned around until I located the vet and asked him countless questions. I didn't really listen to his answers. I wanted him to assure me she would be fine. He didn't. He told me that I could see her early in the morning. I didn't sleep well. I prayed that Mollie was sleeping comfortably in her cage. When I slept, I dreamed she was running through our backyard again—without her tail—but nevertheless running, barking at planes, guarding us.

The next morning we waited for the clinic to open. Suddenly the vet was bringing Mollie to us. She looked alert. The vet brought her outside to see if she'd go to the bathroom in the grass. Jerry and I fell to our knees and put our arms around her. We talked to her and asked her questions. I suppose vets get used to people like us. She sat erect, looking almost normal. She watched a plane overhead, but did not bark. "I love you, Mollie Sunshine," I whispered.

The vet assured us, "She's not in pain. I've never seen a dog so broken up in so little discomfort."

"Well, we have been praying and asking God not to let her hurt."

The vet nodded. "That's it then. Try to keep her moving," he said over his shoulder as he went back inside to the busy clinic. For over two hours we hoped Mollie would go to the bathroom.

Nothing happened. Finally the vet suggested we take her home for the weekend. Perhaps at home she would relieve herself in her own backyard.

At home Jerry took her to her beloved backyard—her world. He laid her in a favorite spot—under a large oak tree. The cats, Joshua and Jessica, came over to rub against her. She gobbled up everything I gave her to eat. I didn't bother with dog food. She got steak, hamburger, roast beef. As it became hotter and the gnats and flies bothered her, we brought her into the cool den by the fireplace, another of her favorite spots. She looked perfectly normal lying there, as though she might bound up the steps any minute.

Surely by tomorrow she would relieve herself and we could go ahead with plans for the surgery. It was going to be an expensive operation. We decided to cancel our upcoming vacation in order to have the money for the surgery and then to be at home with Mollie and take care of her.

By Saturday night she still hadn't gone to the bathroom. She would lick her paws and groom herself after eating. She couldn't reach her hind part, so it began to look a bit rumpled. I would brush it, and she would appear in good shape again. Our married daughter, Julie, came by to see her. Julie had worked for the vet who was treating Mollie. Mollie lifted her head high as she recognized Julie bending over her. Since she couldn't wag her tail, she sort of gave Julie a smile. Julie knelt for a long time and didn't say anything. "Looks good, doesn't she?" I asked hopefully.

Still looking at Mollie, Julie answered softly. "No, Mama. She's putting on a brave, wonderful front for you. See how tired her eyes are. It will be highly unusual if she comes through this. I've seen this type of injury before." Julie got up and walked upstairs without looking back. After Julie and her husband left, I went back into the den. Mollie put her head in my lap. She sighed and looked deep into my eyes. She wasn't smiling. My tears came suddenly and unexpectedly, and deep agony exploded inside me like a volcano. My tears spilled onto Mollie's face so that she blinked her eyes. Jerry came and sat by me. We didn't say anything. We just held Mollie and made terrible noises crying.

Sunday morning we got up and went immediately to the den. Mollie was unmoved, like a statue. I decided that I simply could not leave her and go to church that morning. The rest of the family stayed home too.

On Monday morning, Jerry gathered Mollie in his arms and put her back under the oak tree. She looked perfectly content. A plane flew overhead, and she looked up. One of the cats came over and lay by her in the grass. I began to pray that Mollie would give up. I couldn't watch her try so hard anymore. Jerry came in, and we stood at the kitchen window. "Why won't she give up? Lay her head down and stop that ridiculous smiling?" I said. "What in the world does she have to smile about?"

We were running out of time. I phoned the vet and told him we were bringing Mollie in. I drove, and Jerry got in the back seat, holding Mollie. She laid her head back on his shoulder like a child, and I wondered if Jerry might be remembering the first time he brought her home on Christmas Eve. Looking at passing cars as I drove, I saw that none of them contained dogs. Suddenly I envied people who didn't allow themselves to love a dog in such a ridiculous fashion. Why were we dog people anyway? Why couldn't we love rocks or butterflies?

In a few moments we were in the familiar examination room. Mollie was on the sterile, steel table, which she didn't like. The vet came in and said, "Hey, Mollie." He examined her, and then in a direct manner for which I will always be grateful, he said, "She has absolutely no control over her bladder or bowels. They are totally destroyed. If we operate, you will have to give her an enema daily and she will have chronic kidney infections and endless pain. She will require constant attention. You really have no choice."

I heard myself say, "No!"

The vet said quietly to Jerry, "You will need to sign some papers."

I heard my husband say, "Of course." I was grateful for his courage and quick action. They left the room, and Mollie and I were alone, my hand on her. She was half sitting up, looking directly into my eyes. All my emotions seemed frozen. I knew they would thaw out at home, but I was grateful that for now I stood like a mannequin. No feelings. No movement. No thoughts. No words. When the vet came back in the room, I moved toward the door to leave. *Don't look back*, I told myself. *Don't you dare look back.*

I looked back. Mollie and I stared at each other. I knew she wanted to wag her tail because that impossible smile crossed her face. Not understanding how it was possible, I walked mechanically out of the room.

At home, Jerry and I still had Mollie's fur clinging to us. We brushed ourselves off. The clothes didn't matter. It was our hearts and spirits that needed help.

Jerry changed into office clothes, kissed me and left for work. I didn't manage my usual "Have a good day." In my heart I just wanted him to get through it. The children were off playing, our daughter at work. They had taken it much better than Jerry or I. I was almost angry with them for being able to handle it, when I couldn't.

I was alone, standing at the kitchen window, wanting to look out into the backyard, but afraid to. *This is ridiculous. I can't be afraid of my own backyard. I have to live here.* But I knew I was afraid. I couldn't make myself walk out into a yard without Mollie. I flung myself on the sofa in the den and stared at the ceiling. My emotions were alive again. I cried out, calling Mollie's name over and over. *I'm some kind of a nut*, I thought as I sobbed. I couldn't get myself together. I had to have some kind of relief. The grief that held me in a vise seemed to be cutting off my breath, as though I were being held under water.

Then I remembered in Psalms (34:18) it said that the Lord is close to the brokenhearted. "God," I called out, as though He were up in the kitchen, "please come to me. It doesn't matter that it's just a dog. My heart is broken. You promised to be close to me. You promised! Please come and start a healing process in me. I need You."

Almost instantly my grief shifted into another gear. A lower one. I felt it. I wasn't panicky anymore. My crying stopped as if a dam had been shut down by the engineer. I got up off the sofa and brushed my hair back out of my face. I walked toward the door. I stepped outside. "Thank You, God."

The yard was still and quiet and very, very empty. I walked over to Mollie's house and shut the door. I picked up her dish, ball, and old sock and took them to the shed. I emptied the water out of the wheelbarrow and put it away.

It was a strange experience walking through the yard alone. Mollie had always escorted me... to the garden, clothesline, birdbath... wherever. But now I walked slowly and victoriously over every inch of the yard. I felt as if I had been helped to win a great battle. Healing surely had begun in my broken heart.

Of course I still miss Mollie, but I am now able to recall the four years of happiness and intense love she brought to us. And I will always hold fast to the tremendous truth that I learned through losing her. God longs to be close to the brokenhearted. But He waits for us to cry out to Him. Then, regardless of what caused the pain, He responds to our deepest, most desperate needs.

℘

CALEB

"Absolutely no! Not now, not next year, never," I told Jeremy, one of our thirteen-year-old twins. Since we'd been forced to have our magnificent collie put to sleep after she was hit by a car and badly injured nine months ago, I had refused even to discuss another dog. With God's help I had made it through the pain of Mollie's death, but I was determined never to suffer that way again.

No more dogs for me. I no longer watched the side of the road for strays to rescue, or petted dogs that wandered through our yard. Even though the rest of the family—my husband Jerry, our boys Jon and Jeremy, and our nineteen-year-old daughter Jennifer—desperately wanted another dog, I held out stubbornly. They might be able to love again, but *I* was not.

Sometimes, though, I found my eyes wandering to the want ads, just "checking" to see if there were "Collies for Sale." For a few seconds I allowed myself to think about having a dog again—but I quickly pushed the idea aside. I would have nothing to do with dogs—ever.

But as hard as I fought it, something was stirring inside me. Almost daily I envisioned a beautiful collie out back—running, jumping, sleeping, even looking in the window at me, its tail wagging. For almost nine months this went on—and it became a joyful habit. When it snowed unexpectedly one day, in my mind a collie pranced in our white backyard. Often when I'd drive into the carport, I'd envision the collie there greeting me. After supper, when there were scraps left over, I mentally gave them to a dog with a long nose and soft brown eyes.

One warm, sunny winter day, my husband went out to the spot where he liked to stretch out on the dry, soft grass. Jerry looked so alone out there without Mollie—she had always followed and sprawled on top of him. In an instant, in my mind, I saw a collie appear—and pounce.

I suppose I missed Mollie most of all early in the morning. That had been our special time together. I'd open the back door just after the sun was up, and she'd be there in a flash, tail wagging. I would sit on the step and she'd put her head in my lap. I'd stroke her long nose and say, "I love you, Mollie Sunshine." Every morning in my mind she was there, waiting to start our day together.

By now I wasn't certain if I was remembering Mollie or imagining a new dog. It didn't seem to matter. The images were comforting, and I could handle a collie who just lived in my mind.

Early one morning, just before time for the school bus, I heard Jon and Jeremy shouting excitedly in front of the house. Holding my robe tightly around me, I hurried out the door and down the steps onto our front lawn. I stopped. There, to my astonishment, stood the collie of my imagination. It could have been Mollie, or Mollie's twin—just standing there wagging its tail!

We all seemed to freeze. The boys didn't move or speak. The dog stood perfectly still, too—even its tail was motionless. I think I might have stopped breathing for a few seconds.

The dog didn't have a collar. The fur underneath its stomach was crusted with mud. He was much too thin and appeared exhausted. But this dog wasn't just an image in my mind; he was *real*!

I dropped to my knees, flung my arms around the collie, and buried my face in its thick fur. Suddenly, something gave way inside of me, and in that instant I knew that the love I'd felt for Mollie wasn't meant to be locked up inside, but meant to flow outward and onward, no matter what happened.

The dog licked my face over and over and put out a paw for shaking. My mind was asking, *Where did you come from? How did you get here?* But my heart was pounding, *Welcome, welcome!*

"Will you feed him, Mama?" Jon asked.

"Of course," I said. "There's the bus, you'd better hurry."

The dog followed me into the backyard almost as though things were familiar to him. He ran around and around in a circle right in Mollie's old tracks. He checked out the doghouse and drank from Mollie's water pan, which we still kept full for the cat.

Can this be? I thought. This dog was doing everything that the dog of my imagination had done. I even had the funny feeling that maybe *he'd* been somewhere imagining a big yard to play in and a family to adore him.

I fed the hungry visitor almost everything in the house.

Finally, he lay down under the oak tree and slept. Back in the kitchen, I stood and watched him. He was there, he was really *there.*

When our cat, Joshua, ventured out back, the two appeared to be old friends. *Joshua and Caleb,* I thought to myself, remembering what good friends the biblical Joshua and Caleb had been. From then on I called the stray collie "Caleb."

Of course, I knew we had to try to find the owner. But I had this delicious premonition that there wasn't one to find. I called all the vets in the area and waited to see if they had any record of a missing collie. Each time the answer came back over the phone, I breathed a sigh of relief and a prayer of gratitude. I checked with the Humane Society and the pound, leaving my name and number at each location. Then I ran an ad in the paper for a week. The days passed and no one called to claim our Caleb.

I have no reasonable explanation as to where the collie came from or how he got to our house. But somehow I'll always believe that "seeing" a collie daily in our yard for so long, when none was there, had something powerful to do with Caleb's finding us.

Caleb's arrival has taught me that often the very thing you try to avoid the most is the exact thing you need the most. Even though I didn't consciously pray for another collie, I believe God knew the desire of my heart and what I really needed, even before I asked. And if someday Caleb too is taken from us, I know that God will once again be there to help me through the pain and grief, and prepare the way for new happiness.

Now Caleb and I start each day together. Early in the morning I slip out the back door and Caleb is waiting, just as Mollie used to be. I sit on the steps and he moves as close as he can and puts his head in my lap. We sit there in the sun together, and I rub his long, soft nose and say, "I love you, Caleb."

What a relief it is to let love flow freely again, and to know with a certainty that—just as it says in Psalm 30:5—weeping often endures for a night, but joy comes in the morning!

℃

TRUSTING

*L*iving in the country is a new adventure for me. One evening, I noticed a small, black fur ball moving through our yard. I approached cautiously. It was a tiny baby skunk! Then I spotted another, and still another. In all, six baby skunks, that somehow had been orphaned, greeted me.

I brought out a can of fish-flavored cat food and the visitors quickly gathered around. I discovered that they lived under our house in a deep, dark hole. A vet instructed he how to move their food out farther from the house each time I fed them, until they discovered the woods—and freedom.

I always marveled at their trust as they waddled and tumbled out of their dark hole, one by one. Spooning out cat food, I remembered a deep, dark hole of self-pity I'd found myself in after I'd become a widow. Although four years had gone by, I mostly kept to myself. One night, feeling so alone, I poked my head out of my hole and called some friends. Almost trembling, I asked if I could join them. I was so surprised when they all exclaimed, "Yes, yes! We'll come and get you. We love you!" Tears of gratitude had prevented me from saying anything except, "Bye."

Maybe you've been "hiding" for your own reasons and are ready to come out. Take a deep breath, and with a prayer and God's courage, take that first step. Call a friend who's been patiently waiting; send in the application for that new job; volunteer to lead a church group. Start trusting God.

CHAPTER SEVEN

ON BEING THE MOTHER OF TWINS

TWINS, BUT OH HOW DIFFERENT

My friend Ann and I sat at my kitchen table drinking coffee, engaged in our favorite topic of conversation—spiritual matters. Ann and I often shared with each other what went on at our worship services. It was clear from our discussion that Ann was more open to different styles of worship than I.

I complained, "But, Ann, some people in our church just seem too quiet and withdrawn to be really worshiping. Why, they don't even join in singing the hymns. They just look down at their feet. Others never smile. And one woman who sits near me takes notes all the time!"

Patient Ann smiled. "It's different for different people, Marion. God created us to worship Him in many ways. How we worship is in keeping with our personalities. Some people are naturally outgoing, exuberant, even loud. Others... quiet. It doesn't matter; God understands." She knew I didn't agree, but she finished her coffee, gave me a hug and was gone.

As I put our cups in the sink I kept up my side of the argument: *I don't think she's right, Lord. People should be openly enthusiastic about You. But if she's right, and I'm wrong, I wish You'd show me somehow.*

I was grateful for Ann's unexpected visit. This Saturday was going to be long and lonely. My husband Jerry, usually at home on weekends, would be gone all day because of a strike at the place where he worked. Jerry wasn't a member of the union work force; that meant he had to work fourteen hours a day, plus Saturday. As a result, a kind of gloom had settled over our house. We *needed* Jerry.

Jon and Jeremy, our thirteen-year-old twin sons, missed their father as much as I did. Saturday had always been a special day for them with their daddy. Jerry would do chores with them, or take them with him on errands, or maybe go fishing. They always stuck close to him, talking all the time.

Somehow the day dragged by. The boys cut the grass without their father. Jon even got out the new hedge-trimmer and trimmed the hedge. Jeremy picked the ripe tomatoes from the garden and brought them into the kitchen—a job that usually evoked a lot of conversation between Jeremy and his daddy. Then he polished his father's shoes. Long after they were gleaming brightly, he kept polishing them.

Finally it was dusk. Jon and Jeremy and I sat on the front porch, looking hopefully down the darkening street. It was almost time for Jerry to come home. Tonight he wasn't eating at the company. He had telephoned, asking us to wait for him. At a few minutes past nine, we finally saw Jerry get out of a friend's car and head up the driveway.

Like lightning, Jon leaped over two steps and galloped to meet him. He called to Jerry as he ran, relating events of the day in a loud, enthusiastic tone. Suddenly I felt uneasy about Jeremy. He continued to sit by me on the steps. He had his head down on folded arms. As Jon and Jerry came closer, Jeremy didn't lift his head. Jerry looked down at him and then at me with a puzzled look. I shrugged my shoulders. I didn't understand Jeremy's unusual behavior. Jerry touched Jeremy's red hair and said, "Hey,

Buddy." He didn't ask, as I would have, "Why are you so quiet?"

Jeremy looked up. It was obvious that he was fighting hard to keep back tears. We were all surprised. Jon even slowed down his rapid-fire conversation and pretended to study a fly on the screen.

"Come on in, Jon, and help me get supper on the table," I said. He came without his usual protest. We left Jeremy and his daddy on the front steps.

The minutes ticked by. Supper was ready, but I hesitated to call them in. Instead I peeked out the living room window. Jeremy now stood on a step above his father so that he was Jerry's height. They stood motionless holding on to each other. Jeremy's head was on his father's shoulder and his arms wound tightly around his neck. There didn't appear to be any conversation between them. I knew in Jerry's place I would have asked countless questions. I also knew that he hadn't even asked one.

When finally they came in, Jeremy's eyes were red from crying. We sat down in unusual silence. I was surprised when Jerry asked Jeremy to say the blessing. I wasn't certain he could get through a prayer. His voice cracked, and he sniffed several times. But he managed, "Thank you, God, for this food. Thank you that Daddy is here to eat with us tonight. We pray for a good church service tomorrow. Please let the strike be over soon. Amen."

Later that night I stuck my head in each boy's room. Jon was already asleep, but Jeremy was lying on his back looking out his window. I could see his face in the soft moonlight. "Night, Jeremy."

"Night, Mama."

I hesitated, moving closer. "Jeremy, was anything wrong today? I mean... "

He didn't answer right away, still looking out at the stars. Finally he said, "I missed Daddy a lot today. A lot more than I thought I would. I got to thinking... suppose he wasn't ever coming home again. Suppose every day would be like today. Then when I saw Daddy get out of that car, I was so glad to see him that I... couldn't say anything. I just sat there. But he's a good daddy. He understood, ya know. He really understood."

I kissed him and left him looking out the window at the heavens and thinking his thoughts. My quiet child who loves to ponder things.

When I came back into our bedroom, Jerry was already asleep. I sat for a moment on the edge of the bed, going over the day in my mind. And suddenly my conversation with Ann flashed through my head. I sat up straight, recalling every word I'd said. I remembered my harsh criticism of the way quiet people worship. And I remembered my early morning prayer: *If she's right... show me somehow.* How quickly God had answered it!

I was so ashamed. Hadn't my own sons just demonstrated to me that people express love differently? Jon had run excitedly and grabbed on to his father, talking all the time. Jeremy had sat quietly on the steps with his head bowed. And then finally he had clung to his daddy and cried right on the front steps where anyone could see.

Both boys had expressed genuine devotion. Their daddy understood that, much quicker than I. How grateful I was now that Jerry hadn't asked Jeremy, "Why are you so quiet?"

If Jerry could understand Jeremy's devotion, then surely our Heavenly Father must understand when His children worship Him in different ways. Some are excited and vocal with praise; others only look down and weep in His presence. Some present gifts of good works. Others just cling silently to a loving Father, secure in His strong arms, and cry without shame.

Ann was right; God *does* understand.

CONTENTMENT

*F*or years, grocery shopping was a grueling task. I'd hurry through the store putting anything in sight into my cart. I didn't dare indulge in the luxury of reading labels for fear one of my twin toddlers would jump out of the cart. My two little daughters would cling to my skirt, making walking cumbersome. One day one of the twins escaped and the manager had to announce over the loudspeaker, "Attention everyone. There is a two-year-old boy with red hair probably hiding in a cardboard box somewhere in the store. All shoppers are requested to look for him." That same day the other twin threw a jar of dill pickles out of the cart and broke it.

I never got accustomed to the icy stares of women with one well-behaved child. I hurriedly admired others who shopped without children. They had grocery lists, organized coupons, manicured nails, and carefully applied makeup, and they strolled leisurely through the grocery store smiling at everyone. So unlike me! *That'll be the day*, I would think to myself.

Now—my children all grown—I grocery shop alone. I can take all the time I want and read labels too. Funny thing. I find myself watching women struggle through the store with whining, rambunctious children and I envy them. I do! I want to go back to the way it used to be. I told my daughter Julie, and she happily loaned me her two little ones to take grocery shopping, but she gave me a bit of advice too:

"Mother, you have to be content with who you are in life. Don't look back and yearn for the past," she wisely said. "I love and admire you just the way you are *now!*"

CHAPTER EIGHT

490 TIMES!

"It Wasn't My Fault, Mama!"

"It wasn't my fault," Jon, one of our ten-year-old twin sons, wailed as I loudly accused him of spilling Kool-Aid in front of the refrigerator.

I sighed in silent anger. It seemed that nothing had ever been Jon's fault. Even when he was a little fellow and could hardly talk, he'd shake his head and insist, "No, not me." Now I knew I could make him wipe up the spilled drink, but we couldn't really communicate about it. Just as I expected, he grumbled and wiped it up and went away mad. I was angry, too.

While Jon and I seemed to go in circles about his always insisting he was innocent, Jon and his daddy almost never disagreed. It often seemed to me that Jerry, my husband, wasn't stern enough with the boys, especially Jon.

Jon adored his daddy and was always right on his heels, watching him shave, talking a mile a minute or following him around the house.

One Saturday morning Jerry planned to trim limbs on the oak tree in our back yard. Jon, of course, was helping his daddy.

Jeremy had gone down the street to play with friends.

In about an hour Jerry came in the back door. He slammed it so hard that I knew right away something was wrong. Jon followed without comment.

"What's the matter?" I asked.

"I did a stupid thing. Fell off the ladder. I don't know how it happened, but I seem to have done something to my arm. Can't move it."

Jerry's almost never sick or hurt, so I figured he'd soon be fine. And I was surprised when he said, "You'd better take me to the emergency room."

Jon asked to go and I said he could, leaving our sixteen-year-old, Jennifer, in charge of Jeremy. At the emergency room, we had a long wait. Jon sat close to his daddy and was unusually quiet and well-behaved. Finally, Jerry was X-rayed and a doctor reported the results. "The large bone in your upper arm is broken, about three inches below the shoulder. It's a bad break."

Jon and I were silent in amazement. Jerry was always fine!

The doctor continued, "No work for a couple of weeks. Don't get in the tub, don't drive. Move as little as possible. You'll need a hospital bed because you'll have to sleep sitting up."

We left the emergency room with Jerry in a wheelchair, his shirt draped over his shoulder, the empty sleeve dangling by his side. They had set the arm, and it was strapped to his body.

"I'll go get the car, Jon. You stay with Daddy." Jon nodded and placed one hand on his daddy's good left arm.

Riding home, Jon sat between us, saying almost nothing. But he kept looking at Jerry's empty shirt sleeve.

Back at the house it was almost dark. The cut limbs and overturned ladder were still in the back yard. From the kitchen window I watched Jon walking around where the accident had happened. He tugged at a limb still connected by bark to the large oak tree. It wouldn't come off, so he let it go. He set the ladder up and stood looking at the tree for quite a while. I called him for his bath. He came, still looking over his shoulder at the tree.

As we got ready for bed, Jon came and stood looking at his

daddy sitting up in the hospital bed. "Can you sleep in that thing, Daddy?" he asked, running his hand over the foot of the metal bed.

"Yeah, I'll get used to it, son. You go on to bed. 'Night."

Jerry slept well. The next morning, Jennifer came into the kitchen. "Mama, I have to talk to you," she said.

"Jon came into my room last night. I woke up real late and he was just standing there in the moonlight. You and Daddy were asleep. He looked real scared. You know how nothing is ever Jon's fault? Well, you won't believe what he told me. He said, 'Jen, it was all my fault. The whole thing.' Then he explained that he had pulled at a limb while Daddy was on the ladder, not knowing that it was still connected to the tree. When he couldn't get it off, he simply turned it loose. It snapped back like a slingshot and turned the ladder over. Remember how Daddy kept saying the ladder seemed to have been knocked right out from under him?"

"Oh, Jen, I never suspected. Jon's been quiet, but I didn't know this. I'll have to tell Daddy."

When Jerry came downstairs I told him. A silent pain shot through his eyes—much more pain than when he'd broken his arm. After breakfast everyone had left the table except Jon and Jerry. I was at the sink, thinking how I'd start with a lecture.

Jerry spoke, "Jon, Jennifer told us what you told her last night. She had to, son. We needed to know." Jerry's voice was so gentle, I turned to look at him. The grave expression on Jon's face became even more set. He dropped his head and seemed to slump in the chair.

I looked back at my dishes. "Jon," Jerry said, "understand this. We're just going to talk about it once. The accident was just one of those things that happens sometimes when people are working together. You were my helper and you're a good worker. It just happened. So don't blame yourself. Let's forget it. I'm going to be fine, and we'll cut more limbs together, okay?"

Out of the corner of my eye I saw Jon sit up straighter. He got up and walked around to his daddy and just leaned against him.

No one spoke—not even me—but I knew this was Jon's way of saying, "Thanks, Dad. I'm sorry." Jerry put his left arm around Jon. After a few minutes, they parted. Jon went outside. Jerry left the table and I cleared away the dishes, wondering if Jerry's few, simple words of forgiveness had made an impression on Jon. Had Jerry let him off too lightly?

The weeks passed rapidly. We didn't discuss the accident anymore. About six weeks after it had happened, I had to get after Jon for continually being late for supper. I used a method of punishment that works well for our boys. I assigned him an essay to write. "You choose the topic," I added sternly. I knew what to expect. A theme entitled, "Football" or "Airplanes."

Jon seemed unusually involved in the essay. He didn't even complain about my assigning it. He said very little. He just sat down at my desk, his head almost touching the paper, and began writing in his left-handed scrawl. After a while he handed me the essay and left the room. It read:

FORGIVENESS

"When you forgive somebody, you mean that you don't hold what they did against them. When you do something wrong, you should ask God to forgive you. But He won't forgive you unless you ask Him in your heart. The Bible says you should forgive someone who has done wrong 490 times. That's seven times seventy. When they nailed Jesus to the cross and spit on Him and called Him names, He said, 'Forgive them, Father, for they know not what they do.' Now if Jesus can do that, then surely you can forgive somebody when they do something to bother you.

"Forgiveness is a sign of kindness and love. When you ask God to forgive you, you must forget completely about it. When you sin, you must always ask for forgiveness, because if you don't you will be asked in Heaven why you didn't. When you forgive somebody, do it because you love them, not just to be good.

"So the next time you forgive somebody, remember why you're doing it. And always forgive others."

I gave Jon his first A on an essay even though it had misspelled words.

"Thanks, Mom," he beamed when he saw the grade. I nodded, wishing there was a higher mark than an A.

That night at supper I somehow spilled Jon's glass of milk, all over the table, his plate and him. I sat there for a moment in silent disbelief, thinking, *Mothers don't spill milk.* Jon smiled with the milk dripping down his shirt and said quietly, "That's okay, Mama. I have to take a bath anyway, and you know I don't like milk. It wasn't really your fault." Then he jumped up and grabbed a towel.

Everyone at the table lowered their eyes, but I saw them smiling. I smiled too and felt happy on the inside even though the milk was dripping all over the just-waxed kitchen floor. Forgiveness must work more miracles, large and small, than anything else in the world... or in the home.

FORGIVENESS

My husband, Gene, and I were first-time visitors in the Sunday school class. We were dressed appropriately and smiled warmly as we were introduced. We had our Bibles. No one could possibly know that we'd had a misunderstanding en route and that I had unforgiveness in my heart. The teacher was detained and someone asked, "Who will volunteer to teach the lesson?"

God seemed to say to me, *You and Gene are to teach this lesson.*

I argued silently, *I'm angry, Lord. I can't teach today.*

I glanced at Gene. Smiling, he said, "For some reason, I believe God wants us to teach the lesson." I nodded. No one else volunteered.

Gene explained to the class that since we hadn't studied the material, we'd just share what God was doing in our lives now and in our new marriage. He instructed me to speak first.

Facing the class I heard myself say, "I have unforgiveness in my heart. I need to ask my husband's forgiveness." I glanced at him. He smiled and nodded a quick *"everything's-okay-I-love-you"* nod. I saw several couples smile and reach over and hold hands. I felt differently on the inside, as if God had reached down and removed the junk from my angry heart and put love in its place.

Gene and I taught the Sunday school lesson that day, but I'm sure the lesson I learned was more powerful than the one we shared with the class. God wants our insides and our outsides to match.

CHAPTER NINE

MAKING AMENDS

THERE ARE LOTS OF WAYS TO SAY YOU ARE SORRY

*L*ooking at the clock for the umpteenth time, I calculated that my husband was now an hour-and-a-half late for supper. I had fed the children and myself. The kitchen was a mess and his plate at the table didn't look too inviting.

I knew he had had a lot of work to do today as well as for the past few weeks. He said his work should lighten up in a few more weeks. But I had been pretty patient, I thought. Greeting him warmly each night, even when he worked sixteen hours; sitting with him while he ate; keeping quiet because I knew he was too tired to talk; not bothering him with my daily problems. I had even asked the children not to engulf their father with math problems and financial needs, or to share their victories of the day with him until after he had eaten.

But I had had the flu the week before, gotten out of bed in two and a half days, and hadn't popped back to my old "happy home-maker and helpmate" self. I dragged through each day and couldn't seem to get caught up.

Tonight, supper was a tremendous effort that I thought I couldn't get through. It was as though a ball and chain were attached to me. My teenage daughter helped some. One of the seven-year-old twins spilled his milk and I cried silently as he smeared it around on the floor with a dry towel.

Feeding everyone was finally over once more. Everyone, that is, except my husband. Somehow I couldn't face the kitchen that looked like a battleground. It had been a nice dinner—two hours ago. Jerry could have called and said he would be late again. I got up from the table, leaving the four children sitting there finishing up, and escaped to the living room sofa. I lay on the sofa, thinking, I'm not a short order cook. I shouldn't be expected to plop hot meals on the table at a moment's notice. Feeling terribly sorry for myself, my anger toward my husband flourished.

It felt so good to lie down. I drifted off to sleep into a world without crumbs or responsibilities.

I heard Jerry open the door. *Get up*, part of me urged—*greet him.*

Big deal, an ugly side of me insisted. *Stay put.*

I was tired and angry by now. Rest felt wonderful. If I kept my eyes shut, I would be back asleep in that neat orderly world in a moment.

"I'm home," Jerry announced.

"Lo," I mumbled.

"What kind of greeting is that for a husband who has worked all day for you and the children? You wouldn't believe my day."

"Ummmm."

"Where's my supper?"

"In the kitchen—of all places."

"Is it cold?"

"Speck so."

Julie, our thirteen-year-old daughter and peacemaker, piped up, "I'm heating it, Daddy."

A pang of guilt shot through me, but the ugly part of me said, "Good for her. She needs to learn to do things around the house."

I drifted back to sleep while Jerry ate alone. I vaguely heard Julie and Jennifer doing the dishes. It didn't take much effort to allow myself to go deeper into sleep. *I've been sick*, that trouble-making part of me rationalized. This was not my usual behavior, and a small part of me kept shouting, *get up. Make things right.* But the stubborn nature won and I went soundly to sleep. I awoke to find my husband standing over me, speaking in an un-friendly voice.

"What's wrong with you?"

"Tired and sleepy."

"Well, get up, can't you?"

"No."

Maybe I would have, but out of the corner of my eye I saw a briefcase bulging with work. That settled it! I got up, eyes half shut, and stumbled upstairs to bed.

"Where are you going?"

"Bed."

"At 8:30?"

"Yep."

"Come sit with me." The angry tone remained in his voice.

"And watch you work?" I went to bed.

Julie tiptoed into my room and suggested, "Mama, why don't you go sit with Daddy?"

Guilt shot through me once again, but I sighed, feeling help-less to respond to that part of me that still cried out to make things right again. I drifted to sleep.

The next morning Jerry was gone when I woke up. I barely re-membered him kissing me good-bye. I felt wonderfully rested, but not so wonderful about my actions. All day, thoughts seemed to follow me around.

You must say you were wrong and that you're sorry. You have to do something. I remembered we had been married for twelve years before I had ever said the words, "I'm sorry. Forgive me. I was wrong." For three days I had tried and couldn't get the words out. It was one of the hardest things I had ever done. I can still re-member the look on Jerry's face and exactly where we were standing in the house when I apologized. His face sort of lit up, then melted into a fantastic grin, like it did the first time he looked at one of our newborn babies. He accepted my apology instantly and insisted much of the problem had been his attitude.

Over the next six years I had said that I was sorry more often and with less difficulty. Now the time had come again, I knew God was urging me to apologize to my husband.

"I'm going to do it, Lord. I have to do it." But God seemed to keep saying something else to me. Finally, I thought I understood Him. *There are lots of ways to say you're sorry.*

Maybe this wasn't a time for just words, as important as they were. Something else—but what? As soon as I opened my mind to the "but what?" ideas flooded my brain. First: Put a sign on the door that says something like "Welcome Home Husband."

Second: Cook a super-special supper (even if he's late again).

Third: Wax the kitchen floor.

"Wax the kitchen floor," I nearly shouted. I have a cute little sign that hangs in my kitchen. It says, "I don't do floors or windows—the housekeeper." It's more than a decoration. It's my declaration. But I began to daydream about waxing the floor.

Fourth: Wear something that's not "house clothes."

I couldn't make up my mind to do any of it. Suppose I did all this and Jerry came home late again. Wouldn't my sign look ridiculous? Suppose his supper got cold again? Suppose someone spilled milk on my waxed floor?

As the afternoon wore on I developed a big burst of energy and began waxing the floor. The children tiptoed around me and oohed and aahed. Julie got down on her hands and knees for a closer look and said, "Beautiful, Mom."

Excited about the floor I went to extra trouble in preparing supper. About 5:15 I ran upstairs and put on white slacks that I usually wear out and a "good top." I worked on my hair, put on lipstick, curled my eyelashes, and dotted on my favorite perfume. Julie walked by and grinned silently at me. She gave me an "I approve" signal by making a quick circle with her thumb and forefinger. Might as well go all the way, I thought happily. I made the sign. It said, "Welcome Home—Husband, Father, and Breadwinner!" Then I drew a stick figure wife leaning on her broom and clapping her heels together for joy. Flowers bordered the sign.

Supper was about done and in my enthusiasm I realized I had gotten it ready thirty minutes early. Just then I heard a car door slam and ran to the window. I gasped aloud. My husband was home early! I heard his steps, then a pause at the door. He opened it laughing, kissed me, and handed me a box of chocolate covered peanuts, my favorite.

"You're early," I squealed.

"Yeah. I just decided to come on home for a change."

He looked down at the floor. The children all said, "Mama did it, Daddy."

"Nice," he nodded.

After supper as I munched my peanuts, I thought how marvelous God's timing is. When he speaks to one of his children about an apology, he often prepares the heart of the one to receive it. Or better still—leads both to say, "I'm sorry."

Neither of us had said the words this time. God had suggested something much better and we learned there are a lot of ways to say you're sorry.

THE BLUEHORSE
TABLET OF LOVE

*F*rom upstairs I heard the unmistakable thud of
something being spilled on the kitchen floor.
Running down the steps, I saw seven-year-old Jon standing there
holding an almost empty soft drink bottle. Most of the sticky
drink was spilled on the floor. I assaulted him verbally for
spilling the drink, which he wasn't allowed to have with his
breakfast anyway.

His twin brother, Jeremy, ate his cereal silently. Jon wailed, "It
wasn't my fault. Jeremy... " That's when I really lost my temper.
Nothing had ever been Jon's fault!

After cleaning up the mess I sat him down to a bowl of cereal.
Embarrassed, probably not wanting me to know how sorry he
was about the spilled drink, he laughed and clowned around as
he began eating. Pow! The bowl sloshed across the table onto
the kitchen floor and into the hall. Only Jon could manage that!

A rage began in me that I couldn't control. I screamed and
slapped out at him. Trying to dodge my hand he pulled away and
overturned his chair and fell into the mess he had made.
Completely exasperated, I cleaned up the cereal remembering
that before his daddy had gone to work he had spanked Jon for
fighting with his brother and for whining. That made me angrier
and I continued to tell him how clumsy he was and would always be.

He watched silently, standing perfectly still, as I cleaned up
the cereal. I knew I should insist that Jon do it, but in my anger I
didn't even want him to have the satisfaction of repairing the
damage. "There's still a bowl of sugar on the table, and more
milk. Why don't you pour that on the floor, too?"

As Jon and Jeremy went out the door to wait for the bus, I cautioned Jon, "If I see you starting any trouble outside, you'll come back inside. No roughhousing. Stand still. Trouble just happens around you."

The boys hadn't been at the stop three minutes when I peeked out to check on Jon. I don't know what provoked him, but he was hammering Jeremy on the head with his fist, like one of the Three Stooges. I opened the door and yelled for him to come inside. When he reached the steps, I jerked him through the door and pushed him against the wall. "Why—why, do you have to make trouble all the time?"

He started crying and said, "I don't have a tablet for school. You got the wrong kind yesterday and I have to have one today."

His telling me this just now compounded my fury. "Dummy, you don't even need a tablet. You would lose it. Stand at the window and look at the other children behaving." I pushed him away from me forcing his face against the window.

"I'm hot in this raincoat. Lemme take it off."

"No. Just stand still." I can't remember all I said, but I remember that the words felt bitter and hot coming out of my mouth and I couldn't seem to stop them. Then I saw the bus turning the corner and opened the door and pushed Jon outside, as he screamed back at me, "I have to have a tablet." There was open terror on his face. After I shut the door, it seemed to me he was really saying, "I have to have love." And I knew I couldn't honestly give him the love he wanted right then.

He climbed onto the bus with the rest of the children and if I had been a man I probably would have pounded the front door with my fist. Instead, I sat down at the kitchen table with a cup of coffee and a pounding heart.

Washing my cup in the sink I thought, I'm a Christian—a Christian mother. How can this be happening to me? I don't deserve God's forgiveness and I can't even ask for it.

Gently, God spoke to my heart. *You must ask. I can't forgive you until you ask.*

"I can't. I can't. I don't deserve forgiveness."

What you deserve doesn't count. Ask.

I tried, but couldn't form the words—Lord, forgive me.

I'd planned to meet an out-of-town friend for lunch. She had been my Sunday school teacher in another town. I had looked forward to today. Now, I didn't even want to get dressed. It would be so long until the boys were home from school, and I could make it up to Jon somehow. What kind of day would he have now? What chance did he have with the send-off he had gotten this morning?

Then I felt the icy indifference and pride around my heart melt into a great pool of need and I cried out, "Oh, Lord, forgive me. Please forgive me, even though I don't deserve it. I ask Your forgiveness and I need Your help."

You have it. Ask Jon's forgiveness.

"I will when he comes home."

No, go to the school, now.

Get him out of class?"

Yes, hurry.

"But, Lord.... "

It's the only way.

"I don't know.... "

But by then it was as if a magnet drew me to the school. Dressing quickly, I smiled, imagining Jon's surprised face when he saw me there. As I ran out to the car another thought plunged into my mind. "Why don't you take him the Bluehorse writing tablet?"

I will! I will! That's a wonderful idea.

I drove up to the school with the tablet and practically ran inside. The secretary was out of the office for a moment so the principal called Jon over the intercom, "Jon West, come to the office now, please."

Oh, dear, I thought. Jon would think he was in trouble again. I waited for him anxiously. Then I saw him coming before he saw me. Unmistakable fear in his eyes, he walked—defeatedly, chewing on one lip; but he came quickly to whatever awaited him.

Love for him so filled my heart and overflowed that I blinked

69

the tears away and prayed, "Thank You, Lord, for helping me come. How close I came to not coming." Jon's eyes traveled from my face to the Bluehorse tablet and his face exploded into an understanding grin.

"Mama, you brought me the tablet! Thanks."

I knelt down to his level and gave it to him and of all the ridiculous things—my tears plopped right down on the tablet for Jon to see. He looked up at me silently for a moment, and I couldn't say all the wonderful things I had planned, so I just said, "I'm sorry. I was wrong. I love you."

"That's okay, Mama."

I knew the unwritten rule that forbids asking for a kiss from a seven-year-old in front of people. And I knew the principal and other office workers were right behind us. Students roamed the halls. "Would you give me a kiss?" I whispered.

He reached up and gave me not only a kiss but a tremendous bear hug. Then he turned with the Bluehorse tablet tucked under his arm and headed back for class. There was an unmistakable bounce of security in his walk.

That afternoon Jon handed me his school papers. I took them expecting the usual large amount of incorrect math problems circled in red. *100!* Big red letters. And the teacher had written, "Jon really tried today and did beautiful work. I'm so proud of him!"

SPRING CLEANING

everal years ago I'd been praying for a long time about the problem that existed between my daughter and me. Jennifer was sixteen years old and we just didn't seem to see eye to eye about anything. She thought I had become too strict. I thought she wanted too much freedom. I thought the fault was hers. She was certain it was mine.

I missed her coming into the kitchen, sitting on the tall stool and talking to me in hushed tones. She no longer popped into my room, modeling a new combination of clothes, asking, "How does this look, Mama?" All my questions brought only curt, two- and three-word replies.

One spring day, I prayed again, "Help us, Lord. Get us back together."

Outside, the grass was green, fruit trees had bloomed, and I watched a sparrow hopping around her baby bird. Then suddenly I wasn't looking through the glass door but at it. *How long it has been since I've cleaned it!* I thought. Winter's dirt and grime and mud from our collie's paws covered it. Immediately I called Jennifer and asked her to help me clean it.

She came with a bottle of spray and paper towels, lacking only enthusiasm. "You get the outside and I'll do the inside," I said.

We began spraying and wiping. When we'd hit a stubborn smudge, one of us would clean while the other watched. It was good to be doing something together, even though we remained silent.

Finally, only one spot was left. I stood back and watched Jennifer wipe from the outside. The spot was still there. Jennifer motioned for me to rub from my side. I sprayed and wiped. The spot stayed. Pointing back to her, I mouthed, "It's on your side."

She shook her head and pointed back to me. "No," I said in a

71

loud voice so she could hear me through the thick glass. "It's yours."

She shook her head again and pointed back to me.

I shook my head, protesting.

She nodded with exaggerated movements and then, as the realization set in that neither of us was right or wrong, Jennifer began to laugh. She couldn't stop. Happiness covered her entire face.

Then I laughed too, and it seemed the laughter went all the way down to my toes. It felt wonderful. Finally, with both of us smiling, we bent our heads in silent determination and attacked that last stubborn spot with new vigor.

CHAPTER TEN

LISTENING

GOD DOES SPEAK TO US

O f course, God doesn't tap you on the shoulder and exhort you like your boss, in deep, commanding tones. No, He makes Himself known in various ways. Here's how I came to learn to make myself available to Him.

I never wanted anything in life but to be a wife and mother. I believed this was my calling. When I married Jerry, it all came true for me. By 1968 I was the mother of two young girls and infant twin boys. All four were active and demanding. Suddenly I was up to my ears in diapers and formula and laundry; some days I was so harried and dragged out I never got out of my bathrobe.

Jerry and I were both believers, and when I got the children dressed and we trooped off to church each Sunday, we looked like a picture-book family. We were, except for me. I was drained—running on empty. I began to resent that Jerry went off to work all week to an interesting job with people he enjoyed while I endured daily bedlam at home.

On the morning of March 4, 1972, I told Jerry, "I've got to be alone for a while. Please take the children."

"Sure, sure," he said brightly. "I understand. Maybe it'll cheer you up."

"That's easy for you to say," I said through clenched teeth. Jerry got the message. He quickly collected the children and herded them outside to the yard. It's fortunate he did or I might have screamed at him. I was screaming inside.

I felt like a failure as a wife, mother, and person. I went into the den, shut the door and whimpered, "Help. Lord, please help me. Take over, I can't do it anymore. There's got to be something more for me in life."

I stood stock still. I wasn't absolutely sure what I was doing. But I listened. Oh, how I *listened*.

And then I began to feel something, a feeling of warmth. I felt a love so intense that it seemed to fill and overflow me and permeate the den and reverberate throughout the whole house....

I didn't need to hear words; I could sense Jesus saying, *I've waited a long time for you to do this. I'm pleased and I'm going to help you. I love you.* Although I didn't see anything visible, I knew that Jesus was with me now in a way that He'd never been before, and I felt He was smiling. I smiled back. I'd almost forgotten how to smile. I wondered how I had sung "And He walks with me, and He talks with me, and He tells me I am His own"[1] almost all my life at church and never once heard Him "say" anything to me before.

Shortly after that experience, I began thinking more and more about my writing—maybe I should write a book. The idea kept returning. Could it be that God was instructing me to write a book?

"I can't," I told Him. "I don't have the time or energy or know-how. I have four small children. I can't even spell. You know how tired I am after the children are asleep. My typewriter is ancient. I want to, but... Tell you what, Lord. You know that nice editor lady at *Guideposts* who writes me the encouraging rejection letters, Dina Donohue? Well, if she were to write in her next letter (if there is another letter) 'Dear Marion' instead of

'Dear Mrs. West,' I'd know You were speaking and telling me to write a book... and I'd do it."

A letter from Dina Donohue (another rejection) arrived that week. I was standing at our mailbox waiting and looking for it. I read it still standing by the box: "Dear Marion, I cannot call you Mrs. West any longer, for I know you far too well." I laughed, cried, jumped up and down in the yard and ran around in a joyful circle as my astonished children gaped.

"God wants me to write a book!" I fairly screamed to them and the neighbors. No one in the world, no theology, no argument, no logic could have convinced me that The God of the Universe had not spoken directly to *me*! It was a long road, but my first book was published four years later.

Sometimes even as I learned to listen for God's voice ("My soul, wait thou only upon God," Psalm 62:5) there have been long, dark, almost unbearable times when He didn't speak—or at least I didn't hear Him. When discouraging silence prevailed, I learned that there were always such verses as John 14:18: "I will not leave you comfortless," and Psalm 147:3: "He heals the broken-hearted" (RSV), and many more definite promises. I had to *choose* to stand on them and *believe* them no matter what—as if they were being written for me today.

Once when I was having trouble connecting with God, I asked Him, "Why is it so difficult?" No answer came. Months passed. One night I picked up a book to get my mind off the threatening depression I sensed I'd be facing the next day. Then five words by Oswald Chambers suddenly seemed almost to leave the printed page and invade my defeated spirit like a conquering army rushing to the rescue: "All noble things are difficult."[2] I sat straight up in bed reasoning: *If all noble things are difficult... then I must be doing something noble!* Almost instantly the suffocating depression was lifting. But then I thought, *Why get so excited over five words? Millions of people read this book.* I tuned this out. Belief is for those who want to believe. I had heard from God. I went to sleep savoring, rejoicing in those five words.

Shortly after I began "hearing" from God, Jerry's and my old argument about breakfast resurfaced. Or maybe it was I who argued. Jerry only asked that I cook breakfast, but I hated messing up the kitchen early in the morning. One night after my prayers but before drifting off to sleep, I sensed the words *Cook breakfast for your husband* flashing across my mind.

When I turned to Jerry I saw he was still awake, so I told him, "Jerry, I'm cooking you a good breakfast in the morning." He was so excited that he woke up all during the night wanting to know if it was morning yet. That dutiful obedience put a longed-for new spark in our marriage. Over breakfast Jerry looked at me as if we were dating again. Blessings always follow obedience.

So many times I haven't understood at all why God "told" me to do something, except in retrospect. At another low point in my life God seemed to be telling me to help a quadriplegic: *Teach him to paint.* "Look," I said, "I can barely paint myself. How can I teach him?" I protested all the way to the hospital where I did volunteer work. When I got to the man's room, he was strapped on a Stryker frame, face down, with his back to me. *This is absurd,* I thought, but I did as God told me and said to the back of his head, "Hi, would you like to learn to paint?"

"Yep. When do we start?" That was in the days before Joni Eareckson had made mouth painting a nationally known technique. I had nothing to go on except instructions from God. The young man began to paint marvelous pictures with a brush held in his teeth. They were framed free of charge by a businessman who recognized his talent. An article about him appeared in the paper. He learned to type by tapping keys with a wand held in his teeth, and went on to lead a full life. How could I stay depressed after I had witnessed a young man make a new life for himself like that?

God's voice is gentle, never pushy. Even when He spoke to me years ago as I stood frying chicken for supper and a dangerous situation was at hand, His voice was calm. I kept "hearing," *Go find your boys. Now.* Finally, I went, hands still covered in flour, to look for them. I thought, *How silly to stop cooking just to look for the boys.* I found Jon and Jeremy in the washroom, Jeremy was crouched in the dryer with the door shut, wearing a space helmet. Jon was about to blast him off into outer space by pushing the "on" button.

There have been times when I've misunderstood God's messages. But even the biblical Samuel missed God's voice a couple of times. However, Samuel was willing to learn to listen. The third time God spoke to Samuel, he answered, "Speak, Lord, for Thy servant heareth" (1 Samuel 13:9). I think God just wants us to be willing to learn to *listen* and that He is pleased when we fully *expect* Him to speak. John 10:27 says, "My sheep hear My voice, and I know them, and they follow Me," and in Isaiah 30:21 it says, "And thine ears shall hear a word behind thee saying, 'This is the way, walk ye in it." Ezekiel 12:25 says, "For I am the Lord: I will speak." I believe God likes to speak. But there are times when I goof. I blow it. Later, when I realize my mistake, I confess, "I'm sorry, Father. Forgive me. I was wrong."

It's all right, child. I know you want to hear from Me. That's all I want. Keep listening. Expect Me to speak. Don't tune Me out. You are making remarkable progress. I long to tell you so much more.

"Speak, Lord, for Thy servant is listening."

℃

SUPERMARKET SAMARITAN

uk! I thought. *Why doesn't someone do something about that child?* Carefully and deliberately I walked around him, glancing down with open disapproval at the mess he'd made at the entrance to the store where I had come to buy a loaf of bread.

Chocolate ice cream dripped down his arms and onto his clothes, knees, and feet. Melted ice cream surrounded him on the hot pavement. Bits of chocolate stuck in his curly blond hair.

Inside the store I bought my bread, still looking back at the child, annoyed because he just sat there dripping ice cream all over. Where was his mother? Somebody certainly ought to be taking care of him!

A Silent Voice suggested, *Why don't you help him?*

But I chose to ignore that question. I had two boys at home and I wiped enough messy little hands and faces each day. This child wasn't my responsibility!

Just then a delivery man came into the store. I noticed him at first because he wore such a bright red shirt. After he completed his delivery, he asked the checkout lady for a paper towel. I knew immediately why he wanted it. Suddenly I wished I had asked for the towel. I wondered how many others had passed by the little boy and only frowned at him with disapproval.

The delivery man went back outside. Stooping down, he gently, almost playfully, wiped off the little boy's hands and face. As he talked to the child in a friendly way, the little fellow burst into a bright, sticky smile.

The man didn't really get him all cleaned up, the way a mother would have. A mother probably would have gotten the towel wet and rubbed too hard and looked tight-lipped as she worked. And so I was glad it hadn't been a mother who had stopped to help the little boy.

The man didn't make a big thing of it. He tossed the paper towel into a trash basket, got back into his truck, waved, tooted his horn, and drove off.

As I left with my loaf of bread, I looked down at the child once again. He was still a bit sticky, but when he smiled up at me, I smiled in return and said, "Hi." I had gotten a lot more from my shopping expedition than a loaf of bread.

CHAPTER ELEVEN

FEAR VERSUS FAITH

LOOK OUT FEAR, HERE COMES FAITH!

*F*forced myself to remain calm so I wouldn't lose control of the car.

"Pray, Jeremy, pray!" I cried out to my fourteen-year-old son sitting in the backseat. In one split second, an afternoon outing to a football game had turned into the most horrible nightmare imaginable: My husband, in the seat beside me, appeared to be dying.

Jerry had come home from work early so he could see Jon, one of our twin sons, play in the first football game of the season. It was rare for Jerry to be home early. I was delighted to be able to be with him. I'd just as soon we weren't going to a football game, but it was a sunny Thursday in September and I was happy. Carefree. I felt sort of a hint of apprehension when Jerry first came home. He said that he felt odd. He never complained and was never sick. He's probably just a little tired, I reasoned. But when we left the house to pick up Jeremy at school, Jerry said, "Why don't you drive?"

I brushed away his strange comment. But as I drove, for some reason I didn't understand, I kept looking at him. Something about him seemed different. I couldn't put my finger on it. Then as we waited in the car in front of the school for Jeremy to come out, I asked Jerry to roll down his window. "It's hot," I said. I watched in total disbelief as my husband tried over and over to figure out how to roll down the car window. He touched many different things in the car. He even leaned over the backseat. *Dear Lord, what are we in for?* I thought. Jerry and I stared at each other in amazement.

Jeremy came out from school, jumped in the backseat, and I drove away. "Do you want me to head for the doctor's?" I asked Jerry, forcing my voice to remain calm. But even then I knew there wasn't time. Something monstrous was bearing down on us and it was coming fast. I didn't know what "it" was, only that it was imminent and that we desperately needed protection.

"It's not my heart," Jerry said, looking stunned. "My normal blood pressure is one-twenty over eighty. I've just had a physical." But his eyes didn't look right. They were too set. He didn't seem to hear me. As I drove, trying to figure out what to do, Jerry suddenly fell against me hard. Unconscious. His coloring was bluish; he was having trouble breathing.

"Jerry!" I screamed. At the same moment I caught a glimpse of Jeremy's face in the rearview mirror. It was crumpled like tissue paper. "Daddy, Daddy," he shouted. His face reflected my own feelings. The car seemed to fill up with Fear, overpowering Fear, just as if we'd suddenly plunged into a river and were filling up with water. Our only small "air-pocket" of hope was prayer. "Pray," I said to Jeremy again. "Pray, pray!" He dropped his head and his lips began to move. I prayed aloud, eyes wide open, as I drove with one hand and held Jerry up with the other. I could not let him fall to the floor. If he fell, my faith would topple too. He was very heavy, but I held him erect. Was my husband going to die sitting beside me on a sunny afternoon? Was our life together over so quickly?

All this took place in a matter of seconds. Then something I'd read the day before forced its way into my confused mind; in the

Bible we are told eighty times to "fear not." I made a decision not based on feelings. No matter how difficult, I would "fear not." Then and there, I chose Faith over Fear. Again joining Jeremy in prayer, I said aloud, "Dear Jesus, help us. We need You. I trust You. Jesus, Jesus, Jesus... "

Immediately a plan came into my mind. *Keep driving. Very fast. You can do it. I'm going ahead of you. Blow the horn. Keep praying.* I didn't dare look down to see how fast we were going. I didn't even glance at Jerry. I knew where we were headed now. To a nearby ambulance stand. I could see it clearly in my mind. My faith began to grow as my arm on Jerry's chest suddenly touched the area of his heart. There was a strong, steady beat. *Thank You, Jesus.* Faith, like a scrawny plant, stood erect and bloomed. I kept praying.

Scriptures on faith, a topic Jerry and I had been studying in a new Sunday school class, began coming to me as if on a ticker tape. *What time I am afraid, I will trust in Thee. God hath not given us the spirit of fear; but of power, and of love, and of a sound mind. Be strong, fear not: behold, your God will come. Fear not: for I am with thee. Be not afraid, only believe. There is no fear in love; but perfect love casteth out fear. God is our refuge and strength. Therefore will not we fear. Fear ye not, stand still, and see the salvation of the Lord.*

The ambulance attendants had heard my horn blowing from quite a distance. They were outside waiting for us. Almost before I stopped the car, Jerry was being lifted out and placed on a stretcher. I picked up Jerry's glasses from the car's floorboard and answered the attendant's rapid-fire questions, not sure all the while if Jerry was just unconscious or dead. Yet a great sense of calm seemed to cover me. Looking at him I thought: *You can't be dead. No one simply dies wearing blue jeans and a shirt that says "Adidas" on a beautiful afternoon in September.* Just then one of the ambulance attendants said that he had a good pulse.

Faith and I rejoiced. Fear skulked away. I knew Fear would return. We piled into the ambulance and headed for the nearest hospital. In the emergency room, as people worked with Jerry, he came to and asked, "Did we miss the game?" For him that was a very normal response.

"We'll make the next one," I said. I wanted to add that I'd never complain about not liking football again, but there wasn't time. Whatever had happened to him, was happening again. Fear taunted me: *He's not all right.* Was he slipping into unconsciousness? *See how bad he looks.*

What time I am afraid, I will trust in Thee.

The doctor took me into a room and explained that Jerry would need all kinds of complicated tests. I made the decision to transfer him to another hospital where the needed equipment was available. He looked me right in the eyes and said, "Something has triggered two seizures in your husband. We are probably dealing with a brain tumor or a stroke. You need a neurologist, maybe a neurosurgeon." I heard his words, but somehow the words *brain tumor* and *stroke* whizzed by me, like badly thrown footballs. I didn't reach out for them... those words couldn't be for us.

Brain tumor, Fear screamed at me.

What time I am afraid, I will trust in Thee.

Then we were in the ambulance again, speeding to another hospital. Friends had arrived and taken Jeremy with them. Our older daughter Julie had come to the hospital and now rode with us on our second ambulance ride. I happened to glance in my purse and see Jerry's billfold and glasses. They looked out of place. *Your husband's not a well man. You have to take over,* Fear chanted.

What time I am afraid, I will trust in Thee.

We met the neurologist, a woman whom Jerry and I both liked immediately. She asked us all kinds of questions. We answered each one. Jerry touched his nose countless times at her command and began right away to undergo tests on a "stat" basis. A spinal tap was first. The doctor spoke of a possible stroke. We got word that the CAT-scan was normal. No sign of a brain tumor! Jerry winked at me. Faith was winning this round. As Jerry was being admitted to intensive care, he only asked one question: "Mannie, did we win the ball game?"

I had anticipated the question, made a quick phone call, and had the answer. "Yep. Twenty-seven to seven. Our favor. Jon made several good plays."

He smiled happily. It was just as well I didn't know that his condition for the next few days would be listed as critical. I made the difficult decision to go home and sleep and be with the children. On my way home Fear insisted that I should have stayed. *What if...* Fear suggested.

What time I am afraid, I will trust in Thee.

I woke up several times during the night. Fear hung heavy in my room and tried to tell me that all was not well with Jerry. I got up and read the 91st Psalm and went to sleep thinking, *I will not be afraid of the terror by night....*

The morning brought unspeakable joy. Seeing Jerry. I arrived at the hospital just as the sun was coming up. Jerry seemed in good spirits, but very groggy from sedation. We were overjoyed that he was transferred to a private room.

As the days passed, we had long talks. Jerry spoke openly of his love for me, looking right into my eyes. I, being a hopeless romantic, loved it. I knew he loved me in his own quiet way. But what joy to be told daily. I felt rather like a teenager in love for the first time. Rather than concentrate on his illness or any problems, I found myself constantly thinking how much I loved him. It was *so* much more than I had thought I loved him. "We are really one now," Jerry said one day as I held his hand. I loved spending ten or twelve hours a day with him. We even had our own little revival on Sunday morning in his room.

I had brought some inspirational tapes. Jerry isn't much of a tape man but he agreed to listen to one. He had on new red pajamas and looked good. The doctor was still doing a lot of tests and hadn't told us much. The results of some of the blood tests were not what the doctor wanted. And Jerry ran a fever from time to time. But Fear was not in the room that morning. The minister on the tape asked, "What do you need Jesus to do for you right now, *by faith*?" And then in an emotion-filled voice the minister sang, "No one ever cared for me like Jesus... I would tell you how He changed my life completely... But I'll never know just why He came to save me...."[1]

I knew something marvelous and powerful was about to happen. It was coming from the Source of Faith. I found myself remembering a day ten years before when in my utter desperation I had surrendered myself and my life to the Person of Jesus Christ. Like most people, I had come to Him before in bits and pieces, afraid to commit myself totally. But one day I did it. I said to Jesus, "Here's all of me." I shed tears of joy. And my life was never the same again.

Jerry was crying now, softly, joyfully. I didn't have to ask any questions. I understood. I watched as Faith embraced Jerry and transformed him. "He can have me... all of me," Jerry said simply.

After that experience, we didn't expect to hear from Fear anymore. We should have known better. The very next day, late in the afternoon, Fear came disguised as depression. I saw it the minute it touched Jerry. The sparkle left his blue eyes. His shoulders sagged. He stared out the window, not speaking. He was grim. "Please don't be sad. Don't let depression get you down," I said. "We have to stay above that." I knew he was thinking about the future. There were so many unanswered questions. I couldn't seem to reach him. Fear moved about the room freely now. "Jerry, we have to praise God. The Bible says to praise in all situations, whether we feel like it or not." We both knew the principle well, but doing it was something else. His sadness was reaching me too. Fear couldn't win now. Faith was far out in front. "Let's sing, Jer." I was near tears for the first time since this whole thing started. There was no response from my husband.

"Jerry, please. Look at me."

Nothing.

Fear closed in for the kill. I couldn't see Jerry too well for my tears.

"Jer, would you whistle?" My husband sings off-key sometimes, but he can whistle beautifully. Lots of times he just starts whistling a tune and I guess the name of it. It's sort of an old game we've played since we were dating.

"Please, Jerry. For me."

He turned and looked at me and saw my tears. His eyes said clearly that he didn't want to whistle. But then the first sweet, clear notes penetrated the room. I spoke the words to the now familiar tune. "No one ever cared for me like Jesus.... "

Jerry sat up in bed, the sparkle back in his eyes. He smiled at me and kept whistling. I smiled back and sang the words softly. Fear cowered somewhere in a corner. Faith stalked the room like a giant.

Late the next afternoon, just as the last rays of sun shone through the window, we were both silent for a long time. It was a good silence. I felt we were thinking the same thoughts, and I loved that. Jerry broke the silence. He looked at me, positively beaming as I sat on his bed. He said with certainty, "I'm all right now. I'm all right."

"Yes! That's exactly what I was thinking." I laid my head on his chest and we held on to each other. I had the distinct impression that the unseen arms of Faith held both of us like rescued children.

Jerry was released from the hospital on a beautiful, sunny morning, with word from the neurologist that he most certainly could attend Jon's game that day.

Our next test of faith came that very afternoon. Once again we were picking up Jeremy from school and planned to go to Jon's football game. It was Thursday, three o'clock, exactly like one week before. We sat in front of the school. Without thinking, I said, "Will you roll down the window, Jer? It's hot."

Then I remembered. The whole scene tried to flash before me. Jerry didn't respond for a split second. Fear was waiting for any opportunity to attack. Fear lunged into the car and insisted, *It's about to happen again!*

Then Jerry, laughing at my apprehension, rolled down the window and winked at me. I laughed too. A gentle breeze blew in through the open window, bringing with it sweet faith. Jerry reached over and held my hand.

We know there will be more medical tests, and I suspect our faith will be tested again and again. Meanwhile, life goes on as normal—no, much better than normal. When a husband and wife fall in love all over again, after being married almost twenty-five years, nothing is ever normal again.

Whatever other tests we have to face, we'll face them head on. We've already gotten through the toughest one. We have looked Fear right in the face and said, "Look out Fear, here comes Faith!"

ℰ

SURRENDERING

arly one morning I noticed a bird lying just outside our patio door. I brought him into the house and took him to the bathroom to wrap him up in a towel. His eyes were closed. He was limp but seemed to be breathing. No blood. Suddenly he flew out of the towel. Frightened, he flew around in circles, screamed at me, and finally landed on the shower rod. He was worn out, and so was I.

Standing on the rim of the tub, I dropped some water into his open panting mouth and said softly: "Look, bird, I'm your only hope. If you don't let me save you, you don't have a chance. Let me hold you and then I'll set you free. Please trust me...."

The situation seemed familiar, but I couldn't figure out why. Just then the weary bird relaxed and allowed me to cup my hands gently around him. He remained perfectly still as I walked through the house to the edge of our yard and set him high in a pine tree. Immediately he flew off. A part of my heart soared with him as I realized why the situation had seemed familiar. When I feel like that poor bird, trapped and frightened, God reaches down to help me. But only when I *surrender* can he set me free.

CHAPTER TWELVE

CARING

THE LOVING ARMS OF GOD

For the first time in my life I didn't care about anyone else in the world except my husband Jerry. And myself. Usually I welcomed the opportunity to become involved in someone's life. But not now.

I eased the car into the special section marked "Radiation Therapy." The hospital let radiation patients park free. Despite the cold November air, we walked slowly because Jerry couldn't walk fast. Inside the familiar waiting room we sat in green leather chairs with others awaiting their daily dose of cobalt. We met there each day, the same people, almost as if we were waiting our turns in a beauty shop or some other normal place.

Jerry always entered the waiting room smiling and made it a point to speak to each person. Inevitably he started a conversation. I'd bought him a warm fur hat since he was bald from the brain surgery that had only partially removed the menacing tumor. Already his memory failed sometimes, and he forgot to remove his hat in the waiting room. I removed it for him, and he didn't seem to mind.

It had been more than two months since that day in September when the first horrendous symptom came crashing down on Jerry. Two massive seizures. I told myself that by now I should have become adjusted to the idea that my husband of twenty-five years was walking around with a malignant brain tumor.

But I hadn't. The "adjustment" simply would not come. Hundreds of times I tried to adjust. I tried mentally picturing myself standing in the ocean. It was an actual scene from my childhood, the time a giant wave had caught me suddenly from behind and flung me around and around like a towel in a washing machine. That day in the sea my feet had touched solid ground at last, but now, in the vivid picture in my mind, as soon as I stood, another giant wave came and then another. They continued to knock me down. They meant to destroy me. I couldn't stand or breathe and I didn't see how I ever would again. Not ever.

Across the waiting room Jerry sat with two other men. His rich, spontaneous laughter brought me back to reality. Now the man sitting by Jerry was laughing too. The third man leaned way over to join in their conversation. I almost resented Jerry's ability to still be sociable and fun. He never stopped smiling or trying to encourage others. I sat frozen like a store mannequin, staring straight ahead.

"Mr. West," came the familiar soft tone of the nurse's voice calling him over the intercom to the treatment room. I watched carefully to see if he needed my help to get up. No, he was managing alone today. An elderly woman across the room smiled at me. I glanced away, pretending not to see. *You're old*, I thought with resentment. *All the people here are old. We aren't. We are just in our forties.* The waves came crashing in on me mentally, and I couldn't stand or get my breath. I was under the water again, thinking, *All I want in life is to grow old with Jerry. That's all I want.*

I was staring at the beige wall, determined not to let anyone catch my attention or start a conversation, when God spoke to me. It seemed I hadn't heard from Him in so long. God and I used to have daily conversations. Exact words came to me from Him. Silently, but clearly. And I loved to speak to Him, too. But since Jerry's surgery and the grim-faced doctor's report, I hadn't listened for God's gentle voice. And my words to Him seemed stilted, as if we weren't friends anymore. I never stopped hurting or fighting off fear. And God wasn't saying anything. But today, He *was* speaking. The message from Him came again, loud and clear and as distinct as the nurse calling Jerry over the intercom.

I want you to go to the woman in the hall and speak to her about Me. She's in a wheelchair. You'll know her. You can see her from where you're sitting. Tell her about Me and that I love her.

There were several women in wheelchairs, but I knew the one. Frail, she had probably been beautiful once. She clutched the sides of the wheelchair with open apprehension. Most of her hair was gone. She had that gaunt, hopeless look. Her bright pink robe didn't do much to make her look cheerful.

"I don't want to," I told God. "I don't care about her. She's old and I just don't care. What about Jerry and me?"

Obey me. I know what's best for you. Go over now and talk to her.

"She's not going to respond. Look at her. She doesn't care either. Neither of us cares about anyone anymore."

Go on, Marion.

It was one of the most difficult things I'd ever done, and I'd done some almost impossible things in the last two months. I bent over and spoke softly, "Hello. My name's Marion. What's yours?"

She stared ahead, as though I weren't there.

Keep trying, the Silent Voice urged.

I touched her hand. I wasn't in any mood to make small talk. "God loves you."

Very slowly her cold blue eyes met mine. She turned her head slightly. She spoke softly too. "I don't believe in God."

I wasn't surprised, but something stirred within me. I was beginning to care about her. Just a little. It felt good. "That doesn't keep Him from loving you. God loves you very much. What's your name?"

She moistened her lips with her tongue. It was an effort. "Thelma. (Name has been changed to protect confidentiality.) I'm dying, you know. I've never believed in God or asked Him for anything, and I won't start now. I'm a stubborn old woman."

"I like you," I said and almost smiled.

"Why?" she gasped.

"Because you're honest. I'll see you tomorrow. Okay?"

She nodded.

Jerry came out of the treatment room, walking that unsteady, confused walk that direct radiation to the brain always caused. I placed the fur hat on him, held his arm, and we left. It always felt good to leave. He was smiling, as always.

I moved about the house in my robotlike fashion, still trying to imagine standing up as the giant waves washed over me. I couldn't stand against such destruction. It was impossible. No one could. But still I tried to picture it in my mind. The idea was so real to me, and I wondered what it would be like, to be able to stand in those waves.

Finally, it was time to go to bed. It was the only time that my mind rested from the agony of Jerry's illness. Mercifully, I could sleep and it was a welcome relief. Jerry was already asleep beside me. I'd halfway been trying to think of something I could take to Thelma. A way of saying that God cared about her. Something she could hold on to and take back to her hospital room. I knew by her bracelet that she was a patient in the hospital. I thought of taking her a Bible, or a statue of praying hands. God interrupted my thoughts: *No, no, no. You don't take something like that to someone who doesn't even believe in Me.*

He was right, of course. I was still debating about backing out of this thing with Thelma. She certainly wasn't encouraging our friendship.

The instructions came quickly: *Look up in the top of your closet, way back in the left-hand corner under some stuff. Get the beautiful, handmade shawl, the ivory one. Give that to Thelma and say, "This isn't a shawl. It looks like a shawl, but it's not. It's the arms of God, loving you." Tell her it's from Me. Then wrap the shawl around her with your arms and hug her, a little longer than necessary.*

You'd have to know the kind of closet I have to really appreciate the instructions about the shawl. I hadn't seen the shawl in several months. Messy closets have never bothered me, and Jerry seemed to understand and tolerate my side of the closet. I didn't turn on the light, just tiptoed to the closet and reached up on the shelf, way in the back, left-hand side under some stuff. My hand went right to the soft, luxurious material, and I pulled it out with amazement. God and I were really talking again!

The next morning we arrived for Jerry's cobalt at ten sharp. I looked in the hall at the patients lined up awaiting treatment. Would Thelma really be there? She could come anytime during the day. But there she was in the bright pink robe. I got Jerry seated, removed his hat and hurried over to Thelma. "I have something for you."

"I'm not going to take it. Why should I?" she snapped. "I don't know you."

Standing behind her I pulled the shawl from the bag and carefully placed it around her frail shoulders. I did it slowly and deliberately, and enfolded her in my arms... a little longer than necessary. "It's not from me. It's from God. Now it may look like a shawl, but it's not."

I waited a moment. She bit instantly. "Well, what is it then?" Already she was stroking it as one would a kitten.

"It's the arms of God, holding you and loving you."

I came around to the front of her wheelchair. She stared at me. Her mouth a small, round O. I seized the unguarded moment. "Thelma, He loves you so much. Receive His love. Receive Him. Let Him into your heart and life now. Trust Him."

"But I've been so stubborn... for so long."

"Doesn't matter. He sent you the shawl."

"Could you tell me how to— "

Right in the middle of that sentence an orderly pushed her back to her room. She looked over her shoulder at me and mouthed a *thank-you*. I wanted to run after her, but Jerry was coming out of cobalt, walking very unstably and looking for me.

The weeks crept by. Each day the same. The agony never left. We continued with the radiation treatments, but didn't see Thelma again. Waiting each day, I wanted to see her. It would take only a few minutes to run up to her floor. Jerry offered to go with me. I knew the floor so well. Even where her room was. I could see the floor in my mind. Smell it. Hear the sounds. But I could not go back on that floor. Not yet. Jerry had been hospitalized there several times. The long, shiny hall didn't hold good memories for me. I couldn't even face the ride on the all-too-familiar elevator.

I needed to hear from Thelma. I knew that one of my dear friends worked on Thelma's floor. In fact I found out that she was caring for Thelma daily. I learned that Thelma had been far from a model patient, but one day she showed up on the floor wearing a beautiful shawl and insisting that it wasn't a shawl at all... but the loving arms of God. And that He loved her! She told her family and strangers about God's love. Thelma insisted that some strange woman had given her the shawl. I thought that perhaps people were beginning to think Thelma was strange, but from what I knew about her, it didn't bother Thelma what people thought. The reports were that she was never without the shawl.

I sent her a copy of a book I had written. Inside I wrote: "Stubborn old women are God's specialty. He loves you. So do I." An avid reader, she devoured the book in a few hours. She began greeting people. Even smiling. Though she became worse physically, her attitude brightened daily. "As sick as she is," my nurse friend said, "Thelma's eyes have a new sparkle."

Little bits of new faith laced with joy insisted upon taking residence in my heavy heart when I thought about Thelma. She reminded me of the absolute truth of Luke 6:38: "Give, and it will be given to you; good measure, pressed down, shaken together, running over, they will pour into your lap. For whatever measure you deal out to others, it will be dealt to you in return."

To me it simply meant that whatever you need desperately, you must give away. It sounds foolish, but it works, even if your husband has a malignant brain tumor. If you need money, you give it away. If you need love, you give that away. And in my case I needed tremendous faith, so I had to give away what little I had.

God began pouring the faith back into me in an unmistakable way. I saw myself back in that ocean scene knocked over by giant waves. I was under the water, struggling, unable to breathe. But the scene changed in an amazing way.

I was standing. The waves were pounding me viciously, shaking me, trying to knock me down again and again. But I stood like a small rock, almost without effort. And I knew that if I'd never obeyed God and reached out to unlikely Thelma then I might never have stood in the ocean vision or in real life. But I knew for certain now, from seeing myself stand with those giant waves washing over me, that I was going to stand no matter what came against me. Not in my strength, of course. I had none left. But in God's.

Thelma died in January, wrapped in the soft shawl... and in the arms of the God she had come to know. She learned a lot about how to give out of her need in the short time she had left. My friend who nursed her told me that Thelma decided to leave her sparkling blue eyes to a blind person... someone she'd never met.

DOROTHY'S TIGHT SHIP

orothy Miller had been a nun. She gave it up to become a mother. Never married, she adopted ten severely retarded, brain-damaged, emotionally disturbed children. Doctors insisted one underweight girl would only be a vegetable. Dorothy proved them wrong. There were spina bifida children, Down's syndrome and other diagnoses I didn't even begin to understand.

Dorothy ran a tight ship. There was firm discipline, along with unrestrained love. No pity was allowed. Dorothy taught the children to help one another. It was amazing to watch their feeding, tooth-brushing, and getting-into-leg-braces routine.

One Sunday, after I was newly widowed, my teenage sons and I were having a heated argument while eating in a restaurant. I ended up crying, leaving my food untouched. Just then Dorothy and her brood came in—smiling, laughing, limping, some pushing wheelchairs. She saw me and waved, and they got seated. One of her boys kept watching me. Finally, he came over, patted my shoulder, looked me directly in the eyes and said with a slight speech impediment and a perfect smile, "I tan see ooh having hard time. It will det better."

"Thank you," I responded, greatly encouraged, half laughing, half crying. He was right. It did get better. I still marvel over the compassion Dorothy Miller instills in each of her remarkable children. It's something I can learn—and be reminded of—from them.

CHAPTER THIRTEEN

NEVERTHELESS

ONE SIMPLE WORD FROM GOD

*T*he night before Jerry's brain surgery were the most horrible hours of my life. I'd had a cot set up in the hospital room beside my husband of almost twenty-five years, but I could not sleep. I could feel fear moving around inside me, slowly but forcefully, like a full-term baby.

All my life I'd been hounded by fear—thoughts beginning with the words *What if...* ? "What if Jerry loses his job? What if one of the children has an accident?"

Now the what-ifs stretched and kicked and elbowed me. What if it's malignant? What if they can't get it all? What if Jerry dies? What if I have to watch him suffer for months and months?

I knew Scripture. I knew how to pray. I'd told others in similar situations, "Just stand on the Word. Jesus is the healer." Now there was no room in me for anything but the what-ifs.

Seven A.M. nurses woke Jerry to prep him. He'd slept all night without even a sleeping pill, and soon he had the staff laughing at his jokes. I heard the stretcher wheels coming down the hall.

Jerry opened his arms and we hugged hard. As they rolled him away, I clung to his hand and walked alongside him to the elevator. *Jerry, oh Jerry, you are part of me. The best part. I'm having brain surgery, too. Only they aren't putting me to sleep.*

The waiting room was crowded with family and friends and people from Jerry's office. Our married daughter was there with her husband. Our twenty-year-old daughter, Jennifer. Our fourteen-year-old twin sons. All the people dearest to me in the world... except one.

And that one was strong, healthy, athletic! Jerry was forty-seven and had never been sick a day in his life.

I asked if I could see the room in the Intensive Care Unit where they'd bring him after the operation. "Of course," the nurse smiled. Too nice. Everyone was being too nice.

I knelt down by the bed. Three hot tears slid down my face and spotted the sterile covers. "Please, God, I'll do anything! Just let him be all right."

But Jerry was not all right. The tumor was highly malignant, and doctors were able to remove only part of it. They gave him only months to live.

In the ICU cubicle Jerry and I talked about Jesus the healer, and all the while I was silently telling God *I cannot live without him.* Whenever Jerry had a business trip, he'd wait until the last moment to tell me. I always hit rock bottom when I knew he had to be gone, even for one night. *I can't. You need to understand that, God. I grew up without a daddy, and I can't grow old without a husband.*

Already the fear of our house without Jerry had taken hold of me, and I knew I couldn't go home that night. I couldn't turn into our driveway or walk up the steps past the roses Jerry had planted. Friends had to take me and the two boys to their house that night. I realized I was walking a beaten, humble walk, and I'd started to whisper when I talked.

Had I but known it, I had come to the most enviable place any human being can reach. Because I was defeated and desperate, I was only a step away from the unimaginable joy of Nevertheless living. But I didn't know it, and it would be seven devastating months before I took that step.

Jerry took the step right away. He reacted to the bad news from the doctors by drawing even closer to God. And to me. He came home five days after his surgery able to express his love as never before. The intimacy, the deep sharing, for which I'd begged him over the years, he gave me now in abundance.

Which only increased my anguish. Every evening about six I became almost physically sick. That was when I'd been accustomed to sit in a chair by the window and watch for his car—a habit I had formed in childhood when I watched for Mother to come home from work.

Now, although Jerry was right there at home, I would go into the living room at six o'clock and look out, hurting, terrified. The cars moving past all had husbands in them. *I can't live for my children*, I'd tell God. *Jerry is my world. I'm sorry. I know that's not right, but he is.*

It wasn't exactly like praying. God seemed far away. The what-ifs were the only voices I could hear.

Christmas was awful. I'd stand in line at the drugstore to get a prescription filled for Jerry, while "Joy to the World" piped through the air and wives talked about what they were getting their husbands. *Only four months ago*, I thought, *I was like these women. Illness was foreign to us. Oh, God, why can't we go back?*

But there was no going back. By March Jerry had headaches almost continuously. I chased after every cancer treatment I heard of. I read about a new "wonder" drug and got some of it shipped to us. "The patient's wife," the doctor wrote in a report I saw later, "is phoning medical centers all over the country. She is, of course, desperate."

That desperation, had I but known it, meant that I was on the royal highway to Nevertheless living.

We had set up a hospital bed in the recreation room downstairs. One evening as Jerry was undressing there, he toppled over backward. He fell stiff like a store mannequin, eyes wide open. With the help of Jennifer and the boys, I got him into the car and to the hospital, where they discovered brain swelling.

For the next three days I drove despairingly back and forth between the house and the hospital. And it was on one of these trips, on a spring evening, May 11, 1983, that God did something in my life that I cannot understand, let alone explain. The greatest change, the greatest miracle, of my life occurred—Nevertheless living began.

The brain swelling had gone down some and Jerry was to go home next day. The sun was setting as I drove home. I'd come to hate sunsets. *You knew I didn't want to be alone, God. You knew that.*

And suddenly—it was as though the sun's rays came right inside the car. Everything around me was golden. I felt golden, too. And not at all alone. Something very close to joy seemed to have entered the car with me. For a moment I wondered if the car was just going to float up off the highway.

Then into that golden silence, God spoke a word. That was all. One word. I knew it was from Scripture, but it wasn't even a verse. It was a single word.

Nevertheless.

I knew it had to be a special word, though I didn't yet know it would become a lifestyle. I was sure only that it was a kind of promise. It was even a powerful little phrase: never the less.

Never the less with God, no matter what. Always the most. Though I was alone in this automobile, nevertheless God Himself was right here beside me. Though doctors pronounced Jerry incurable, nevertheless he would be gloriously healed. Perhaps not here on earth as we had all prayed. If Jerry's physical body should die, nevertheless he would go on living in another, greater dimension.

I gazed out the window at the glorious sunset. "Thank you," I whispered.

"What if you're losing your mind?" It was the voice of fear—

fear that had been with me so long that even in this radiant moment it could bully and bluster. "What if you've finally flipped under the pressure?"

I am not the God of What-If, I heard in the golden twilight. *I am the God of Nevertheless.* It was the moment when I first spoke aloud my new word, "Nevertheless," I told the fear-voice, "I know that this is real."

Fear was silent.

The next morning I put on my best clothes when I went to bring Jerry home. No one, except Jerry, understood my overnight change, but it didn't matter. Somehow it didn't even seem to matter that I might be left alone, a widow. I was excited for Jerry.

As his body grew thinner and weaker and fear renewed its attacks, "nevertheless" could always send it scurrying. I began to research this word in the Bible, wondering why no one had ever told me about this principle before. I found it used more than ninety times, always with tremendous power:

"I said in my haste, I am cut off from before Thine eyes: *nevertheless* Thou heardest the voice of my supplications" (Psalm 31:22).

"Master, we have toiled all the night, and have taken nothing: *nevertheless* at Thy word I will let down the net" (Luke 5:5).

"I am crucified with Christ: *nevertheless* I live" (Galatians 2:20).

I engaged two Christian nurses and knew I could keep Jerry at home until the end, though doctors told me no one keeps a brain tumor patient at home. As his abilities declined, Jerry's love for God grew to unbelievable proportions. I would sit beside him on the bed and we would pray and laugh and listen to praise music on the phonograph.

July 16 was a Saturday. Jerry's breathing was labored, and fear tried again. *Your husband is dying.*

"Nevertheless," I shot back, "God is in control. This is the re-creation room."

Knowing that the end was close, *nevertheless* about 11:30

that night I lay down on the sofa. Here was the what-if I'd been so terrified of. Now that it was actually happening, I was drowsy, relaxed....

At 12:45 A.M. Sunday morning Jennifer called, "Come quick!" When I got there, just two steps, it was over. Jerry's form, his earthsuit, didn't seem to be a big deal. My husband wasn't here anymore. He was in glory; running, leaping, more whole than ever before.

I miss him dreadfully, of course. Nor has it been easy being a single parent. And all the things I had to learn—how to get the house painted, how to fill out insurance forms. *Nevertheless* I managed—and each time the what-ifs were a little easier to silence.

On my birthday, a year after Jerry died, I went out to the backyard just as the sun was rising. The day was cool and new and smelled like hope. "Thank You, Father, for today. Thank You that I'm not afraid of the future. Oh, I know there's plenty I could be worrying about. Nevertheless You are in charge."

The dew shone so bright on the grass that I thought, *This could well be the most joyful day of my life so far....*

❧

NEVER GIVE UP

During my husband's illness, I faced deep moments of despair... and an ebbing faith. Although Jerry and I frequently prayed together—and apart—I seemed to battle doubt continuously.

One night when I was especially restless, a dream came to me. Jerry and I and the children were pioneers stranded in a covered wagon on the prairie. The enemy—wild Indians—was attacking. There was no hope; we faced certain death. But then—just as in the cowboy movies—the cavalry appeared on the horizon. The soldiers were riding hard and fast, coming straight to our rescue even as the enemy bore down on us. And the Indians were driven off. Then the riders dismounted and embraced us, expressing great joy at finding us safe. Some of them I knew—others were strangers. My husband and I and our children cried out in gratitude to the cavalry and we all sang praises to God around the campfire.

Upon awakening, as I pondered the dream, a gentle silent Voice seemed to offer an explanation. "You really do have a serious problem, Marion. You can't handle it alone. The cavalry in your dream is the Body of Believers who have banded together to intercede on your behalf. They mean business with the enemy and their prayers are reaching Me. I know that the foe seemed unconquerable to you and your little family huddled there in the covered wagon, but remember this: The soldiers who joined together to rescue you are in My army—the army of the Lord Jesus Christ—and it is because of the Calvary two thousand years ago that they ride today, and they ride in victory.

"Never give up... for I promise you that in the midst of your very peril—in life and in death—I will always be with you now and forevermore."

CHAPTER FOURTEEN

KEEPING THE HOMEFIRES BURNING

FEEDING THE FEW

"ther mothers get up in the morning and cook breakfast!" Jon, one of my sixteen-year-old twins, bellowed up the stairs.

"Well, I'm not other mothers!" I yelled back, and pulled the covers up to my chin. I hated cooking breakfast. While my husband was alive, I had done it, but ever since Jerry had died—over a year and a half before—I just didn't make the effort. Sometimes when I was cleaning up the boys' breakfast dishes, I'd think, *You should get up with them in the morning*. I didn't like that idea any more than I liked cooking breakfast.

The relationship between Jon and Jeremy and me was poor in other areas, too. They resented my being their authority. Sometimes I resented it myself. Being the final authority was hard.

"You're too strict. Daddy was never like this," Jeremy complained one day. He was almost crying. Jon chimed in, "Yeah, if you don't give me more freedom, I'm moving out when I'm nineteen."

"You're moving out at sixteen if you don't watch your mouth," I blurted out. I didn't mean it.

One morning after breakfast the boys saw me moving chairs

down into the den. "Are you having that stupid Bible study here again?" Jeremy asked.

"You know it's not stupid! People get help here."

"Good for them. *We* don't. You never have time for us anymore. You are always doing things for other people, Mama... even strangers."

"Help me move the chairs," I said, remembering my position of authority.

"Why can't your good Christian friends help you?" Jeremy asked.

I forced him to move the chairs, but, as he left, he said, "I know there won't be any supper tonight. There never is when you have your big-deal Bible study."

We were back to arguing about food.

After Jerry died, I had a hard time getting back into the routine of cooking. We ate out a lot. One evening Jeremy said, honestly and without apparent anger, "Aren't we ever coming home from school to smell supper cooking again and sit around the table and be a family?"

I wanted to assure him that we would. I wanted to be a family and sit around the table too. But for some reason I seemed almost afraid to try.

I continued to have the Bible study, I also attended other prayer meetings and Bible studies and got involved with helping people. Sometimes the boys would come home and a stranger and I would be sitting at the kitchen table talking or praying. After the company left, Jeremy would ask, "Why can't they go somewhere else for help?"

"You know I like being involved with people and helping people."

"Me and Jon are people. You don't do much for *us*.... "

"That's not true, Jeremy. Anyway, I have to have some kind of life besides cooking and puttering around the house and saying hello and good-bye to you two. I can't just cling to you boys. One day... "

I finished the sentence in my mind. *You and Jon will be gone too. Just like Julie got married and left and like Jennifer has just married and left. Then Jerry died. In five years our family has gone from six to three. Soon it will be just me. I need to have somewhere to go. Something special to do.*

Another voice spoke in my thoughts. I knew Whose it was. *Could you be, in a sense, leaving the boys before they leave you? They really need you now. I can handle your future.*

My reaction to that suggestion was to attack the oven with a powerful cleanser and make a mental list of people who had been helped at the Bible Study in my home.

In December of 1984 I decided to go on a mission trip to the slums of the Philippines. That seemed really worthwhile. Jon and Jeremy were openly opposed to my going.

"What if you don't come back?" Jeremy asked quietly.

Jon answered, disguising his concern just as his father would have. "Then we'll know they made missionary stew out of Mom."

"Jonnn!" Jeremy hollered. Jon laughed, but I saw beneath his witty answer.

I arranged for a neighbor to stay with the boys. Just as I was about to leave for the airport to start my trip, a phone call from school informed me that Jeremy was in trouble again and would be suspended two days for using inappropriate language. I made a quick trip to school. I had seldom seen Jeremy so upset. I hated leaving him like that. But I did.

I phoned home from the Philippines several times. Once, Jeremy answered. "I'm learning so much, Jeremy," I said. "You'll probably have a new mom when I get back home."

"I don't want a new mom. I just want my old one. Come back home now... please."

I tried to sound cheerful and reassuring for Jeremy and for me. "Guess what? Yesterday I fed eight hundred hungry children breakfast and told them about Jesus."

There was no response.

It was nearly Christmas when my plane landed back in Atlanta. Jeremy met me at the airport, pushing through the crowd almost rudely, and we held each other for a long time. "I thought you wouldn't come back," he whispered.

At the house, he showed me the tree he had bought and decorated himself. "Sit down at the table, Mama. I'll make you a bowl of tomato soup," he said.

The kitchen was warm, homey, and comfortable. Jeremy watched as I ate the soup as though it were a gourmet dinner. For some strange reason, two tears slipped right into the soup. I was startled and confused. Since just before Jerry died, in July 1983, I had been unable to cry over anything. My tears seemed trapped deep inside me. Yet now two went *plop, plop* right into my soup.

In January, Jeremy mentioned that Jon was getting pretty good at basketball. He played on the school team. "They're in a tournament now, Mom. Most all the parents come to the games."

Jeremy knew I liked basketball about as much as cooking breakfast. Of course, when Jerry was alive, I had attended all the boys' sporting events. Jerry had insisted that I go. He was the most enthusiastic parent at any ball game. Once he was voted Dad of the Year. One time he even flew home from an important business meeting to see a football game. He was always in the stands cheering. I hadn't been to any kind of game since Jerry was gone. I hadn't even asked who won.

One morning about five o'clock, God seemed to speak to me. *There is a reason why your boys keep getting into trouble. They are becoming more and more rebellious because they have a rebellious mother.*

I sat straight up in bed, fully awake, and whispered back to Him as the first hint of a new day entered the room. "What! Look at all I'm doing for You."

Then God gave me some unmistakable instructions that I didn't like nor understand at all. *Go to Jon's game this Friday night.*

"Basketball over a dynamic Bible study? It's not logical... or even spiritual."

But what was it I'd told someone last week? "God is not always a God of logic. What is important, though, is complete obedience."

I didn't want to go to that basketball game at all. I don't like noise or sports. Feeling rather foolish, I called off the Bible study and went to the game.

Jon's school was losing by seventeen points at halftime. Suddenly Jon began to make basket after basket. He scored thirty points, and in the last two minutes of the game, his team won. I was on my feet screaming, clapping, cheering... and I'd never in my life even said a mild "yea" at a game.

Jon hadn't asked me to attend the game. He seemed surprised that I was there. I went back the next night for the second game of the tournament. On the final night some kind of award event was scheduled, and at the last minute I went. They were calling out boys' names for awards. The announcer said, "And now for the most valuable player of the year in Georgia Christian schools in this association... voted on by all the coaches in the tournament... Jon West."

The applause was deafening. I sat motionless, stunned. As the crowd rose to their feet cheering, I thought *I almost didn't come. I could have missed this.* My vision blurred. The salty tears tasted wonderful. I clapped till my hands hurt.

Driving home, Jon held his plaque quietly. Finally he said, "Daddy would have been proud of me. He'd smile all the way home, even in the dark car. The men at his office would have to hear about the game tomorrow. And we'd have to talk about every play when we got home tonight, ya know?"

"Yes, I know." He had his daddy pegged perfectly.

"Hey, Mom, did you feel a little proud of me? That I was your son? I mean, did you clap or anything? Are you glad I'm not a nerd or something? They say I might get a scholarship. You think God could swing that?"

"Oh, yes, I'm sure He could. And it's so much fun being your mother. I had no idea you were so good. I'm terribly proud of you. And I'm coming to your baseball games when they start."

I discontinued the Bible studies in my home and decided that I could not make the return trip to the Philippines that some of the group would be making. I always tried to be at home when the boys got in from school. I began learning to listen, and now we are able to talk more about nitty-gritty stuff. The rebellion in the boys has diminished—Jeremy hasn't gotten a single demerit at school, and Jon never mentions moving out.

Of course they aren't perfect, but their response to my authority is different. Recently, when I confronted Jon about something, both of us were all set for me to give him the lecture of the century. But suddenly, as I looked at him, unexpected words burst out. "Oh, Jon, I love you so much. I don't want you to get into trouble. I know it's hard for you to make the right decisions, but I want you to turn out okay more than anything in the world. I know I haven't done everything right since Daddy's been gone.... I've made some big mistakes, but please know that I love you.... "

He grabbed me, all six-feet, one-inch of him, in a bear hug. "I love you too, Mama," he said. "I'm sorry about what I did. I was wrong. I know it was wrong. Go ahead and punish me. I really want to do what is right. You're a good mom. Just keep on saying 'no' and loving us and we're going to be okay... all of us."

A few months ago, I popped out of bed early one morning with a strange new desire. I went to the kitchen and made oatmeal, bacon, toast, and hot chocolate for the boys. Standing at the stove stirring the thick oatmeal, I started crying. *God what is this? No one cries over oatmeal.* But I felt wonderful, happy, secure, excited... obedient. All the opposites of rebellion.

Then a picture came clearly to my mind—one of me feeding eight hundred hungry Philippine children breakfast and then telling them about Jesus. *Oh, God, I* **do** *see. I have to start at home, don't I? With my own children. Never mind that one day they'll leave too.* I poured up the oatmeal, and God poured such joy into *me* that I thought I might do cartwheels right across the floor. But I knew the boys wouldn't understand, so I settled for humming "Amazing Grace."

They came in sniffing the aromas of breakfast, and Jeremy said, "Hey, Jon, she even made our lunch!"

As unto Jesus

few years ago I went through a period when everything I did for my family seemed like an unrewarded duty. *Why,* I thought, *should I be the one to pick up a wet towel? Why should I take time to set a lovely table when my family never comments on it?*

One day I happened to be in the home of a friend who also has four children. As we talked, she picked up a few clothes that her children had left on the kitchen chairs, fixed a casserole, and slipped it in the oven. She seemed so happy that I found myself asking, "Don't you ever feel your family is taking advantage of you?"

"Oh, I did for years," she said, "until I found a little formula. It works with my family, and with strangers too."

"Tell me," I begged.

"Well, I just pretend I'm doing whatever I'm doing for Jesus—to ease His burden. That He's here in my home and He needs me to take care of something or run an errand for Him, or needs a drink of water."

I drove home wondering if anything that simple could really work. In our driveway a bicycle had been left out. "I put this away for You, Jesus," I whispered. Someone had spilled a soft drink in the refrigerator. "I'm cleaning this up for You, Jesus." The phone rang. My son needed a lift. Heading toward my car I noticed the flowers in our yard. "I'll put some on Your table tonight, Jesus."

Suddenly I felt a burst of renewed energy. And I recalled His words... "Inasmuch as ye have done it unto one of the least of these... " (Matthew 25:40).

CHAPTER FIFTEEN

CAUGHT IN DEPRESSION

HOW TO RISE UP OVER DEPRESSION

hen I approached my third year of widow-hood and the last of my four children were about to leave home, I felt very melancholy. It wasn't the first time I had felt depressed, but it was bad enough to keep me awake for entire nights. I seldom laughed and I seemed haunted by thoughts of "how it used to be." All my anticipation for life was gone. Finally, like a drowning person, I cried out, "Do *something*, God!"

The next day I happened to see a small ad in my church paper for a secretary at the church counseling center. I had the strangest feeling that God was telling me to answer that ad. My church was twenty-five miles away, in downtown Atlanta, and I hated driving downtown. Furthermore, I wasn't a secretary and hadn't worked outside the home in twenty-eight years. But in spite of my reluctance, I still felt God nudging me.

I got the job. And I was a disaster. I made one mistake after an-other—even wrote down phone numbers wrong! I had the feel-ing that everyone would be relieved if I quit—including me. The one good thing about it was that I began to take an interest in the people who came in for counseling. I prayed for them. I began to notice their progress and rejoice over their victories.

Slowly things changed for me. I was exhausted when I got home, but content at night, and sleep came again. So did laughter. I began to anticipate the next day. After several months I began to understand why God had wanted me to take the job. Doing something difficult—something for which maybe I wasn't even qualified—had helped me because I was helping someone else.

I've learned some things about depression since then; that you can't escape by running away, that it can attack men and even children. I know, too, that if depression persists, it's wise to seek professional help.

But I've also learned there are things you can do on your own to confront depression:

1. Arm yourself for the battle. I read encouraging passages of Scripture and try to memorize them (Isaiah 61:3 or 40:31, or Psalm 34:17, for instance). I also read from a favorite book, *My Utmost for His Highest,* by Oswald Chambers. Or I listen to inspirational music, sometimes singing along. Of course, I don't *feel* like turning on the tape player. But this is a battle.

2. Try to pinpoint why you are depressed. For instance, I miss being a wife, and I think that if I were a wife again, I wouldn't be depressed. But I must remember that I was a wife for twenty-five years, and there were often times when I felt depressed then. I explain to myself that people, circumstances, and things don't make one really happy. Joy comes from choosing to believe that God is working in my life in *all* circumstances.

3. Do something for someone else. Dr. Karl Menninger of the famous Menninger Clinic once said there's one sure way to avoid having a breakdown, a solution so simple that almost no one will believe it works. You simply walk out your front door and find someone—anyone—who needs help, and you help him or her.

Reaching out, reminding ourselves that we're not alone, is the first step back. We may not be immune from ever feeling depressed, but our powerful God is always standing ready to help us fight the battle against it. After all, He promises us that "sorrow and mourning shall flee away" (Isaiah 51:11).

❦

Sprung from the Depression Trap

Depression and loneliness work together like the jaws of a vise. Once I'm caught in them, all the spiritual principles that I thought I had down pat disappear like a vapor. And soon enough the enemy whispers: *You are alone. No one likes you. You have no purpose in life. No talent. You'll never taste joy again. You aren't a good mother.*

Relief has never come to me suddenly or triumphantly, but rather in seemingly inconsequential bits of interaction with others. And it comes only after I have said to myself: *Okay, depression and loneliness, so you have me again. I've been through this before. I don't know how to get out of this trap. I'm just going to stand still. I'm not even going to battle you.*

Just giving in seems to help me. Then a sort of whirlpool principle takes place. When the struggle is given up, the swirling waters of futility take me to the bottom, and the vise-like grip is suddenly sprung open and I am shot back to the surface... where people are and I'm wonderfully a part of life again.

Sometimes the simplest little acts trigger release. Recently I hit bottom in a whirlpool of depression-loneliness. Within ten minutes I had three phone calls. Two were separate calls from my sons, just telling me where they were going after school and what time they would be home for supper. The third call was from a friend with some good news about a newborn grandchild. Pow! Without any effort I broke out victoriously from my prison of futility. Others needing me and wanting me to share in their lives... what healing there is in a cycle of caring and love!

CHAPTER SIXTEEN

NEW STEPS OF FAITH

LEARNING TO LAUGH AGAIN

When my husband of twenty-five years died, it seemed that laughter died too. I observed others laughing. I recalled laughter, but I couldn't laugh. It was scary to think that I might never laugh again. When my oldest daughter married, she told me, "Know what I miss the most about being away from home? Hearing you and Daddy laughing." Maybe it was the thing I missed the most too. I had always been too serious a person and Jerry had taught me much about laughter. There were times when laughter probably held our marriage together. I knew it was a powerful force. I even knew of a hospital where a room designed just to laugh in had been created on the cancer floor!

A *Guideposts* reader wrote me, "Are you laughing again? You must learn, if you aren't." She had been widowed too, and I respected her advice. We began to correspond. In her next letter she told me how hard it was for her to laugh. One night she was having dinner with a man she knew well but they weren't having much fun. Suddenly, to her own surprise, she spit a watermelon seed across the table at him. Stunned at first, he suddenly burst into laughter and spit a seed back at her. And then for the first time since her husband's death, she laughed, long and hard. (She later married the man whom she'd spit the seed at!) Mercifully watermelon wasn't in season or I may have gone around spitting seeds at everyone.

However, one blisteringly hot day, my daughter and some friends and I met at a renovated, pink, marble mansion for lunch. As we walked around the perfectly manicured gardens, we spotted a fountain with a statue in the midst of a miniature pool. Everything was quite proper and elegant, until I decided to climb into the pool and wade a bit. Fortunately, no one else was around except my small group, and my daughter suddenly joined me as we burst into laughter. It helps to find laughter in childlike, even unconventional ways.

Before long, I was brave enough to talk to others who had suffered a deeply painful experience and learned that, yes, they, too, had lost the ability to laugh and wanted to learn again. Knowing I wasn't alone helped tremendously. Even though I don't usually enjoy movies, I heard about a particularly humorous film that had been playing for over two years. I invited someone who wanted to learn to laugh again to go with me. Quite simply, our aim was to laugh. At first I only smiled in the dark theater while other people roared. But then tears began streaming down my contorted face. I laughed until my stomach hurt. My friend was laughing too. We laughed all the way home. As I told others about the movie, I laughed.

I have found that it also helps to cultivate friendships with people who already know how to laugh. Teenagers (not usually your own) can be excellent choices. A friend's sixteen-year-old daughter phoned to tell me about an incident involving my eighteen-year-old son and herself. They were both riding her horse and fell off in the mud one night in the rain. The young girl giggled first, then finally laughed so hard she only made little puffy sounds into the phone as I listened. Her mirth was contagious, and I soon collapsed on the bed in screeching laughter. Both my sons came to observe me in silent wonder.

Laughter is sometimes appropriate even in heart-tugging situations. It can have a healing, calming effect. I once visited a dying man in the hospital. He could barely speak and was in intense pain. He and his wife had read one of my books and phoned, asking me to come. They were strangers. I had no idea what to say or do. Immediately, the desperately sick man made a stab at humor. I smiled, then laughed. He said something else funny and I laughed again, easily. His pain-filled face was transformed into a wondrous smile as he chuckled softly and squeezed my hand. "It feels so good to laugh," he whispered. "Everyone who comes to see me is so serious." We were no longer strangers.

Our Father must have known how desperately His creations would need to laugh, no matter what life dished out. His Word says: "Then our mouths filled with laughter... the Lord hath done great things" (Psalm 126:2). " ...God hath made me laugh so that all who hear will laugh with me" (Genesis 21:6). "A merry heart doeth good like medicine... " (Proverbs 17:22).

℃

NOT REALLY ALONE

*T*he minister of education at our church handed me a slip of paper and asked, "Will you go by and see her? She called the church for help. I've been, but a woman should visit with her. It involves a divorce." I took the scrap of paper, said I would be glad to go by, and stuck it in my sweater pocket. I didn't plan to go right away, but that piece of paper seemed to get heavier and heavier in my pocket. I woke up the next morning having already decided to go meet Rhyne Sommers. (The names in this story have been changed to protect confidentiality.)

I drove slowly down the unfamiliar street, admiring the beautifully manicured lawns and rustic mailboxes. Finally, a house number matched the number on the paper in my hand. I pulled into the driveway and smiled at the house. It welcomed me with country charm, which included a deacon's bench and lots of hanging baskets. Flowers lined the rock walkway. I was nervous about meeting Rhyne. I had no idea how to help. Just before I rang the doorbell, I prayed, "Lord, I don't know anything about helping someone who's going through divorce." For a moment I nearly prayed that no one would answer the door. I took a deep breath and pushed the bell, once, twice.

It opened suddenly and a little girl about four-years-old looked up at me. She was such a beautiful child, the kind I had seen on the front of Mother Goose books, with long golden hair and inquisitive eyes, that for a moment I didn't say anything. I just stared at her.

"Hi," she broke the silence.

"Hi, is your Mama at home?"

"Yes." She turned around and called, "Maaamaaa... "

I stepped inside the door and felt comfortable in the warm, friendly den. The child called her mother again and looked at me, seemingly a bit worried, a little tense. Her expression suddenly seemed much older than her few years. "Mama is coming," she reassured me.

Rhyne Sommers joined us. She made very little effort to smile or pretend that things were fine. She appeared ready to collapse. The little girl looked up at her mother gravely. Rhyne thanked me for coming, introduced herself and her little daughter, Emily. We went into the living room to talk.

I suspected that Rhyne wasn't the complaining type and that talking about herself was difficult. Sitting erect, her mouth grimly set, eyes puffy, she looked at me and then down at her hands, tightly clenched together. She seemed in such utter despair that I wanted to run out the door. "Lord, help me. What do I say?"

Tell her about yourself—problems you've been through and

how I was sufficient. Just talk about yourself for a while.

I began telling her about some rough experiences I had been through, and felt her absorbing every word. We looked at each other more and more as I spoke, slowly becoming friends. She nodded often, smiled a time or two, then began talking, so softly that I had to strain to hear. "Right out of the blue, Richard told me that he wanted a divorce—wants to be free. I thought our marriage was wonderful," she said hoarsely. Tears spilled down her face and dampened her blouse.

"Asking for help of any kind is difficult for me," she almost smiled. It was my turn to nod. I understood that. Rhyne admitted that while she believed in God and had been in church almost all of her life, that now she needed something else—a more intense relationship with God. She added, "I guess I made Richard my god."

We talked for almost two hours and then went into the kitchen so she could write down my telephone number. I couldn't help admiring her gracious home and charming kitchen—even the way the sun shone into the kitchen through the spotless window and streamed across the shining floor seemed perfect to me.

Rhyne and I exchanged telephone numbers and while she wrote I thought of something that seemed like excellent advice, wise and scriptural. "Rhyne," I began almost glibly, confident my illustration would help her. Then she looked up at me and I noticed that her hand shook as she wrote. I saw the deep agony in her eyes—like a doomed animal in a trap. I didn't share my advice. We just looked at each other. Tears slid down her face and she made a great effort not to cry or lose control. A knot developed in my own throat, and the next moment we were in each other's arms, sobbing. No words were adequate. So we just cried together in her beautiful kitchen as the sun streamed through the quaint kitchen window as though her world were not falling apart.

I called Rhyne the next day and we talked comfortably. She started coming to church and Sunday school regularly. We visited and talked on the phone often. Sometimes we prayed together, or shared Scripture. One Sunday we were sitting together in church and during the invitation hymn I stole a quick glance at her. I hadn't intended it, but our eyes met. She smiled, squeezed my hand quickly, and walked down the aisle. Rhyne was baptized that night and even with her pretty, short hair wet, she was beautiful. Something new shone in her blue eyes.

Rhyne's husband, Richard, still wanted his freedom. That she loved him dearly was quite evident even when she spoke his name, but she agreed to the divorce. Mostly she didn't complain about her suffering. Then, she called one afternoon and was crying. "Oh, Marion, it hurts so bad. I don't think I can do it. I'm not going to be able to give him up. I can't. I just can't. Even if I give him the divorce, I can't let go of him in my heart."

Her defeat and despair came over the telephone and seemed to fill my kitchen. Rhyne was at her lowest. I suddenly believed that if she would take one small step of faith now that God would meet her deepest need. "Listen, Rhyne, will you come to the prayer meeting tonight?" It was Wednesday and she had started coming to our regular midweek prayer service at church.

"No, I don't feel like coming."

"Please. Forget how you feel. Come, not just to be in the church, but just to make one move that you don't feel like making or even understand. Just trust God, please."

"I don't know."

"I'll be looking for you."

"I don't think I'm coming. You don't know how I feel."

We hung up and I prayed that God, Who knew exactly how she felt, would get her there someway.

I sat in the back row at church praying she would come even though the service had started. I sat alone that evening. Announcements were made and we were singing. Finally, I heard the door open softly. I continued singing, joyfully. I just knew it would be Rhyne. She slid into the pew by me and put her hand under half the hymnbook that I held. She leaned over and said, with utter joy, "I believe!" Then we sang, "Be not dismayed what'er betide, God will take care of you… "

The next week Rhyne agreed to meet Richard at the lawyer's office to sign the final papers. She told me, "The night before I was to sign the paper I got this tremendous desire to make Richard his favorite fresh apple pie. I know Jesus gave me the idea and helped me do it. I made it with joy, just like nothing was wrong. I couldn't have done that. When he came by the house I served him fresh, hot apple pie. I don't understand it," Rhyne marveled. Then, she continued, smiling. "And when I had to drive to the lawyer's office, I was scared. There was nobody to go with me. But I started singing 'Jesus Loves Me,' and I didn't feel alone anymore!"

I stared in amazement. She laughed a little, "I can't explain it. I just know Jesus is with me, all the way. He's even keeping the bitterness away."

One morning she stopped by my house with some home-made pumpkin bread. She wore a bright red sweater, and her cheeks were flushed from the cold. She had a smart new haircut and never seemed to stop smiling. Looking at her, I thought, you've passed me in our spiritual walk. You're teaching me now. How grateful I am to know you.

One night at church I asked Rhyne how she would feel about my including her remarkable story as a chapter in my new book. I was all ready for her to say no. I would have understood. But her face lit up and tears brimmed her bright eyes. "Oh, yes, please share my story. Tell others who may be going through it. Tell women who feel shame, who've had their pride crushed publicly, that Jesus will get them through it. He will put them back together. They don't have to be alone."

I nodded gratefully and we left the church. I watched Rhyne come out of the nursery with Emily. It was a dark night—no stars or moon. But I had the warmest assurance that the One Who loved Rhyne the most and had healed her heart, climbed right into the car with her and Emily and went home with them.

𝓒

A FUTURE AND A HOPE

My favorite work of painter Bob Judah was a collection of roads he'd known and loved since his boyhood days. Bob's friendship with the roads dated back over seventy years: paved, dirt, rocky, slick, obscure, open—they led me through an adventure of seasons and locations. I marveled my way through fresh fallen snow, then instantly wandered amidst piles of bronze and golden leaves. Deep within some cool woods a subtle but glorious hint of spring blossomed, and I also followed a dirt road through lush green trees and startling summer sunlight. No figures on the roads, not even animals. Yet, Bob had somehow painted life, emotion, and something almost spiritual into the pictures.

"Bob," I said to him once, "all the roads have a curve in them! They beckon me—make me wish I could go around them. Seems like there's something waiting for me around the curve, something good."

Bob looked pleased. "That's right. When you get discouraged about the future, start believing that God really has something for you—just around the next curve—and keep moving toward it."

Now when I'm traveling, I find myself looking for "Bob Judah Curves." And when I get disheartened, I try to create a road in my mind, reminding myself that just around the next curve is something good... something from God.

CHAPTER SEVENTEEN

LEARNING TO TRUST

THE ONE THAT MATCHES MY HOUSE

After thoroughly examining my old car, my son-in-law, who is a top-notch mechanic, devastated me with the sudden announcement, "You need a new car. Go buy one." I was in my third year of widowhood and felt somewhat like Alice in Wonderland, having to do all kinds of things that I simply didn't know how to do.

My husband had always bought the cars. I have no interest in automobiles whatsoever. I could never understand why he bought new tires when the old ones still rolled around perfectly. I don't like mechanical things. Instantly, a hint of fear began to follow me around. And I had just written a book on how to live fear-free. I also spoke on the subject. Now here I was about to run from the fear of... buying a new car.

Some women might have liked that opportunity. Not me! I decided to go into the yard and weed my tiny flower garden.

It was no use. The fear hunched over each flower with me. I had often told people, "When you are afraid of something, do the very thing you fear. *Never* run from fear."

I stood up and wiped my hands on my slacks, jumped into our

old car and headed for the nearest automobile dealership, the one where Jerry had often talked about getting a new car.

I talked to the Lord on the twenty-minute drive. "You know I don't know how to buy a car. I'm doing this because I don't want to battle fear again. I'm not a car person. I don't know anything to ask about or look for in a car. I want to do this quickly and get it over with. I'm starting to be afraid. You promised in Your Word to be a husband to widows. Be one now and show me how to buy the car You want me to have."

As I neared the automobile dealership, a thought came to my mind. It was beige. Just the color beige. And I thought God asked, *What do you know about cars? Let's go with what you know instead of what you don't know.*

I almost laughed. "Lord, I only know the color I'd like. Beige. You know how much I love beige. How good it makes me feel." Many of my clothes are beige, my sheets are beige. I have beige pets, beige stationery. I live in a beige house.... "Oh, Lord, do you mean I can simply look for a beige car? Could it possibly be that simple? Do You already have my car picked out, knowing how much I love beige?" Such relief and confidence welled up in me that I felt for certain God was answering in the affirmative.

I parked at the dealership and was on my way to the elegant showroom when across the lot, gleaming in the bright sun, I saw the beautiful beige top of a car. *It's yours,* the thought kept running through my mind like an excited child. Once inside the showroom I realized I should probably have changed clothes. But when fear is closing in, there's not always time to dress properly. There was dirt on the knees of my old pants.

An astute young man in his twenties came up. I noticed that all the salesmen wore spiffy blue blazers. "May I help you?" he said and seemed to be overlooking my inappropriate clothing.

"Oh, yes. I believe I want that beige car out there." I pointed.
"An excellent selection. Let me explain some of the features. I'd like for you to look under the hood at the fuel injection—"

"Oh, no, I don't want to do any of that. All I want to do is take the car home for the weekend." It was late Friday afternoon.

"I beg your pardon?" His flashing smile vanished.

"I have to take it home to see if it matches the paint on my house. If it does... it's my car! I believe God has selected that car just for me."

"God... wants you to have that car." He lowered his voice.

"I think so. I need to see if it matches the paint."

"Yes, er... well, we don't usually allow people to take cars home for the weekend. Perhaps you'd like to think about it and bring a paint chip on Monday." He had regained composure.

"No, I might be afraid again on Monday. I've never bought a car before. I can do it now. I *know* I can. Just let me take—"

"Excuse me a moment, please."

He came back with other men dressed in identical blue blazers. They all wore the same smiles. These men were older. One glanced at the dirt on my slacks. "We'd like to assist you in buying a car," he said.

"That's my car out there, the beige one. I know it is. I just need to take it home—"

The young salesman finished the sentence with an I-told-you-so tone of voice: " ...to see if it matches the paint on her house. She thinks God wants her to have this car."

"Where do you go to church?" the man in charge asked.

"First Baptist, Atlanta."

He looked stunned. "My aunt goes there. It's a good, solid church."

I nodded. They wanted to go out and have me look at the car. When we got close to it, I was surprised at how elegant it was. I would have never, never selected such a car for myself. "This is the top of the line," the young salesman said. "It does have two thousand miles on it. It was a demonstrator. Just came on the lot yesterday. Let's take a drive in it."

It wasn't necessary, but I went with him to be polite.

A short time later I drove the magnificent beige car off the lot for the weekend. Some of the salesmen stood and waved to me. I already knew it was my car and was wonderfully happy that buying a car could be so easy. I still had to go back and do the paperwork, but I felt confident, not at all frightened. I was ecstatic that God had indeed shown me a simple way to buy a car. In the driveway I sat and marveled. My car and the house paint could have come out of the same can! Fear was nowhere around.

I drove back early Monday morning to buy the car. I didn't read the contract, but I did notice that the price was an uneven number. I asked the smiling young salesman to change the numbers to that the amount would end in zeros. "I hate uneven numbers," I explained. The amount would reduce the price of the car somewhat. But he came back in a few moments with all the numbers in the neat zeros except for the first two.

The manager there insisted that I look at some brochures, **and** he explained certain features of the car. I smiled, but I wasn't really listening. I was thinking that when the car rolled off the assembly line, God already had selected it for me.

Months later I parked in downtown Atlanta one day. Just as I was getting out of my car, someone parked beside me. To my astonishment it was my car's twin.

The driver of the other car and I looked at each other and smiled. He came over and said, "Well, it certainly seems like you did your homework. I searched for six months, read every consumer report and did a tremendous amount of detailed research to see what new car was the best buy for the money."

I smiled and listened.

"Did you select your car yourself?"

I nodded.

"I'm impressed. I wouldn't think a woman would... well, you know, really investigate the automobile industry and come up with such an excellent choice. Congratulations."

"Thank you. The color's nice too, isn't it?"

Walking away from my new car, I realized that a new truth had come with it. When I have to do something hard, something scary, I can zoom in on what I *do* know about the situation, however insignificant it may seem, and not concentrate on all that I don't know. Then I can call on my Heavenly Father, a God of the nitty-gritty, and He'll help me.

LEARNING FROM MY CAT

*F*ear was creeping up on me as I sat in my living room. I needed to confront a neighbor who I felt had slighted me, and as I tried to pray about it, confusion mounted and my prayer felt empty. Suddenly, our new stray cat Minnie jumped on my lap. It took me a moment to realize that she was fearful. She stood almost paralyzed, staring at something with her ears flattened and her eyes widened.

Finally, I located the source of her fear. Minnie had seen my china cat sitting under a table. The statue looked quite lifelike. I picked it up to let my cat see that it wasn't real. She immediately buried her head under my arm and refused to look. I stroked her and talked to her and gradually she lifted her head, still clinging to my arm. Ever so slowly Minnie sniffed the large china cat. Then she cautiously placed one of her paws on the statue's pink nose. She looked at me in astonishment and then with pleasure. She began to purr. I put the china cat back under the table, and Minnie hopped down and sauntered over to sniff it once more... maybe even to become friends.

Watching her walk confidently around the statue I thought, *Father, I do believe You can teach me about fear and trust, even from a cat!*

I went to the door. I would call on my neighbor and reach out past my fear. And with His help, maybe even find the way to restored friendship.

🍂

CHAPTER EIGHTEEN

RESTORATION

MARION'S MARRIAGE

*A*s I approached my fourth year of being a widow, my son Jon said to me one day, "Mom, you should attend singles meetings. Go somewhere. How will you ever meet anyone?"

I sat at the old oak kitchen table with Jon as he devoured a sandwich. "I can't, Jon. I just can't take a casserole and go to a singles meeting. I didn't like boy/girl parties when I was thirteen. I still don't like them. God's going to have to send someone to me."

"That's crazy, Mom. Do you really think you can just sit here day after day and someone will knock on your door and say, 'Hello. I'm your Christian husband-to-be, sent by God.' "

I brightened. Sounded good to me. "Yes, Jon! That's exactly what I'll do."

"Aw, Mom, be reasonable. You have to date."

I'd dated some. I didn't even like the word for someone my age who'd been married for twenty-five years. Jon left for work and I sat alone, thinking. "Lord," I said, "I do not want to date. I just want to be a wife again. And I don't want to get married simply for companionship. I want a real romance. You select him. You know me better than I know myself." About the middle of last March I added a list of some qualifications for the husband I wanted:

1. God must be first in his life. I want to be second.
2. He's well-read and loves books.
3. Further along than I am spiritually.
4. I'd like to be a minister's wife, but I'll leave that up to you.
5. He has a deep sense of humor so that we can laugh a lot.
6. He's able to communicate and have long conversations.
7. Cares about people, especially people who are hurting.
8. He will allow me to write and speak as long as You want me to.
9. He needs me.
10. There must be romance. Sparks!

In the weeks that followed, thoughts that I believed were from God eased into my mind. *I'm going to answer your prayer for a husband. The answer will come very quickly—so fast it will scare you if you don't trust Me completely. The answer will come through a phone call from a Guideposts reader in response to an article.*

"When will I know for certain, Lord?" I asked.

By your birthday.

So by July 8th I should know something.

In April *Guideposts* published my article on depression. The article evoked responses from quite a few men going through the pain of losing their wives. Phone calls and letters became fairly common—from the Atlanta, Georgia area, as well as other states.

On April 8th I received a telephone call from a professor of sociology at Oklahoma State University in Stillwater. He lived on a small farm with some cattle, a grown son, and a red dog. He was also a minister. Our conversations quickly became a regular thing, three or four times a week. I was corresponding with several other men too as a result of the article and had gone out with several from the Atlanta area. But pretty soon the professor/minister/farmer and I were writing almost every day. Our letters weren't love letters exactly, but there always seemed to be something between the lines, and I easily understood the unwritten messages.

Sometimes Gene Acuff enclosed a blank sheet of paper without explanation. "What's the blank paper?" I finally wrote.

His answer was immediate: "Things I want to say to you that you aren't yet ready to hear."

Gene planned to come to Atlanta to see me. He says that I invited him, but I didn't. "What do you want to see?" I asked. "Where do you want to go?"

"I just want to see you. No parties, no big plans. I want to walk with you, talk and laugh. I want to sit in a porch swing with you and I'd like to go somewhere under a tin roof and listen to the rain with you." I was smiling as I held the phone. I smiled a lot when we talked. We were talking six to eight hours weekly. My mother said I had a certain light back in my eyes again.

Of course, I carefully told myself this wasn't serious. We didn't really know each other. We'd just get acquainted, have some good conversation and good food, and relate our experiences of grief and loss. Gene's wife of twenty-five years had died in February 1987 of an eleven-day brain-related illness. His loss was much too recent for us to be serious. I had no way of knowing then that when Gene read my article on depression in the April *Guideposts*, God spoke to him: *Check your wife's Bible. If she has the same Scriptures underlined that Marion used in the article, phone her right away.* She did and he did. Although neither of us understands it or can explain it, he says God told him then, *She will be your new wife.*

On my fifty-first birthday, I went to get the mail as soon as I saw the mailman put it in the box. I knew a letter from Gene would arrive. He'd already sent me a dozen red roses. There had been some mention of photographs. So far, all I had was a very small family portrait taken several years ago. I wanted some new pictures but wouldn't ask for them.

There were two letters, one so thick I knew it was the promised pictures. I was late for an appointment and it was terribly hot, so I sat in my car with the air conditioning going full

142

blast and read the letters. Just as I opened the pictures, God seemed to say, *Put the tape lying on the seat in the tape deck.* I glanced on the seat. Yes, there lay a tape. Several days earlier all my Christian tapes had been stolen. The police returned them a few days later and by mistake included a country-and-western tape, which I'd meant to give back. I'm definitely not a country-and-western music fan. But I knew Gene was, and I had this funny feeling that something big was about to happen. Playing this tape seemed absolutely crazy, but this whole adventure with Gene Acuff was crazy, so I put the tape in.

Jim Reeves began to sing incredibly sweet songs about love, including an old favorite I hadn't even thought about since I was sixteen: "Evening shadows make me blue, when each weary day is through... how I long to be with you... my happiness."

Tears blurred my vision, and I whispered aloud over my pounding heart, "God, you can't possibly be speaking to me through a stolen country-and-western tape!" I had the photographs in my hand. I looked intently at Gene's smiling face and then at his dog. The dog was smiling too! His expression clearly said, *He's pretty wonderful.* Gene wrote, "If I could take you out on your birthday, I'd pick you up in my old '41 Chevy, and we'd go to a 1950s movie and eat popcorn and drink Cokes from the little bottles, and of course we'd eat Milk Duds at the movies."

"Milk Duds," I screamed over the music, my heart melting like hot butter. No one knew of my passion for Milk Duds. How could Gene Acuff know? Jim Reeves was singing "Have I Told You Lately That I Love You?" I was humming along and trying not to cry on the photograph—as I drove to my appointment an hour late.

That night Gene phoned, and as we were about to hang up he said for the first time, "I love you, Marion." "Thank you, ' bye," I answered curtly and hung up. He said the same thing two nights later and I said the same thing. Only this time I hid under my pillow after hanging up and said, "Oh, God, I don't know how to handle this." The third time he told me he loved me, there was a long silence. Then Gene asked, "Are you going to say what I want you to say?" I took a deep breath. I knew I loved him. It was as though I were a child about to jump off a high dive that I'd tried to jump from many times during the summer. "I love you, Professor Acuff. I really do love you." I had often wondered what his response would be if I ever said those words. His response wasn't to me at all: "Thank You, Lord. Oh, thank You. Praise You, Lord Jesus."

July 27, the date of Gene's planned arrival, finally came. The waiting had been almost unbearable. I had lost twelve pounds and was hardly sleeping. The phone rang at noon, right on schedule, and a voice I knew so well said, "Hello."

"Where are you?" I asked.

"Stone Mountain Inn."

"I'll be there in ten minutes." Driving to the inn, I could hardly believe it was finally happening. We were actually going to meet. Stone Mountain Inn is a resort just ten minutes from my house. I pulled in the driveway. Someone honked at me. Looking in the rearview mirror, I recognized Gene. I thought about sitting in the car and letting him come over. But just like in the movies, we moved very fast toward each other. I left my car running in the middle of the driveway, the door open. My sunglasses dropped on the pavement. Just as we embraced, I remembered some strict advice I'd given my girls when they were growing up: "No public display of affection, *ever*." But right then in the middle of the parking lot in broad daylight with people all around us, we kissed. I lost count of the times.

I had planned a picnic for just the two of us the next day at my cousin's one hundred and fifty-year-old renovated farmhouse located on six hundred acres in northeast Georgia. It is sort of a getaway for them and furnished in antiques. I thought Gene would feel at home there. There were even cattle and three swings and a tin roof. Sitting on a quaint love seat in front of a stone fireplace, Gene started to ask if I would marry him in December.

I suddenly experienced a full-fledged ulcer attack. The stress had been unbearable. We were deeply in love and knew God had brought us together. But he had to return to Oklahoma to teach, and I didn't see how I could just pull up stakes and go with him. My two boys, almost twenty, lived with me. I was paranoid about leaving them alone for even a night, certain they would break some of my rules. Also, my two married daughters and two granddaughters lived nearby. Jennifer, the younger daughter, was expecting her first child. My widowed mother lived less than an hour and a half away. All my dearest friends, my world, was in Georgia. I'd always lived there. And I was booked to speak for the next six months.

Gene had to move to the far end of the love seat. Every time he came close my stomach pains intensified. He held onto my foot and asked me to marry him. I found I could tolerate foot-holding pretty well. I said yes. We talked about maintaining two separate residences and commuting often. Two days later, in exactly two minutes, we selected an engagement ring.

Then it was Sunday. Our week was over. Gene left crying, and I went to my room, crying, and fell across my bed begging God to "do something." He somehow knocked me out. Totally. Meanwhile Gene, en route back to Oklahoma, phoned, but my boys couldn't wake me up. When I did wake up four hours later and they told me he'd called, I somehow knew I must clear my calendar. I started phoning people, asking to be relieved of speaking engagements. In eleven years of speaking, I'd never done such a thing, except when my husband, Jerry, had brain surgery.

Later, Gene called again from Tennessee and asked, "Could you marry me Wednesday of next week?" I checked my calendar and said yes and wrote "Marry Gene" on August 12.

As it turned out, the date was moved to August 14 at seven in the evening. A small ceremony was planned. Gene never asked me to leave my boys. He was content to have a marriage in which we commuted for a while. But God told me clearly, *Quit hovering over your boys. You are trying to be their god. Let Me be God to them.*

Gene and I honeymooned at my cousin's old restored farmhouse. We sort of identified with it. The farmhouse never expected to be whole and alive again with meaning and purpose. Gene and I understood something about restoration. We thought the farmhouse might like us too. Together we were almost 107 years old. The night before we left the farm, God sent the rain we'd so often talked about on the phone and written about. It was our first time to see rain together. As we listened to it on the tin roof, Gene said quietly, "Your formula works, Marion."

"What formula?"

"The restoration formula from your book, *The Nevertheless Principle*."

Oh, yes! Yes, it did work. I could remember the formula almost word for word. When I was slowly watching my husband die from a brain tumor, I carefully examined my restoration formula: "No matter what is taken away from you, if you keep your eyes on Jesus and praise Him, He will restore it to you. You will be joyful to the exact same degree you have hurt. What you have lost will be replaced... joy for mourning... beauty for ashes.... God, I don't see how it could possibly work now. I don't see how You will ever come to me again in any shape or form. But I won't limit You, so I'm going to remember this moment for the rest of my life. And if and when You restore the years that the locusts have eaten, I will tell people about it and write about it. I am committing to You to remember this agony, and if You can come up with some kind of joy to the equivalent that I hurt, You are truly a God of miracles."[1]

On August 22, 1987, Gene and I headed for the Atlanta airport and a new life together. I'd often said after Jerry was gone that if God ever asked me to simply walk out on everything, I would. But I had assumed that it would be for the missions—Africa, not Stillwater, Oklahoma. But God had recently given me an old familiar Scripture with a marvelous life-changing message: "The Lord is my shepherd: I shall not want.... He leadeth me beside the *Stillwaters*. He restoreth my soul.... "

146

SMALL BEGINNINGS

*A*bout two years after my husband died, my grand-daughter Jamie announced one day, "Nanny, you need a husband. I'm going to ask Jesus to send you one."

"Okay, Jamie," I said. Jamie was only three-and-a-half. She didn't really understand that prayer—and romance—don't work that way. The next day she told me with uncontained enthusiasm that she had talked with Jesus and He told her He was sending me a husband who would look like Grady (Jamie's pet name for my late husband).

Two years later, someone entered my life quite suddenly—without warning. We wrote and talked by phone for two months before I saw pictures of him. Jamie and I stared at the photographs in stunned silence. This professor/minister/farmer from Oklahoma bore an amazing resemblance to the husband I'd lost four years before.

When Gene Acuff arrived in Atlanta from Oklahoma, Jamie went straight into his arms. "I knew you'd come," she said softly, arms still tight around his neck. Jamie beamed throughout the entire ceremony when Gene and I were married shortly thereafter.

❦

RESTORED

n July 1985, after my husband's death, I attended a family picnic at my cousin's farm in Georgia, six hundred magnificent acres of green hills dotted with cattle, lakes and a shell of a 150-year-old farmhouse. My cousin Jo and her husband John were restoring the house piece by piece. As I looked out an upstairs bedroom window at unbelievable beauty and serenity, I thought to myself, *This house is going to be restored... alive again!*

I wanted that, too. I asked God, "Could You restore me, too? I want to be a wife again."

Two years later, when I returned, the house was completely restored. The wrap-around porch was rebuilt with three swings, and the house was furnished with antiques. I looked out that same bedroom window and remembered my prayer. I was now corresponding with a man from Oklahoma whom I was soon to meet for the first time. In one of our conversations, he'd asked, "Is there somewhere quiet we can go? Somewhere with a tin roof where we might listen to rain? Somewhere with a porch swing?" We went to the farm together for a picnic one day and it was there, in the parlor, that he asked me to marry him.

On August 14, 1987, having just been married, we returned to the old farm for a week's stay. In the mornings, just as the sun came up, I walked to that same bedroom window, amazed and without adequate words to praise God for my restoration.

CHAPTER NINETEEN

A TIME TO BE HEALED

AN UNSUSPECTED FRIEND

*D*uring those first weeks in Stillwater, Oklahoma, I'd awaken early and tiptoe alone to the patio to watch the sun rise over the barn. Its sudden explosion of radiant light reminded me of our sudden love. The dark, lonely days were really over! Watching the sun, I learned that intense joy, as well as intense sorrow, produces tears.

On those brilliant mornings my prayer was always the same: "God, I don't know how to thank You. I didn't think there would ever be anyone, and You sent Gene to me. Thank You. Oh, thank You."

But I'd overlooked the obvious in my fairy-tale romance. I was moving into the home where Gene and his former wife, Phyllis, had lived, dreamed, loved, and raised their children. I didn't deal with the fact that Phyllis had been gone only a short time when Gene first phoned me, or that we had gotten married just six months after her sudden death. Gene had assured me, "I've worked through the grief."

When I stepped inside the country home with him and met some of his children and grandchildren, they smiled, hugged me and said appropriate things, but I could see the unmistakable grief in their eyes and beneath their warm smiles.

It made me wonder, *Is Gene grieving too?* My luggage suddenly looked out of place sprawled on the floor—and I felt out of place too. Even then I knew I didn't want to deal with grief again. My own had nearly destroyed me.

Shortly after arriving, I found a place of solace in my new home. When Gene looked sad or attempted to remember Phyllis, I learned to retreat to a beautiful pink bathroom with wallpaper much like some back in the home I'd left in Georgia. Fixing my eyes on the sweetly familiar paper, I'd reason: *Maybe I can live in this lovely bathroom. It's roomy but cozy. I just can't go out there and battle grief again.*

We'd been married about two months when I decided to make Gene a cup of hot, spiced tea. As I handed him the cup, a look of sadness crossed his face. He took the steaming tea to the kitchen table and set it down. We both stared at it mutely, and I knew—Phyllis had made that same kind of tea. I didn't want him to tell me about it. And he didn't.

Gene suggested we go for a walk. Each day we walked around the pasture with Elmo, Gene's golden retriever, and Bobby, a stray kitten we'd taken in. The sun was low and the air nippy, so we bundled up, held hands and walked fast. Gene said, "You walk faster than Phyllis." Then he was silent.

I thought, *Only a few months ago he was walking in this same pasture with another wife.* I knew he needed to talk, but I was afraid that he would and I'd be involved with grief again.

Then, without warning, a silent voice spoke clearly to my heart: *Marion, you need to grieve for Phyllis.* I wasn't even praying or asking God anything, and the strange message so startled me that I slowed my pace.

"What's wrong?" Gene asked, slowing down also.

I insisted nothing was the matter and quickened my step. I wanted to examine God's instructions more carefully before sharing them with Gene.

I waited a week before telling Gene I believed God wanted me to grieve with him for Phyllis. A look difficult to explain crossed his face: pain, laced with enormous relief and gratitude.

I had no idea how to grieve for someone I'd never known,

someone I didn't even want to think about, but I wanted to be willing to follow God's instructions.

The very next day I was searching for some Scotch tape and discovered a cabinet where Phyllis had kept all of her gift-wrapping supplies, right next to the pink bathroom. It was crammed full of fancy paper, ribbons, new greeting cards, tape, gift lists, mailing supplies. From that first moment, I adored the cabinet. Most of my cabinets and closets back in Georgia were jumbled, just like this one. There were days, while Gene lectured at Oklahoma State University, that I went to the "clutter cabinet" not really needing anything; I just opened it and simply stood there, inhaling the lovely feeling that was always there for me.

As I searched through the cabinet, I realized what a giver Phyllis had been. There were lists of things she planned to buy for people. She really cared about people. On lonely days I sometimes longed to actually crawl inside the cabinet. And as I continued to ramble through the clutter cabinet, I began to "know" Phyllis.

Gene encouraged me to open drawers, look at scrapbooks, do anything necessary to make myself feel at home. I admired the many lovely antiques and touched some of them gently. I picked up some of Phyllis' books—we liked the same books. Thumbing through her Bible I discovered that we had underlined many of the same passages. I dusted her grand piano and antique organ carefully, almost reverently.

While looking through a drawer one day, I found a lipstick—hers. I held it tightly in my hand, feeling I had no right even to touch it, but unable to put it down. Finally I pulled the top off. My heart pounded. It wasn't some harsh red or bright purple, but a lovely shade of coral. I leaned toward the mirror and applied some of her lipstick, and a thought struck as powerfully as lighting, a memory from high school: *Only best friends use each other's lipstick.* I slipped the tube of lipstick in my skirt pocket and sort of patted it most of the day. I carried it wherever I went for weeks. Somehow it gave me courage.

The first snow of the season came unexpectedly early. "Gene, let's go out in the snow!" I begged.

A startled look came over him. "Phyllis used to beg me to play in the snow with her," he said. "She loved it. I never wanted to. I had to work outside in the snow with the cattle, and so snow never meant fun to me."

All the time he spoke, he was putting on his boots, gloves, warm coat, and bright-orange hat. Elmo joined us outside. The fresh snow crunched beneath our feet. Gene stopped suddenly, looking down the road in front of the house as though he saw something in the distance. "The last time it snowed, nine months ago, Phyllis wanted me to walk down that road with her. She begged me to. I didn't. I remember so clearly that she and Elmo walked without me... I watched from inside."

I squinted my eyes and looked down the white country road, and I could almost see them.

Back inside, we were getting out of our coats and boots when I looked at Gene and recognized such open, raw grief, I almost gasped. He managed with great difficulty, barely above a whisper, "I keep thinking she's coming back." No tears, just quiet, desperate agony.

Holding his face in my cold hands, I silently asked God what to do. I was shocked at what came out of my mouth. Gently but firmly, looking Gene right in the eyes, I said, "It's over, Gene. She's never coming back. Phyllis is gone. *Really* gone. She's okay now, but she's never coming back."

He broke and cried long and hard. We held on to each other and I cried too. When the tears were over, he said, "You two would have liked each other."

But the struggle was far from over. The following July 4, 1988, was one of Gene's most difficult bouts. Phyllis had loved the Fourth, and she and Gene had always had friends and family over with lots of food and fireworks. She was a marvelous hostess and cook. Gene and I chose to spend the Fourth alone, almost anticipating that grief would track us down this day. We were quiet, both seeming to realize that no words would help. This day simply must be endured. Gene sat in his favorite recliner, sometimes speaking in broken sentences and sometimes remembering quietly. I sat close by on the sofa. We hurt together. Instead of driving us apart, the shared grief was bringing us even closer.

One day the following month, Gene and I went swimming in his daughter Jo Shelley's pool (she lived about three miles from our farm). Now that I "knew" Phyllis, I could see her radiant smile in Shelley's expression. Gene didn't really enjoy swimming, but he hadn't made the time to swim with Phyllis, so now he wanted to swim with me. It was a scorching, cloudless day and we were hanging onto a raft, still discussing grief, and Gene asked, "Why does it have to hurt so much, Marion?"

I felt God guiding me to an explanation, and I said, "Gene, this might be the answer: Grief is to healing what labor is to delivery. To prevent it or even slow it down would be unnatural, disastrous. Grief is really our unsuspected friend who introduces us to healing."

After that, we talked more openly about grief. I told Gene about the time I was flying to speak to a group, Jerry had been dead two years and I hadn't hurt for several days. I had assumed that my grief process was finally over. I felt confident, secure. Then a man in the seat next to me opened a complimentary pack of peanuts and rolled them around in his hand for a moment before popping them into his mouth, slowly, one at a time. Jerry had eaten peanuts exactly like that. I was pulled back into fresh, smothering grief.

"Did you ever think you were losing your mind?" Gene asked suddenly.

"Oh, yes! That's a real part of grief. It will pass."

When we were about to celebrate our first wedding anniversary, I went to the clutter cabinet for ribbon for Gene's gift. A few bright ribbons fluttered to the floor, along with a card I'd never seen. I picked up the card. On the front were two smiling bears, one holding a bridal bouquet. It read, "Congratulations. God has given you the best—each other. 'Delight thyself also in the Lord: and He shall give thee the desires of thine heart' " (Psalm 37:4). Phyllis had bought the card for someone else, but just for a few precious, crazy moments, the card was from Phyllis to me.

That evening I pulled out the card and told Gene what had happened, and he smiled. There was no grief. At last Gene had worked his way through it—to joy.

Oh, grief will visit us again from time to time, but now we can meet it head on, because that unsuspected friend has brought us healing at last.

❦

THE HEALING TREE

*T*hat golden Sunday afternoon in autumn I was feeling lonely and depressed. For some reason I had begun to doubt myself as a wife and mother. No one really seemed to need me. Our oldest daughter was married and expecting her first child. Our nineteen-year-old daughter and I had been having some personality clashes. The thirteen-year-old twin boys seemed to look to their father for everything. He was fun-loving, always the one to say yes to them, while I mostly said, "No. Absolutely not. Brush your teeth. Pick up your clothes. Take out the garbage. Don't tilt your chair back.... "

Now Jerry, my husband, was watching a football game again. And it was such a pretty day. He'd gone to a high school game with the boys on Friday night. I'd stayed at home alone. Then Saturday he'd listened to a game on the radio. Now he was going to watch another game on TV. I sat across from him in the den, glaring at him. He knew the look well. It meant "Please don't watch that game. Talk to me. Or at least glance my way now and then." But he was absorbed in the television, even talking to the players as if they were in the room with him.

Glancing out the window at the unbelievably blue sky, I asked somewhat hesitantly, "Do you want to go for a walk in

155

the woods?" There was a special place in the nearby woods where we sometimes walked and talked. For me, going there was always like a mini-vacation.

"No," he said, still looking at the screen. Our nineteen-year-old rolled her eyes up in her head momentarily as though it was a ridiculous suggestion. The boys laughed. Sometimes I felt that they were all against me. No one even looked up as I picked up the car keys and went out the door.

I drove to the woods that I loved so much, and began to wander. Looking up, I could see patches of sky through the trees that seemed to hug one another high above me. The only sounds were my own footsteps, the murmur of water in a nearby brook, and an occasional plane droning overhead. I sat on a log for a while, then moved on, then sat on an old stump. Then I was up again, pressing on as if looking for something; I had no idea what.

At a distance, standing apart from the other trees, at the edge of a brook, I could see a tall black walnut tree. "I feel like that tree," I muttered, "all alone." I went and sat beneath it. *Yes, I said to myself, this is a very special tree. It's as though God put it here just for people who happen to be walking through the woods feeling sad.*

I leaned my head back against the tree's solid trunk and looked up into a limb directly above me. Some of its leaves were brown now, and shriveled. A wind stirred, detaching a few of the brown leaves and twirling them in the air. The time was right for them to leave the branch. *And how easily this old walnut tree lets those leaves go, I said to myself. If only I could let go as easily, as naturally.*

"O Lord," I prayed out loud, "teach me about letting go."

On impulse I picked up a tiny branch that lay near me. "God," I said, "this branch symbolizes my husband. I want to let go all those things about him that bother me. I want to accept him just as he is, even if that includes football every day. I give up trying to change him. Give me a fresh, new love for him. Straight from You. Now I set him free to be all *You* want him to be, not what *I* want him to be." I cast the branch into the water and watched it move downstream.

I picked up a smaller one. "God, this fragile stick is Jennifer. I let go of her too. I will stop trying to control her life. I want to smile just looking at her and not offer so much advice. Let her be all You want her to be. Show me how to give her up again." I let go of that stick and it began its journey downstream.

Next I picked up a fat stick. "Lord, this fat stick is Julie—pregnant. She doesn't seem to need me so much. Not nearly as much as I thought she would. She's so efficient and self-confident. Help me re-release her to You. Don't let me be meddlesome or interfering." I threw the Julie stick in.

I picked up two sticks and, holding one in each hand, I prayed, "Lord, these are Jon and Jeremy. I don't know why they fight all the time and do things that upset me so much. They're so loud, and I love quietness. I don't know why I can't think of fun things to do with them like their daddy can. Please, Lord, don't let me be jealous of my own husband. Don't let me press the boys into a mold of what I think they should be. Keep me from being so fearful that they will get into trouble. Help me let them be themselves." I threw the twin sticks in.

Reaching over, I took one more stick from the ground and held it awhile. "Lord, this is me. I'm so stiff and unyielding. Not very lovable. And I'm not nearly as nice as I once thought I was. So much in me is ugly and selfish. So demanding. Well, I'm giving up trying to be a superwife and supermom, Lord. Please figure out a way to use my failures. They're so many. I'm tired. You take over. Do it Your way. Just love my family with Your unconditional love. I don't know how anymore." I dropped the me stick into the stream and it joined the others and they all disappeared together around a curve.

Finally I looked at my watch. I'd been in the woods almost two hours. I stood up and started walking toward where I'd left the car. But I turned to look at the tree because something stirred within my heart. What was that elusive feeling? Happiness! Yes, I was happy again.

I smiled at the tree. This old walnut had restored me. It was a healing tree. And why not? Why couldn't God have created a healing tree for me?

He did, you know!

I walked faster... almost running toward home.

CHAPTER TWENTY

MAMA KNOWS BEST

MAMA'S PLAN

I suppose it was the reality of my first grandchild, Jamie, starting school that triggered the bittersweet memories of my first year of school. The year was 1942. "Miss Edna" was that marvelous old-fashioned kind of teacher who gladly put her entire life into teaching. I loved school: the smell of chalk and colored crayons; the way the old wooden floors smelled after Jim, the janitor, had waxed them; and having my own desk that was just my size. There was, however, one overwhelming problem with school. Mildred. (Name has been changed.)

Daily when I walked the short distance home after school, Mildred would taunt me, hit me, and scare me. I was absolutely terrified of her. She had failed first grade and was a year older than I. Mildred didn't have any friends, so she seemed to concentrate on making enemies. Because I was one of the smallest children in first grade, she had selected me as her number one enemy.

As we walked home after school, she would continuously step on the back of the heels of my shoes and cause the shoes to slide down. Then, when I stopped to adjust them, Mildred would slap me hard on the back. As soon as the dismissal bell rang each day, my heart started to pound and I blinked fast so I wouldn't cry.

Pretty soon my mother figured out something was wrong at school. I didn't want to tell her about Mildred. I sat close to the radio listening to *The Lone Ranger*, pretending not to hear her questions about school. Mother continued to question me, and finally I sobbed out the whole story. "You can't do anything, Mama. *You can't.* Everyone will think I'm a baby."

It was impossible for Mother to pick me up after school. She had to work. My father had died a few years earlier. I didn't have any sisters or brothers to watch after me. I couldn't imagine what my mother might do. I was certain there was no answer— no answer at all for a problem this big.

The next day at school, Miss Edna leaned over my desk and whispered, "Marion, dear, could you stay after school and help me with a project? I spoke with your mother last evening and she said it would be fine with her." Her blue eyes were understanding and she smelled like Jergens hand lotion. I decided right then that all angels must have blue eyes and smell like Jergens hand lotion. I nodded eagerly.

I remained joyfully at my desk when the dismissal bell rang. Mildred looked confused for a bit, but filed out with the others. After a while Miss Edna said that I'd better be going on home. She stood on the front step of the school and waved to me. I skipped up the hill without any fear whatsoever. Then, just as I got to the top of the hill, I heard familiar footsteps behind me. Mildred had waited for me. She immediately stepped on the back of my shoe and slapped my back. I cried. I couldn't help it.

When my mother saw my face after she got home from work, she questioned me. I begged not to go to school and I didn't sleep much that night. The next morning she said, "Marion, I'm going to walk up the hill with you today. I believe we'll see Mildred." Mildred walked from way across town to school. She never bothered me on the way to school, only afterward.

"Oh, Mama, please don't do that! Don't say anything to Mildred. It will just make her mad. Let me stay home by myself. Please, Mama."

"Hurry and get dressed, Marion." Her voice was gentle, but quite firm.

"Ple-e-ease, Mama."

"Trust me, Marion. I have a plan." My insides were in turmoil. Why couldn't my mother understand that no plan she had dreamed up was going to work? We bundled up against the bitter cold and started walking up the hill. Maybe we wouldn't see Mildred, I hoped. But my mother had this confident look. I knew the look well, and I had a sinking feeling that we would see Mildred and that Mother would use her "plan."

Sure enough, just as we got to the top of the hill and I had to go in one direction to school and my mother in the opposite direction to her job at the bank, we spotted Mildred. We waited a few horrible moments as she approached. She pretended not to see us, recognizing that I had my mother with me.

"Hello, Mildred," Mother said quietly. Mildred stopped, frozen as still as a statue. Her hands and face were bright red from the intense cold. Her oversized coat hung open. There were only two buttons on it. The rest were missing. Underneath she wore a cotton dress, as though it were summer. I was so wrapped up I could hardly walk. I even had to wear undershirts.

Mother stooped down to Mildred's level. She didn't say anything at first. Instead she rapidly buttoned Mildred's coat and turned the collar up around her neck. Then she fastened back this stubborn piece of hair that forever hung in Mildred's face. I stood off to one side watching our breath lingering in front of our faces in the frigid morning air, praying that no students would happen by and that my mother's plan would be over quickly.

"I'm Marion's mother. I need your help, Mildred." Mildred looked intently at my mother with an expression I couldn't identify. Their faces were inches apart. My mother's gloved hands held Mildred's cold ones as she spoke. "Marion doesn't have any brothers or sisters. She sort of needs a special best friend at school. Someone to walk up the hill with her after school. You look like you'd be a fine friend for her. Would you be Marion's friend, Mildred?" Mildred chewed on her bottom lip, blinking all the time, and then nodded.

"Oh, thank you!" Mama said with certain confidence and gratitude. "I just know you are someone I can depend on." Then she hugged Mildred long and hard. She gave me a quick hug and called to us as though nothing unusual had happened. "Bye, girls. Have a good day." Mildred and I walked on to school, stiffly, like mechanical dolls, both staring straight ahead without speaking. Once I cut my eyes over her way. Mildred was smiling! I'd never seen her smile before.

We walked up the hill each day after school together, and pretty soon we were talking, laughing, sharing secrets. Mildred started tying her hair back the way Mama had. Sometimes she even wore a hair ribbon. Someone sewed buttons on her coat, and she buttoned all of them and always wore the collar turned up. Somehow I started calling her "Mil." The others did too, even Miss Edna.

"Hey, Mil, sit by me," someone called out at lunch. "No, Mil, sit with us," someone else begged. Mildred shot them a happy smile, but she always sat with me at lunch. My mother usually included something in my lunch especially for Mil—even notes of gratitude. Mil always let me in front of her in the line at the water fountain.

Valentine's Day was a very important event in first grade back in the '40s. We made huge valentine boxes and set them on our desk for a valentine exchange. I pulled out an enormous valentine toward the end of the party. Everyone stood up to see better. It was store-bought! And had obviously cost a lot. Most everyone had made their valentines from red construction paper, lace and glue. Ahhhs and ohhhs floated out over the classroom and seemed to linger, suspended in the air, as I opened the magnificent valentine. Printed neatly in bold red letters inside the card was: "From your best friend."

I looked over at Mil. She was sitting with her hands folded on top of her desk and smiling the biggest smile ever. She had a red ribbon in her hair. Mildred smiled a lot now. She was getting good grades now too and didn't stuff her papers inside her desk anymore. Her eyes darted over and met mine. Right then I knew my mother's plan had worked.

I didn't understand Mama's plan back in 1942, or for years afterward. But along the way I discovered where my mother had got her remarkable plan. And I've learned that the plan works in all kinds of impossible situations: "Love is patient... kind... does not act unbecomingly... is not provoked, does not take into account a wrong suffered... believes all things, hopes all things, endures all things. Love never fails" (1 Corinthians 13:4-7).

❦

ONE SINGLE ROSE

When my mother was a little girl, the family homestead burned down and almost everything they owned was lost. To this day she has a vivid memory of the family riding away from the gutted house in a horse-drawn wagon, her father, silent and inscrutable, sitting up front. The children looked to their mother to understand better how to deal with their loss.

My mother says she will never forget the expression on her mother's face. She was serene, smiling slightly and appeared totally unshaken. In one hand she held a single rose—the only thing she had been able to rescue.

As the children watched, she lifted the flower to inhale its lovely fragrance and then she allowed each child in turn to sniff at the delicate petals. No words were spoken. While the wagon carried the family away from their devastated home, the children and their mother focused their attention on the pristine beauty of a single red rose.

When as a child I heard that story, I thought my grandmother had made a poor selection as she ran out of the burning house. But now that I am a mother and grandmother myself, I am astonished by the wisdom and faith of this remarkable woman. Very simply she gave her children the essence of faith: to let go and let God in, for if we are but quiet and listen, we will find Him speaking to us in even our most difficult moments.

❧

CLOSE BY

When I was about four years old, my mother made arrangements for our next door neighbor to keep me while she worked. I didn't like being separated from my mother, but my father's death made her working a necessity. When my mother came home to lunch each day, she would come next door to see me for a short while. But I began to cry when the lunch hour was over and she had to return to work.

So she stopped coming to see me around noon. I did all right as long as there wasn't that middle-of-the-day reunion and separation again.

Only when I was grown and had children of my own did I learn that she sat at our kitchen window each day and watched me playing next door without letting me know that she was close by. I thought she was far away at work.

Sometimes there are days when God seems far away. It almost seems that He doesn't love me. But I remember how my mother watched me playing. She longed to come and hold me close for a few minutes, but realized it was best for me if she didn't.

I'm sure that God must be close enough to touch me many times each day, probably when I feel the most alone, but for some reason I can't understand, He doesn't always reveal Himself to me.

Nevertheless, He's close by—watching and loving me, His child.

CHAPTER TWENTY-ONE

HELLO'S AND GOODBYE'S

THE HARDEST BATTLE

Julie West Garmon
Julie West Garmon is the
oldest daughter of Marion Bond West

he doctor had been very matter-of-fact after my ultrasound, but a certain sentence she said locked in my mind and played over and over again: "Your baby's head is so low, I can't get accurate head measurements." I was thirty-two weeks pregnant and an earlier ultrasound at six weeks had revealed that my baby should be born May 28, 1989. Without asking any questions I quickly left the doctor's office, and by the time I got into my car and started driving I knew a mighty battle had begun in my mind.

I tried to reassure myself that *of course* everything was alright. I told my husband, Ricky, I was certain everything was okay. But since I had worked for a pediatric group before having children, I was familiar with a term that kept racing around in my mind. "Anencephaly," meaning an absence of most of the brain. I couldn't forget about it and spent hours searching through medical books from the library. Everything I read fueled the fierce battle going on inside me. My suspicion was too agonizing to share with my doctors or even my husband. Some days the fear would advance unexpectedly and quickly defeat any peace I'd tried to gain. Other days fear hid quietly. But just as day always turns to night, fear always returned to attack my thoughts.

At an Easter egg hunt, I spotted a friend who had recently delivered a baby with anencephaly. I found it impossible to allow myself to even look at her. If this happened to her, surely it could happen to me too.

Days passed, even clumped-together weeks, during which time I convinced myself that my baby was healthy. Looking down at myself, I reasoned that since I had normal arms and legs, of course my baby would be normal too. But when I was alone or at night in bed, the all-out battle started up again.

Decorating the nursery seemed to get done in slow motion. I had a hard time taking the plunge and becoming enthused. Friends asked why I hadn't "fixed-up" the room sooner. Pretending to be too busy with other things, I responded that I still had plenty of time. But deep in my heart I felt somehow strangely unattached to this nursery. My husband, our daughters, Jamie, seven, and Katie, five, and I finally chose an adorable border of geese, hearts, and teddy bears. We painted the furniture red and the walls bright yellow. My husband insisted there was a possibility that we might have a boy, and wanted bright, primary colors. After we completed the nursery, I took a deep breath and rationalized: "There! A wonderful nursery, even more elaborate than the first two had been. Surely this would help produce our healthy baby." My sister-in-law gave me a shower in April. While driving home I thought: "The trunk is filled with marvelous, happy, baby things. This has to be a good sign!"

Twelve days past my due date, contractions began at nine in the morning. At nine that night we entered the hospital. Within an hour, and after four ultrasounds, I knew I was living out my nightmare. During the third ultrasound I gravely commented to one of the doctors, "I know what you're looking for. You're trying to locate the top of the baby's head. And you're thinking anencephaly." At last, I had spoken aloud the word that had terrified me all these months.

The two doctors performing the scan stopped their frenzied motions, and were speechless. One finally admitted, "You're right. We're ninety percent sure we're dealing with an anencephalic infant." It was as though I was locked in a hideous horror movie and couldn't fight my way out. The labor room seemed to squeeze in on us. It felt as though we were under water with no oxygen. Ricky held my hand tightly, but didn't quite understand the severity of the problem. "It'll be okay," he insisted.

"No! You don't understand, Ricky. The baby will live maybe hours, but not more than a few days. We won't be taking the baby home!" I had begun to speak in whispers. It nauseated me to speak the truth in normal tones.

When Ricky finally understood what we were facing, he looked long and hard out the huge picture window at the pouring rain. We cried in silent unison with the rain. *Will I always hate the rain after this? Will it always suffocate me?*

Gently, and very quietly, small bits of Scripture began to come to me like an occasional leaf in a rushing water. "What time I am afraid I will trust in Thee... " (even in this Lord) " ...Lean not to thine own understanding... In all thy ways acknowledge Him, and He will direct thy path."

"God, this is unreal. People don't come to the hospital to have a baby and no one smiles. Why won't anyone smile at me? Surely I've been wrong all along. Surely the ten percent possibility of error will win out and my baby will be fine." The doctors communicated through a secret language using only their eyes, but Ricky and I understood everything they "said." The battle within me intensified. Mentally, I screamed: "Oh, let us go home and begin all over again. We will start timing contractions and come back later. This can't be real." The room felt incredibly heavy. Even the rhythmic sounds of the baby's normal heart tones seemed to thump: *Bleakness... no hope... you were right all along... bleakness... no hope... you were right all along....*

But deep within me, wedged far below the crushing fear, a tiny speck of faith struggled relentlessly to emerge. Finally, I acknowledged it and decided: "God... I trust You... no matter

170

what. I will learn in the next few hours if all the promises about You are true."

An unsmiling nurse offered something to relax me. I said, "No thank you," having decided to totally use my thoughts to draw me closer to God. She did give me a bitter drink before my epidural. Within a few short minutes my hard trembling stopped. I floated in a pool of golden sunshine. I immediately asked if she'd slipped me a tranquilizer.

"No. Just an antacid before the epidural."

"God, this warm trust I feel is from You! Not any drug.... 'My God shall supply all your needs according to His riches in Christ Jesus.' "

"What about the girls? How will this make any sense to them?" I asked Ricky. Katie had gone with me to several doctors appointments and put the stethoscope to her ears. Smiling, she'd listened to the baby's heartbeat. She already seemed to have a big sisterly relationship with the baby. Whenever she commanded it to move, it did. At bedtime, both girls kissed me and my tummy goodnight.

"I'll handle it," my husband answered with strong confidence. My labor progressed normally. It seemed odd that my body could continue to function with my mind in such a tremendous battle. Somehow, the green scrubs Ricky was dressed in for delivery didn't seem appropriate now. Hospitals should have a different color for people in our situation. We moved into the delivery room. It had always been such a positive, happy place before. Now it seemed as though I was entering a dungeon of some kind. The delivery was long and difficult. I remember thinking: "This is like swimming across miles of water and not knowing if there is a shore. 'When you go through the waters, I will be with you.... ' "

Our son, Robert Clifford Garmon, was born at three-twenty in the morning on June 9, 1989. He lived for twenty-five minutes. After his birth, there were no triumphant, "It's-a-boy!" shouts. Total silence. No one spoke. It was as if each person in the room played a part in a painful pantomime. In the recovery room, I sobbed to Ricky, "Why a son? Why did it have to be a

171

boy?" as though he knew some logical, wonderful explanation.

I asked to see my son. Ricky had examined him thoroughly just after he was born. Robbie had been carefully wrapped in a blanket and had on a little white cap. His face was extremely bruised from the delivery, but perfect. He weighed a little over six pounds and looked a lot like Katie. He came and left so quickly. *Hello, Robbie. Goodbye, Robbie.*

Ricky had to leave the hospital to disassemble the most elaborate nursery I'd ever created and to make funeral plans. Then he came right back to the hospital for me. They allowed me to check out nine hours after Robbie's birth.

Ricky and I drove silently to my mother's house. There we waited for my sister, Jennifer, to bring Katie and Jamie to us. I opened my eyes wide and blinked hard, practicing for when they walked in the front door. My heart pounded in my ears. Ricky had "explained things" to them and told me they were doing fine. But I could picture their sad faces... and feel their tremendous disappointment. I couldn't see myself being positive about Robbie's death with them.

Suddenly, in the midst of my thoughts, they both ran in, each holding a box of Nerds (their latest "favorite" candy). They hopped onto the sofa beside me as though they had rehearsed. Katie said right away, "If Robbie had lived we would have bought him a box of Nerds, but he's in heaven."

Jamie added, "Grady's probably holding him." (Grady is their pet name for my father who died five years earlier.) "I'll bet Grady said, 'Here comes Robbie!' " They sat very close to me, smiling genuine smiles. Their hands rested on my arm.

No bitterness! No anger! No complaints! Smiles and excitement. Total acceptance over such a horrible disappointment? Their reaction to Robbie's death had been one of my biggest worries. *Oh, Lord, You have truly healed my broken-hearted children and are binding up their wounds. Thank You.* I remembered that children's broken bones heal much more quickly than adults' bones do. Maybe their hearts do, too.

Depression found me in the weeks to come. My hardest times were the very first moment of the day and late in the afternoon.

One day I sat on my bed mentally reliving everything. My thoughts carried me through my entire pregnancy. I had to cover all the bases, making sure that somehow I hadn't done something to cause the baby to be born with anencephaly.

Two weeks after Robbie's death, Katie and her Daddy had been playing one-potato, two-potato, three-potato, four... with their fists balled up. Ricky had to go cut the grass. "Maybe your Mother will play with you," he suggested. She looked at me with questioning eyes.

"Katie, I don't feel like playing right now." She shrugged her shoulders slightly, nodded as though she understood perfectly, and went into the den. Out of the corner of my eye I saw her with her fists balled up once again. But this time she threw her arms up high when counting and looked up toward the ceiling, changing, "One-potato, two-potato, three-potato... "

"Katie, what are you doing?" She never missed a beat of her game.

"I'm playing one-potato with Robbie." I quietly struggled to reach her level of faith. Robbie was okay. Really okay. He just lived somewhere else. Even so, I had a lot of emotions to work through.

The next morning I got out a washcloth to wash my face. It was baby blue, and the delicate color brought back the intense agony of losing Robbie, as though I were in the delivery room again. Then I remembered a sentence my grandmother—we call her Goge—had shared with me a week before Robbie's birth. She had no idea I was apprehensive about my baby. The sentence hadn't made much sense then, but now I leaned, rested against the thought, and examined it carefully; *The hardest battles are not fought in the battle fields, but in a mother's heart.*

As I accept Robbie's death, a newfound Scripture flies high in my heart somewhat like a victory flag: "The Lord says you must not be discouraged or be afraid... the battle depends on God, not you" (2 Chronicles 20:15).

Author's Note: Julie and Ricky are expecting a baby this year.

"HI THERE"

never imagined I'd turn away from a child's friendly, open smile. Then my daughter Julie's little boy Robbie died twenty-five minutes after birth. I didn't seem to want to acknowledge that there were babies in the world, so I carefully avoided the baby department in stores, as well as the "new arrivals" section at card shops. For nearly six months, I managed to look away abruptly from babies sending out smiles my way. I never returned even a trace of a smile.

Then it happened without warning. I was eating at a fast-food restaurant and didn't glance at the playground or at any of the children who were excitedly eating their hamburgers. I felt the "beaming" smile on me like a laser beam before I saw it. The little fellow was about eight months old. He had to lean far to the right and put his head on the table in order to catch my eye. He smiled. I stared back at him expressionless. I was getting pretty good at this. Then he waved one tiny hand—quickly, almost timidly. I didn't mean to, but I waved back—quickly, almost timidly. He waved again, and I waved awkwardly as though I'd never waved to anyone before. Then I felt it coming. A smile. It traveled bravely toward my face and for a moment had to pause behind my clenched teeth. Suddenly, I smiled at him. He laughed out loud and I released waves of pent-up smiles.

When I left, I touched his hand briefly, passing by his high chair. God had brought unexpected, much-needed healing through this child—silently, quickly, and thoroughly.

CHAPTER TWENTY-TWO

GESTURES OF LOVE

THE GENUINE BIRTHDAY PRESENT

"Collect call from Jon," the operator said.

"Yes, of course I'll pay," I answered excitedly. Jon's calls from college were infrequent and short. Usually he only phoned to inform me that he'd be home for the weekend. I always hoped that we'd have a real conversation one day. I was excited because I was certain Jon would be coming home this weekend. It was his and his twin brother's nineteenth birthday. Jon had asked several weeks ago, "Mom, plan a real party. Invite all the family and make reservations at some good restaurant, okay?" Jon's a real food person. I'd made all the arrangements—even ordered a cake to be presented at the restaurant. I was so excited. I imagined that Jon and I wouldn't argue this weekend. Just maybe this weekend would be good. Surely, Jon and I wouldn't fight about grades, his newfound freedom, or moral issues. I planned to take Jon shopping for a new bike. All the students at Berry College rode bikes. The campus has the largest acreage in America. I knew he wanted a bike.

"Hi, Jon," I said with real enthusiasm, feeling very motherly.

"Lo, Mom." A long silence told me instantly that everything

wasn't okay. My excitement fizzled quickly. "Er... Mom... I'm not coming home for my birthday."

"But Jon, everything's planned... "

"Go ahead without me."

"But it's *your* birthday."

"I have other plans." His tone of voice told me not to proceed with this conversation. Immediately, I knew I wouldn't approve of his new plans.

Shifting rapidly to my angry, but controlled voice, I clipped curtly, "Very well, Jon. Happy Birthday. Goodbye."

Everyone was stunned that Jon wasn't at his party. "Jon sure missed a good dinner," one of my sons-in-law said, as we left the Japanese steak house. "How come he didn't come?"

I shrugged my shoulders and desperately tried not to be angry or hurt. I didn't succeed with either.

A few days after the boys' birthday Jeremy asked, "Hey, Mom, what are you getting Jon for his birthday?"

"Nothing," I shot back.

"How can you do that, Mother?" Jeremy asked in open disapproval.

The following week Jon phoned again. I had anticipated his call and decided that when the operator said the sweetly familiar words, "Collect call from Jon," I'd say, "Jon who?"

My smug smile vanished as the operator said, "Collect call from Jon West. Will you pay?"

Why was Jon always one step ahead of me? "Yes, yes, of course," I answered impatiently.

"Hi, Mom." *Friendly, cheerful voice. He was coming home.* "I got a ride home." (Long pause) "Okay?"

"Okay, Jon." (No warmth in my voice.)

More silence. Then Jon blurted out, "Do you have a present for me, Mom?" He suddenly didn't sound nineteen anymore. Even though he'd told me loud and clear and often that most of my traditional values were obsolete, it seemed birthday presents were still "in."

"No."

Silence. (Two could play at this game.) "Well... see 'ya around four... okay?" *Hopeful voice full of anticipation. He's trying to con me. I will absolutely not get him a birthday gift.*

Jon arrived at four the next day with a large basket full of dirty clothes and an even larger smile. After church on Sunday, when he suddenly realized that I had not done his laundry as usual, he silently began doing it. He put colored and whites all in together. I shuddered but pretended not to notice. I couldn't believe how he ironed his pants. He took them from the dryer and laid them on the carpet and sort of dragged his feet over them, almost as though he were skating in slow motion. I pretended that everyone ironed that way and went on with my typing. Just as he finished his "ironing," his friend arrived to take him back to school. We hugged briefly and he ran out to the car in the pouring rain. I didn't even tell him to put on a jacket, and I hadn't rushed out and bought cough medicine for his hacking cough.

After he was gone the house seemed very quiet. I turned off my typewriter and sat stiffly on the edge of the sofa and looked at his barefoot prints in the carpet. Finally, I got up and placed my feet inside his feet prints. He wore a size 11-1/2 now. I already missed him, but the anger held on fiercely.

I wasn't at all prepared for the memory that surfaced clearly during Monday's early morning hours. The boys must have been about ten. Their daddy was picking out bikes for their birthdays. I recalled it all vividly. Jerry and I were in the bike shop and Jerry couldn't stop smiling. He selected a blue bike for Jon and a red one for Jeremy. I could see the certain slow smile that I loved—almost a reverence cross Jerry's face as he paid for the bikes. He ran his hand over them gently as though they were alive. I kept complaining about the price, but he was in another world—a world of bikes—and couldn't hear me. I wasn't a bike person.

Suddenly I was wide awake, sitting up in bed. Thoughts of the blue bike that Jerry had bought Jon years ago cemented in my mind. Jerry had been dead almost four years. Thinking about that bike somehow brought me intense happiness. Then in my mind, the bike changed into a large, ten-speed, light-weight one.

I suddenly saw Jon riding the elegant bike *today*. I didn't seem to have control over my thoughts! How could Jon possibly receive a bike today? Unmistakably, I felt something moving around in my heart. Unforgiveness. It seemed to be moving out! Then, like two eager children, hand in hand, forgiveness and joy rushed in. I hopped out of bed and could hardly wait for the stores to open. Finally, at nine sharp, I phoned information in Rome, Georgia, where Jon was in school. I asked the operator for the number of a bike shop. Then I dialed the number. The joy inside me was unbelievable.

A young man answered. I blurted out, "Hello. There's a blue bike there, ten-speed, light weight, large.... "

"We have hundreds of bikes, Ma'am."

"Well this one is for my son, Jon. He's in school at Berry. What kind of bikes do the boys there ride?"

"Tell me about your son," the patient young man said.

"He's six feet, two inches tall, weighs 190 pounds. Very strong (I almost added "stubborn," but then didn't) long legs, athletic... quiet... and he didn't come home for his birthday and I've been angry all this time. I just forgave him early this morning and he *has* to have the blue bike today."

"Hold on a moment, please." I waited in utter delight. I had forgotten how delicious forgiveness felt.

"Hello, Ma'am, I believe I have found Jon's bicycle here."

"Wonderful! Could you put a big bow on it and here's what I want you to write on a card. 'Happy Birthday, Jon. It's a late present, but it's a genuine birthday present. Your daddy would want you to have this. Me too. I love you. Mom.' " The stranger read the message back to me.

"Oh, could you deliver the bike to the college today? Take it to Dean Carver's office. I want someone who knows Jon to give it to him. Dean Carver will know what to say. I'll call him and explain that you are bringing the bike."

"Yes, Ma'am, I can deliver it today. I know the Dean and right where his office is."

At six that afternoon the phone rang. "Mrs. West." I immediately recognized Dean Carver's voice. We'd never met, but had spoken on numerous occasions about Jon. "I wanted you to know that one happy young man just rode a magnificent blue bike out of my office. Literally, Mrs. West. He rode it down the hall and right down the front steps."

"Oh, thank you for giving it to Jon for me. Is it okay? I don't know a thing about bikes."

"Okay? It's quite a bit more than okay. I know something about bikes."

I closed my eyes and imagined the scene that Dean Carver described— "All Jon could say for a few minutes was 'For me? For *me*?' Finally, he confessed that he'd been thinking about having a bike all day. He looked at it for a long time silently and then touched it—well, actually he sort of stroked it. What a smile!"

I knew the smile well.

At six forty-five the phone rang again. "Collect from... "

"I'll pay! I'll pay, operator," I fairly screamed at her.

"Hi, Mom. I got the bike! It's pretty... neat. I rode it back to the dorm, and then all around campus. I can't figure how you picked out such a good bike. You really aren't a bike person, 'ya know. Anyway... I really like it Mom. It's a great, *genuine* birthday present."

"Where's the bike now, Jon? Did you use the lock I sent? Is the bike locked up? Do you have a bike rack at your dorm?" (I was back to my old self, asking too many questions.)

"No Ma'am. I have the bike up in my room with me."

"Jon! You carried a bike up three flights of stairs. Isn't it too heavy? How could you.... "

"Mom. Mom." His voice was gentle. Calm. "It's really light. Doesn't weigh anything at all. Really."

"Oh." I smiled. Jon and I were at last having a real telephone conversation. Maybe the bike was even as light as my heart with all the forgiveness surging around in it.

A TOUCH OF FORGIVENESS

"You never encourage me—all you do is find fault! Why can't you ever encourage me?" Jeremy, my angry twenty-year-old son, screamed at me.

I immediately defended myself in a tone loud enough to match his. "That's not true. I do a lot for you."

His face contorted in anger and he bellowed again, "But you never encourage me!"

I was about to reply when my new husband of one year, Gene, caught my attention. His face turned from me to Jeremy, and then from Jeremy to me, as though he were watching a rapid tennis match. Like a furious hurricane our argument strengthened. Jeremy turned to Gene, "She never encourages me, Gene, you know she doesn't."

Gene walked over and put his arm around me. "I love you, Marion." It was evident in his touch even before he said the words. "But this time you owe Jeremy an apology. He's been doing so many things right lately. Remember how proud of him we are?" In an even gentler voice he asked, "Could you apologize to him?"

Jeremy looked at me from the kitchen stool where he sat. His expression was of surprise—almost delight.

I couldn't get the apology out. It was buried deep inside me, and anger prevented its escape.

"Encourage him, Marion," Gene said softly.

I didn't make a move. I just stood stubbornly by the kitchen sink with my arms folded and stared down at the green and white floor. How could this have happened so quickly? Jeremy and Gene and I were about to go to my granddaughter's birthday party—a skating party. We were late now because of the argument. Gene broke the silence that hung in the kitchen like heavy fog. "I'm going to leave you two alone for a bit." He hugged me and then walked over to Jeremy and put his arm around him. I expected Jeremy to pull away; instead, to my surprise, his head flopped against Gene's chest and remained there. Gene sort of rubbed Jeremy's back soothingly. I could see Jeremy's body relax.

Alone in the kitchen, Jeremy's eyes met mine. Immediately he said, "I'm sorry I hurt your feelings by hollering. I didn't mean to." There was no trace of anger in his face or in his voice. I walked over and held him in my arms. He held me. "I'm sorry, Jeremy. I'm sorry I hollered too. I should be able to control my feelings better... I'm the mother. I love you Jeremy."

Patiently he let me hold him while I cried all over his neck. He shifted from one foot to the other. "I love you too, Mom."

A few minutes later we arrived at my granddaughter's skating party. Seven-year-old Jamie talked me into skating even though it had been twenty years since I'd skated. Immediately, I realized that twenty years is a long time not to have skated. I wobbled insecurely, nearly losing my balance several times. I couldn't even remember how to stop!

It was only going to be a matter of time until I fell. *What am I doing here? I'm fifty-two. I shouldn't be skating. I should be trying to figure out how to encourage Jeremy.* People zoomed by me. Again, I nearly lost my balance....

Suddenly I felt a strong, but gentle arm around my back and someone held my hand firmly. Whoever it was had appeared right out of nowhere, like Superman to the rescue. I turned my head carefully, still concentrating on my balance, fully expecting to see a reassuring Clark Kent. Instead I looked right into the brown eyes of Jeremy. We didn't say a word, but with his arm of encouragement around me, I immediately felt secure and soon we were skating—gliding, it seemed, around the rink. We skated on and on, picking up speed and moving in perfect harmony. No words were spoken. Just frequent glances and smiles were exchanged and I was continually aware of his touch.

Looking straight ahead, I realized a powerful, new truth: A quiet, unexpected touch is more encouraging than a thousand words.

A LOVING TOUCH

Nobody's chocolate chip cookies are as delicious as my friend Lydia's. One day she came by my house with a batch of her cookies, and we sat at my kitchen table while I sampled them. "What's your secret, Lydia? Why are your cookies so good?"

Lydia laughed. "It's so simple that you won't believe it. While the cookies are still very hot, you scrunch them. Simply use the tips of all five fingers at once and briefly push each cookie in. You know you've scrunched them just right when they look like a bulldog's face."

The next week I made a batch of chocolate chip cookies and followed my friend's unusual secret. She was right! What a dramatic difference a touch makes! It transforms a good cookie into a fantastic one.

You'll probably realize, as you touch each cookie briefly, that a touch is an amazing gesture. It can change people, too. When God touches us, He expects us to pass His loving touch along to others. Maybe there's someone you want to reach out and touch today.

❦

CHAPTER TWENTY-THREE

WHEN I'M WRONG, LORD

THE TOWN I PLANNED TO HATE

"Okay, okay!" I said loudly, "I'll commute with you to Perry, and I'll be a dutiful minister's wife, but you should know that I plan to detest every minute of it—including the entire town."

I knew my attitude was rotten, but I hoped my husband, Gene, would back down. Instead, his face lit up. "Thanks," he said, "and as soon as the farm sells, we'll be on our way to Georgia to live, just like we planned."

Until I married Gene Acuff, after being a widow for four years, I'd never lived anywhere except Georgia. When I came to live in Stillwater, Oklahoma, I felt I didn't fit in. Now the farm had been for sale for over a year, and it looked like it would never sell. And without even asking me, Gene had accepted an invitation to be interim minister at the First Christian Church in Perry, a town of 5,000 a half-hour drive away. And to my horror and disbelief, he told them I'd come along to help out! If I felt out of place in Stillwater, I'd really be a misfit in Perry!

In the sanctuary of the church the following Sunday in Perry, I found a seat near the front, determined to sit alone. Just as the service got under way, a smiling couple got up from their seat and came to sit with me as though we were old friends. When Gene started to pray, the woman reached over and held my hand. No one else held hands. For such a petite, older woman she certainly had a powerful grip. She offered to share her hymnal with me, but I pretended not to notice.

Monday we drove back to Perry in silence. At the church I couldn't bring myself to go inside. "I'm going to town," I announced with some independence.

Gene handed me the car keys. "Have a good time."

Feeling like a blob, I drove the three short blocks to "town." I parked and got out of the car, slamming the door harder than necessary. I felt ridiculous—I couldn't even think of anything to buy. Hoping I looked confident, I started across the street against the light. A red truck slammed on its brakes. *Oh, Lord, if he hollers at me, I'm going to cry.* A smiling man leaned out of the truck, motioned me on and waved. "Thanks," I called out.

"You bet," he said.

Oh, my goodness. I hadn't expected a town square. I stood there gazing helplessly as sweet memories of my own hometown square in Elberton, Georgia, poured through my emotions like a balm. There's something marvelously secure about a town with a square. It's almost as though the town has a real heart and the ability to care. A gazebo, bandstand, manicured lawn, giant shade trees, picnic tables, a cannon, little paths—everything! Almost reverently, I sat on a bench and looked around.

Then I caught myself. *So what if the town has a square? I'm still not going to like it.*

I strolled around the square despite the heat. I shrugged off the feelings of brief contentment and entered Foster's corner drugstore. I sat on a stool at a real old-fashioned soda fountain. The hand-lettered sign said Cherry Cokes, and I hadn't had one since I was a teenager. I slurped my large, tasty drink and asked the pleasant woman, "Do you make chocolate sodas too?"

"You bet. Best in town. You'll have to come back."

Back outside, a bright yellow sign beckoned to me: The Perry

Daily Journal. I was surprised that a town so small would have a daily paper. I went in to buy a paper to read about the town I planned to hate.

The minute I stepped inside the glass door, a long-forgotten childhood memory surfaced. Even as a youngster, I knew I wanted to be a writer—and oh, how I longed to meet a real, live writer, any kind of writer! Of course there weren't any in Elberton, except for a veteran reporter who had his own column at our newspaper, *The Elberton Star*. I thought up reasons to go to *The Star* office to buy things from Mr. Herbert Wilcox. Pencils, poster board, even newspapers. He'd smile over his small, round glasses when I entered, get up from his ancient typewriter and ask, "May I help you, young lady?"

As I stood in the office of *The Perry Daily Journal*, which looked amazingly like *The Star* office back in the '50s, a distinguished, white-haired gentleman rose from his outdated typewriter. "May I help you?" he asked. I felt thirteen rather than fifty-three. When I found my voice, I couldn't blurt out, "Could you just talk to me for a while?" Instead, I said casually, "I'd like to buy a paper." Even so, I spilled my change on the counter.

I left the marvelous office reading the paper. The man must have been Milo Watson, editor and publisher of *The Perry Daily Journal* for forty-two years. In large, bold letters I read: Say Something Good About Perry Today! I stopped smiling abruptly. This was the town I planned to hate.

Later that week, Gene asked me to go with him to visit a church member in the hospital. After parking the car we observed an unusual truck parked in the lot. The back was crammed full of iron pipes and junk, and standing on top of it all was a goat! I hesitated. "That goat's fine, Marion," Gene called. He knew my passion for rescuing stray animals.

"Then why has someone tied him to that iron pipe?" I asked. I ran into the hospital ahead of Gene to find the owner and ask questions. By the time Gene found me I was talking to a tired-looking man in overalls.

"Yes, that's my goat. Rather, my wife's. She thinks more of that goat than she does me. Crazy goat hides in the back of my truck and hitches a ride to town. Then he sneaks off and heads for the square." I nodded. The story made sense. "Today some friends of mine noticed him. Out in the middle of the street again, stopping traffic. They chased him down and tied him in the back of my truck. Everyone knows my truck and my goat. We're heading home now."

I smiled quite a bit that day.

A couple of days later, I decided to write a note to a church member visiting Albuquerque. I couldn't find a dictionary at the church, so I dialed the post office. "Do you know how to spell Albuquerque?" I asked. Slowly, patiently, the man spelled it for me.

"Thanks," I said.

"You bet."

People in Oklahoma use that expression a lot. I like it. Short and to the point. No frills.

After we'd been in Perry for a few weeks, Gene came up with an idea. "Marion, tonight in church I want you to share with the people how you planned to hate this town."

"Oh, Gene, I can't. I won't."

"Of course you can. We've been studying how God can change attitudes—"

"Well, mine isn't completely changed," I snapped.

Gene went ahead and announced it in the morning service. That evening I stood looking into gentle, open faces, the kind that simply expect you to speak the complete truth.

"I... I... planned to hate this town," I said. They never flinched or dropped their eyes. "I didn't know Perry would have a square, and sidewalks, and chimes that ring out at noon. I didn't know that paying bills was a social event—that is, you don't mail them, but rather walk around the square, visiting as you leave your checks. People care here—so much that Mrs. Lynch, who's 102, can live alone. Everyone checks on her. The waitresses even know my favorite kind of pie, and before I ask, they tell me if they have it. People sit on their porches and wave to you.... "

I got a lot of hugs afterward. Everyone was so accepting and caring. How, I wondered, could I ever have planned to hate this town?

That night before I went to sleep I confessed, *Dear Lord, sometimes it's a glorious thing to be wrong. Thank you for bringing us to Perry. And,* I added, *for changing my attitude.*

I was beginning to feel as though we lived snugly inside a Norman Rockwell painting when, in December, the farm sold. I'd about forgotten it was even for sale. "Well, now we can move to Georgia, just like I promised you," Gene said. I nodded.

But after we packed up all the furniture and shipped it to my home in Georgia, I found myself saying, "Gene, we can't leave until the church gets a minister."

He stared at me. "But we planned to leave when the farm sold."

"Let's move into the parsonage. We can borrow some furniture."

He smiled slightly. "That could be a long time. Are you sure?"

"You bet."

❦

WHERE'S MY "NEVERTHELESS" GIRL?

The romance between Gene and me and our storybook marriage seemed so perfect that I assumed we'd never have a spat. But one sneaked up over something trite. I was wrong. Unreasonable. Also angry and hurt. Gene picked up on my attitude and initiated a conversation. I fled from the room. "Hey," he called after me. "Where's my 'Nevertheless' girl?" He was referring to a term I'd coined about how to live victoriously no matter what.

"She doesn't live here anymore," I shot back. I marched to the kitchen and sat stiffly in a straight-back chair, glaring at the wall. Gene pulled up a chair directly in front of me. I wouldn't look at him. He spoke as though we were having good eye contact: "I'm sorry. I hurt your feelings. Forgive me."

I didn't dare look at my new husband because if I did even for a moment, I might not be able to hang on to my resentment and self-pity.

"Look at me, Marion." His voice was gentle. He held both my hands. I continued to glare at the plaid wallpaper.

"Marion, I love you. I need you. Don't shut me out."

I gazed into a face fervent with love. Of course resentment and anger made a hasty departure. They can't endure such love. Gene and I looked at each other for a few silent minutes smiling, then laughing, then embracing.

CHAPTER TWENTY-FOUR

FRIENDS, BOTH NEAR AND FAR

THE PEPPERMINT MIRACLE

Wistfully, I decorated the tall tree. I had so hoped we would be in our new house by Christmas. I had hated the cramped, weather-beaten rental house from the moment Jerry drove up the narrow driveway and announced, "Here it is." The backyard was deep in mud that rainy March day we moved in.

"Where's the grass?" three-year-old Julie asked as Jerry carried her through the mud. I held Jennifer, not yet one, in my arms.

"We'll have grass at our new house," I answered. And I thought bravely, as I fought back tears, maybe there'll be neighbors here I'll enjoy and children for the girls to play with.

Soon I discovered eight children lived next door to us, but they were painfully shy and any move toward being friendly sent them running into their house.

I almost never saw their mother. Mrs. Long worked each day. Our houses were so close together we shared a driveway, but an invisible wall kept us from being neighbors. I called to her sometimes, but she seemed too tired or busy to notice me. Maybe she was embarrassed about her husband's loud, arguing manner that she knew I could hear.

Julie and Jennifer were excited about the tree and helped me decorate it. It was one of our loveliest trees, reaching almost to the high ceiling. Its cedar aroma stirred many nostalgic memories for me. The music from the record player sounded like Christmas. Packages waited underneath the tree. Jerry had been whistling "Jingle Bells" for days. My small kitchen was loaded with good food I planned to cook when our families joined us for this special day. Cards from friends that I had read and reread were on the coffee table.

But I felt dark and lonely inside.

This sad feeling will go away. Surely it will. I just miss my old friends and neighborhood. Last Christmas it seemed the doorbell or the phone rang constantly.

Oh, that wonderful moment of opening the door to find a neighbor standing there with a sample of goodies from her kitchen or a small, homemade article gaily wrapped.

I missed a neighbor running over to borrow a cup of sugar or a bit of nutmeg, and the friends that called out to me when I went to the mailbox.

I tried to look forward to spring when we would be in our new house, but it seemed a lifetime away. I wanted to feel the way you were supposed to feel on Christmas.

As I put away boxes that the decorations had been stored in, I fought to keep back the tears. How could I explain to Jerry what was missing? Maybe tomorrow, Christmas Eve, the special feeling would come.

The next day the girls and I wrapped some last minute gifts. As I cooked supper I told them about what Christmas was like when I was a little girl. Even reliving those happy memories didn't fill the vacuum inside me.

Finally, it was time for Jerry to come home. We sat at the window looking for him. It was dark and cold outside. A light drizzle fell. I turned on the porch light and wondered if anyone noticed our door decorations. I felt like we were on a desert island.

"Look, Mama," Julie exclaimed, "Mrs. Long's coming to see us."

I looked, expecting to see her checking her mailbox or perhaps walking to the grocery store that was near us. She and some of her children usually walked and pulled their groceries home in a buggy. But she was coming toward our house. She held her face down to avoid the icy rain.

We moved back from the window and sat on the sofa waiting for the sound of the old doorbell. I answered it on the first hint of a ring.

She wore a wool scarf and clutched her coat tightly about her throat. Little drops of rain clung to her dark hair. Her breath circled about her face. She held something in her hand.

"Come in, come in, Mrs. Long," I said.

"Hello," Julie said warmly, and Jennifer reached up and held onto her coat.

"Here, let me take your coat. Do you think it'll snow? Please sit down."

But she held her coat even tighter and replied, "No, no, I'll keep it on. I just wanted to bring you this." She handed me a bowl covered in tinfoil. A little red bow sat on the top. I opened it to find small broken pieces of peppermint candy filled the bowl.

"Ohhh, we love peppermint. Thank you so much. It really isn't Christmas without peppermint, is it?" I popped a piece in my mouth and gave the children a piece. When I offered Mrs. Long some, she declined.

"I work in the candy factory, you know. I can pick up the broken pieces anytime I want to. I just wanted to come over and say 'Merry Christmas.' "

"Thank you, thank you. Please sit down for just a moment." She hesitated a bit, then sat down, loosening her coat. She smiled down at Julie and Jennifer who sat as close to her as they could get. I noticed the tired lines beneath her warm smile.

She told the children, "Your door certainly is pretty. We've been admiring it."

"You have?" Julie beamed at her, then me.

We began talking about our children and Christmas. She told me she had two days off for Christmas. Then she insisted she had to leave.

"Oh, your bowl, Mrs. Long. Let me empty your bowl."

"No, you can bring it back sometime. And bring your little girls when you come."

"All right. We'll be over soon. Wait just a minute, will you?"

I ran to the kitchen, as she chatted with Julie and Jennifer, and cut most of a fruitcake, arranging the pieces on a colorful Christmas plate. Quickly, I wrapped it in clear wrap and covered it in Christmas stickers. I rushed back to the living room and gave her the cake. "Merry Christmas, Mrs. Long."

She took the cake, "Why, thank you."

As we watched her go back into the dark night, I thought, how easily she could have pushed aside that idea of coming to my house and bringing us a gift of peppermint candy. "Thank you, God, for sending her."

I looked at the small bowl of peppermint candy. It didn't look like so great a gift. But, instantly, I remembered another gift that had been given quietly and humbly on Christmas Eve nearly two thousand years ago.

Somehow the message of both gifts seemed very much alike to me that Christmas Eve—the ageless and urgent message of communicating love.

ℰ

Next-Door Neighbors

When I was offered the opportunity to take a trip back to Athens, Georgia, recently, I grabbed it immediately. More than anything else, I wanted to see the person I had never really known while I lived there, but who had since come to be an important influence on my life—my former neighbor, Grace Fields. I fully expected my visit to be filled with nostalgia, but I wasn't at all prepared for the discovery we made during our reunion.

Grace and I had lived next door to each other years ago, in the '60s. Our backyards in Athens were separated by a chain link fence my husband had erected to keep in our twin sons and the dog. But something more than that chain link fence seemed to separate Grace and me.

A busy young mother of four children, I was shy, often insecure and lonely. Grace seemed just the opposite. She and her husband, Dewitt, were older; they had never had children, and she appeared to have enormous amounts of time. I often noticed her from my kitchen window or as I hung out mounds of diapers; she was usually working in her picture-perfect yard.

Sometimes when I strolled the twins, I met her walking briskly around the block, long before it was fashionable to walk. We spoke politely. She seemed so orderly and mature that it was a while before I got up the courage to pay her a neighborly visit. I took along two children in case I ran out of something to talk about.

We found her on her knees digging in her flower bed with a bright-red trowel. I usually dug with a soup spoon when I had the energy to tend my neglected flowers. Her yard was breathtaking—small, but lush and manicured, enclosed by a quaint wooden fence with a marvelous squeaky gate. I felt like Alice in Wonderland entering another world. Grace wore a wide-brimmed straw hat and a pastel button-down-the-front flowered dress that she called "everyday." Somehow it looked spiffy to me. She was trim and wore well-worn sensible shoes and white socks.

Grace invited us inside for some lemonade. We followed meekly. She and my oldest child, Julie, talked intently and comfortably while I shifted Jeremy, one of the twins, from one hip to the other. She introduced us to her two overweight cats, who lived inside.

I looked around and quietly marveled over a house that wasn't childproof, and I tightened my grip on Jeremy. My eyes lingered on a lovely silver bonbon dish that sat on an antique marble-top table. She had good books on her shelves and some paintings she'd done herself hanging on her immaculate walls. On the floor by the refrigerator were two china saucers from which her cats ate.

After that visit, we came back and forth to one another's homes, but we were careful not to allow ourselves to become vulnerable or close. She always phoned before coming over and assured me she'd stay only a few minutes. She always kept busy, and she seemed to enjoy being alone.

There began to be days when a depressive, deep loneliness and a fierce, unnamed longing seemed to pursue me like an enemy, usually late in the afternoon. Motherhood was more difficult than I'd imagined. I was tired and sometimes cried for no reason I could name. On those days I found myself standing at my kitchen window looking out at Grace's back door, which often was flung wide open so that the sun shone right into her kitchen. That sight never failed to soothe my emotions. An open door meant Grace was at home, and she was the most secure person I knew. I imagined her moving about, full of energy and joy in her quiet, lovely, and organized world.

All those years I lived behind Grace, I never dared to run to her open back door and admit, "Oh, it's so hard being a mother! I'm tired and I want to have time to paint and write. I've always wanted to write." I could not let her know, "I'm lonely and afraid some days," or ask, "Could we just sit in your kitchen and drink hot tea from your china cups and talk? Could we be... friends?"

Then before the twins started school we moved away—Jerry and I, our four children, and our black dog, Muff, which Grace never liked. Just as we were pulling away, I hopped out of the car and ran to my front porch and grabbed my flowering hanging basket and took it to Grace. I don't recall that we said anything significant.

Somehow we began to correspond—at first, little casual cards with careful, guarded messages, and then suddenly long, long letters in which we became less and less reserved. Grace returned some of my letters with misspelled words circled in red (she had been a schoolteacher).

Soon I was pouring out my heart to her, writing details of my thoughts and dreams. She responded with picturesque letters faintly reminiscent of Emily Dickenson. I'd begun having articles, then books, published. Once she wrote, "One of the neighbors brought me your latest article. The whole neighborhood thinks it's quite good. However, I believe some of the letters you've written to me are much better." Grace was one of the few people from whom I could take criticism.

Once, after years of letter writing, Grace added a P.S. to her letter: "Oh, how I miss you." Leaving dinner dishes and dirty laundry, I rushed right out to buy a card for her. It took nearly an hour to find the perfect one—a Persian cat resting in a Victorian setting.

I always answered Grace's letters the day I got them, ignoring whatever responsibility was most pressing. Her responses, always long in coming, were enormously anticipated and unbelievably delicious. How freely she poured her thoughts and feelings into those perfectly typed and spelled letters! I read and reread them.

When Jerry died just after he turned forty-seven, I heard from Grace—not a flowery sympathy card, but a neatly typed two-page letter in which she remembered Jerry with fondness and subtle humor.

After a few years I met and married Gene. And so it was that when he was asked to teach a short course back in Athens, I was able to go along one afternoon—to visit Grace. I was approaching fifty-three and expecting my fourth grandchild. Grace's own husband had died three years earlier.

Her house was just as I remembered it. Once again we sat on her living room sofa and talked. It was as though time had stood still. "Oh, Marion, I had this dress when you used to live here," she said with a laugh.

"Really? I thought it was new. It's back in style now and looks good on you."

After a while we went out to the backyard. She'd just had cataract surgery, so I offered her my hand. She took it, as though we'd always walked hand in hand. In her kitchen she paused to pick up her wonderful old straw hat; she never went outside without a hat to protect her face from the sun.

Grace's backyard was unchanged; woodsy, with violets and ferns, and squirrels and birds so tame they hardly noticed us.

Then we were at my old fence and we stood there holding on to it with both hands as though we were about to catch our breath taking a ride on a Ferris wheel. We did take a remarkable trip—to the past. It happened quickly and quietly, and we both realized it was happening.

The man who now owned the house had just cut the grass. It was late spring, and a wonderful fresh-cut-grass aroma filled the air. But for me, in that instant, it was as though Jerry had cut *our* grass. I was a young mother again, and my children would appear at any moment needing something. I must keep one ear tuned for a cry for help from one of the twins....

We stared long and hard across the fence. Finally, Grace spoke. "Your dog always messed in the path I used when I came to see you. I always stepped in it."

I nodded, remembering. "Under the kitchen window my cat is buried."

"What was his name?"

"Little Kitty."

"Oh, yes. He was a good kitty. Yellow. I liked him."

We continued looking, remembering. Then we walked back toward her house, still holding hands. At her back door the late afternoon sun shone radiantly and formed a square of bright light that looked like a welcome mat on the floor. At long last I was basking in the warmth of Grace's kitchen.

Then we went to her sofa, and she began to tell me things I had not known. The words caught me by surprise.

"Marion, I was just your age now when you moved into the neighborhood," she said. "We'd just moved here too. I'd resigned from a position that meant a great deal to me to help care for my terminally ill mother. I nearly went crazy because I didn't have enough to do. I walked and walked the neighborhood to try to stay busy—and sane.

"You thought I was an old woman, I guess. You seemed to have everything. A young and healthy husband, four beautiful children, youth. I used to watch you from my yard; I knew you were too busy for me. And you had young friends. I was the old lady of the neighborhood. Did you know I cried when you brought me your hanging basket before you moved away? The flowers were half dead, but I revived them."

My heart pounded. All those years while we'd been neighbors, we'd allowed outward appearances and fear of rejection to form an invisible wall between us. We had thought we were too different to be friends. But in our letters those differences had faded.

The Bible says, "Man looketh on the outward appearance, but the Lord looketh on the heart" (1 Samuel 16:7). Finally we had come to see each other as God sees us.

After a long pause, Grace said at last, "Marion, thank you for... for coming to see me—and for being my friend."

To my astonishment, she cried openly. I threw my arms around her and we clung to each other for ever so long. I cried too. When we separated, we just sat, still holding hands, gazing out her picture window. Grace's enormous cat watched us, and the last reflected light of a lovely spring afternoon spilled through the window and surrounded us with a golden glow.

ℭ

FARAWAY PLACES

can remember helping one of our children with a geography assignment years ago. It was then that I realized I would never meet people from faraway places such as California and New York. It was a sad thought because some of those people I would never meet might have become my dearest friends. On the map I let my finger touch the state of Washington and then slide down to a western state. From there I traced the route to New York and then back to California.

"What are you doing, Mama?" Julie asked.

"Oh, just thinking of how there are so many dear people in all those places across the country and I'm never going to meet them. Some of them are probably a lot like me and we could be such good friends. But I'm going to live my life out right here in Georgia."

Only recently have I understood that God has given me a way in which I can make contact with strangers faraway. Through my writing, people in distant places have reached out to me. We have become friends through countless letters, sharing our joys, disappointments, and prayers. I have pictures of my faraway friends, their children and grandchildren—and their dogs and cats too!

Yes, it's as I suspected. There are many dear people out there in the world, just waiting to be friends.

CHAPTER TWENTY-FIVE

ENCOURAGEMENT: FOUND IN ODD PLACES

WHO FALLS IN LOVE
WITH A FENCE?

hen my husband, Jerry, died in 1983, my future appeared overwhelming. I became angry. I decided that life wasn't fair. I hated being alone. By my third year of widowhood my face had become a stiff mask. *Oh, Lord, please don't let me be bitter,* I prayed.

One day, driving down a busy road in the town where I lived at the time, I noticed a new fence being built around a home I'd always admired. The house, well over one-hundred-years-old, faded white with a large front porch, had once sat back from a quiet road when our town was small. Then Gwinnett County, in Georgia, became the fastest-growing county in the United States. The road was widened and traffic lights went up and the town took on all the characteristics of a city. Now the house had hardly any front yard. Still, that dirt yard was always swept clean. Flowers burst forth from ground that appeared too hard to produce anything. Old rocking chairs on the porch moved slightly in the breeze.

I began to notice a small aproned woman raking, sweeping, working with her flowers, cutting the grass out back. She even picked up the litter thrown from the countless cars that whizzed by.

Each time I passed the house, I watched the progress of the fence. It went up quickly. The elderly carpenter painted it snow-white, a picket fence with a gate near the road. He added an overhead rose trellis and a gazebo. Then I noticed that he was painting the house to match the fence! I fairly crept by now, fascinated by the beauty. Cars behind me honked.

One day, I pulled off the road, parked, and stared long and hard at the marvelous fence; it was as if I had been drawn there for some reason. The carpenter had done a magnificent job. I blinked tears away. It was so beautiful. I started my car to leave, but I couldn't. I cut the engine off, got out, and walked over and touched the fence. It still smelled of fresh paint. I heard the woman trying to crank a lawn mower out back.

"Hi," I called, waving.

"Well, hey, honey." She stood up straight and wiped her hands on her apron.

"I—I—came to see... your fence. It's beautiful." I didn't tell her that I was near tears, desperately lonely and in love with the fence.

She smiled. "Come on and let's sit on the front porch, and I'll tell you about the fence."

I swallowed hard to keep from bawling. It was as though she were expecting me. We walked up the back steps and friendly cats followed. She opened the screen door for me; it squeaked like the long-ago, almost-forgotten screen from my childhood. I was nearly fifty years old but felt somehow like a child again. The kitchen was strewn with remains of a fresh garden-vegetable supper. She didn't apologize for the disorder. We walked over worn green linoleum, down a wide hall with wooden floors and out to the front porch.

"Have a rocker," she said, smiling.

I was suddenly overjoyed that I was on the porch with the marvelous white picket fence surrounding me. Cars whizzed by, but I felt protected, secure, at least for now. We rocked, talked, and drank iced tea.

"The fence isn't for me," the woman explained matter-of-factly. "I live here alone. But since so many people come by here every day now, I thought they would enjoy seeing something real pretty. Is anything prettier than a white picket fence?"

"Oh, no... nothing," I said, with absolute assurance.

"People look at my fence, wave to me. A few, like you, even stop and sit on the porch and talk about it."

"But didn't you mind... when this road was widened... and all the newcomers moved in... and there was so much change?"

"Change is an important part of life and the making of character, hon. When things happen that you don't like, you have two choices." I stopped rocking and leaned forward. "You get bitter or better."

When I left she called out, "Come back anytime. And leave the gate open. It looks more friendly."

I carefully left the gate ajar and drove off, thinking about the woman's words. Deep inside me something unmistakable was happening. I didn't know exactly what to call it, but in my mind I saw a hard, cold brick wall around my troubled, angry heart. Now it was crumbling. And this neat little white picket fence was being erected by the Master Carpenter. I planned on leaving the gate open for whatever or whomever God might bring my way.

Author's note: I was married to Gene Acuff one year later.

THE PHYSICIAN'S ROSE

*S*trange, the little things that encourage us and give us hope. My mother was to have surgery by an eminent specialist on the following day. Tests were still being done on her. I sat alone in the hospital hall while she was in X-ray. It was not yet seven in the morning. I watched the hospital come to life as all the people who made it run came to work in full force. I began to think about my mother's doctor. He had the finest reputation in the southeast. He was booked solid. We'd waited two weeks to fit into his schedule. He was unquestionably the best. But all his credentials and fine reputation, his thoroughness, didn't satisfy something deep inside me. I didn't even know what to call this feeling... sort of a gray area of discouragement.

While I was sitting there, the elevator door opened and out stepped my mother's doctor on the way to surgery. He was carrying a perfect pink rose. I didn't expect him to speak or even recognize me. He barely knew me. But *the rose*... the rose spoke volumes to me. The man inside the doctor *cared*, above and beyond his medical skill; he cared deeply. I imagined him out in his garden, before the sun was fully up, searching for the one perfect rose that bloomed to bring to... I didn't know who. It didn't really matter.

Just then the doctor saw me, smiled, and lifted his hand to wave, hurrying on his way. Even after he disappeared down the hall, I kept smiling too.

CHAPTER TWENTY-SIX

CHILDHOOD REMEMBERED

THE LUNCH BOX

*I*n the early 1960s, my husband and I became the parents of two little girls, two years apart. Quiet, obedient, demure children. I quickly assumed the role of a confident, smiling mother with enormous time, energy, and enthusiasm—even patience.

When the girls approached eight and six, twin sons arrived. Superactive, loud, demanding, headstrong. Julie, my oldest little girl, became my faithful helper, folding mounds of diapers, strolling the babies, helping her sister, Jennifer, get ready for school, reading to all the children while I prepared meals. I could always depend on her, and I did. Perhaps too much.

The carefree days the girls and I had known when we enjoyed long, delightful tea parties under the weeping willow tree vanished abruptly. Supermom disintegrated bit by bit and a tired, grim woman replaced her. Sometimes I cried silently from sheer weariness. Julie often saw me and tried even harder to help. She never complained.

It was only after Julie was grown and married that I learned of the hurt she'd felt back then. One day she laughingly asked me, "Remember my school lunches you made, Mom? All my friends took their lunches in cute little lunch boxes, and I wanted to be like them. Did you know I was embarrassed to eat with my friends? Those fancy lunch boxes of theirs were always filled with wonderful things their mothers had put in them."

I leaned forward, our faces inches apart, listening intently. Julie somehow seemed to have become a child again and spoke freely. "Jeannie's lunches were always the best. She had little sandwiches cut into halves, triangles and circles, and packed in small sandwich bags. She had neat little carrot sticks! She always had a folded napkin for whatever holiday was approaching. You should have seen her lunch box near Valentine's Day. Her mother wrote her name on heart-shaped cookies.

"On cold days Claire had hot soup or hot cocoa in a thermos. And their mothers often tucked notes in their lunch boxes.... "

I listened to Julie, fascinated, as she went on. "Sometimes, Mom, you threw a couple of unwashed, unpeeled carrots in a sack—the largest sack I'd ever seen—and spread peanut butter on two hard pieces of bread and threw in an old apple and a crumbling cookie. I folded the sack forever, trying to make it small."

"Why didn't you ever tell me?" I asked, a ball of sorrow beginning to form in my stomach.

She laughed a genuine laugh, and appeared grown-up again. "You were so busy. I could see you were trying as hard as you could with the boys, and you just never got caught up. I knew you were always tired. Anyway, Jen and I had cute clothes with matching hair ribbons. You always helped us with posters, and picked us up when we had to stay late at school and couldn't ride the bus. Remember the raincoats you bought us with matching umbrellas?" She tried very hard to make it okay. After all these years she was still committed to helping me.

I couldn't drop the subject. "What did it feel like when the lunch bell rang?"

"Well... I always dreaded lunch. I hid my sack under some stuff in the cloak room and always... hoped that maybe.... " She brightened. "Once, I found a grocery ticket in the bottom of my sack and for a moment... I thought you'd written a note."

"I never knew you wanted a lunch box," I spoke in a whisper of regret.

Years passed, and from time to time I thought of the lunch box Julie had yearned for years ago. In my mind, she now sat alone in a corner of the lunchroom with a grocery sack almost as large as she, while her friends chatted away eating dainty sandwiches and reading reassuring notes from their mamas.

Last September, Julie's two little girls were in kindergarten and second grade. She phoned me from five states away to tell me they'd just got on the school bus for the first day of school. "Mama, they picked out their own lunch boxes. Jamie's is pink and Katie's is yellow. You know how she loves yellow. I made their lunches last night." Excitement spilled through the telephone, filling my kitchen and my heart. "Triangle sandwiches, Mama, with the edges trimmed. M and M's. Grapes. Cheese. Homemade cookies. A drumstick... everything in separate Ziploc bags."

"Julie, Julie!" I fairly screamed into the phone. "Did you remember the notes?"

"Yes. Oh, yes!" she responded.

One day I was fervently cleaning out the garage. Julie's father had died a few years earlier. I had remarried, and moved to my husband's farm a thousand miles away, so all the things in this garage were unfamiliar to me. I reached down to the bottom of a dusty cardboard box and pulled out something. A tin lunch box! On the front was the lovable, smiling television tiger who gobbled up a certain brand of cereal and growled a happy "Grrrreat!" The lunch box was old—probably from the 1960s. I sat crosslegged on the garage floor and held it tenderly on my lap, as though it had been dropped right out of heaven, aimed just for me.

Dear Lord, is it possible that You're giving me a second chance?

Go ahead, a silent voice urged. *It's not too late.*

I took the lunch box to the kitchen sink and washed it as carefully as if it were crystal. My imagination stirred and stretched, like a sleeping cat slowly awakening. What does a mother put in

214

a lunch box for a grown-up daughter who lives a thousand miles away? Mounds candy bars, Life Savers, gum, a little box of raisins!

Remembering Julie's passion for old, sentimental things, I included some paper dolls nearly ninety years old—in a Ziploc bag. An antique lace handkerchief, a very old hand-embroidered tea towel. Such a tiny space to pack in so much... love. I tucked in a very old, quaint, jeweled hair comb, a small book about friendship published in the early 1900s. In the book, I printed, "Julie, pretend this is a washed, peeled carrot, cut up properly."

In a tiny satin container, I enclosed an antique pin a friend had given me years ago. Some small packages of Julie's favorite cosmetics and hair products also went into the lunch box. When it would hold no more, I carefully placed a folded napkin on the top—a napkin with a big brown turkey and golden leaves and the words "Happy Thanksgiving." Of course I'd hidden in the very bottom of the lunch box a note printed in large red letters: I LOVE YOU, JULIE BABE. HAVE A GOOD DAY. MAMA.

Driving to the post office with the carefully wrapped package, I reasoned joyfully (if not logically): Never mind that the lunch box is over twenty years late. Never mind that Julie is almost thirty. At last, she was about to have a lunch box! *Please, Lord, don't let it be too late,* I prayed.

Three days later the phone rang. I didn't recognize the voice at first. Someone was squealing, laughing, crying. "Mother, I never realized that I'm still seven years old. It was so... emotionally heavy I could barely breathe. Everything is sitting right out on the kitchen counter. When I opened the lunch box it was just as though I was sitting at the long table and I could even 'smell' school and all my friends were watching me!"

"So the lunch box wasn't too late, after all?" I croaked.

"Too late? Oh, never." Then she paused. "Most of all, though, I loved the note you put at the bottom. Back in the second grade, Mama, maybe I wished for a triangle-shaped sandwich or a peeled carrot stick, and, especially, a note. But I always knew you loved me, Mother."

ℭ

BEYOND THE BLACKBERRY PATCH

*A*s a child I often observed women confidently mothering their brood, knowing exactly what to buy in the grocery store, or driving with complete assurance to a destination, with a car full of squealing children.

And I told myself, someday I'll be doing that. I'll be all grownup, married, and have children. But in my mind's eye, I wondered, how can that ever be? For it seemed that I would always be a skinny, shy little girl merely peeking into the awesome world of adulthood.

I used to reason, I can't just stay a child—no one ever does. Growing up must happen sometime. But I can't imagine being one of them—an adult. I can't believe I'll do grown-up things like drinking coffee or sitting around and being still for hours or wanting to take a nap. And I can't believe I'll ever put cold cream on my face. I don't know how to be a mother—and who will ever love me and want me for his wife?

I tried not to think about the future too much, because deep down it frightened me terribly. I didn't like changes. I wanted to hold onto my childhood. I knew I would be content for the rest of my life to continue picking blackberries with the hot sun beating down on my back in the summer and marveling over seeing my own breath before me in the winter.

Zooming down a hill on skates, playing "kick-the-can," till the stars came out, sleeping late, reading all day if I wanted to, going to camp, feeding stray animals, rescuing drowning bugs, carefully cutting out a new book of paper dolls, and smiling to myself in a dark theater over Gene Autry's goodness, was the only life I knew.

I couldn't possibly see how I would give all this up in exchange for methodical grocery shopping, talking politely to other grown ladies, having permanents, and struggling with a child who had temper tantrums in the dime store.

As a teenager I occasionally thought about the future, getting married, and having children. But I decided that the future must be a long way off, because inside I still felt like a child.

When I went away to college, if I had had to choose sides, I would have quickly said I belonged with the children of the world rather than the adults.

In my early twenties, I loved someone who loved me, and we began talking about marriage. The future I had imagined for so long was near—and yet, it didn't seem too different from yesterday.

The other evening I sat on my front steps and watched the sun disappear. The delicious coolness of the twilight touched me as the heat of the day faded away. Supper was over; the kitchen clean. I had even done some extra house cleaning and felt especially good about it.

I watched my husband move the sprinkler. We had just re-seeded the front lawn. (Funny, as a child, I had taken grass for granted.)

Our thirteen-year-old daughter sprinted across the street to her best friend's house. She leaned impatiently against the door and waited for it to be opened, confident that she would be welcomed inside.

Our eight-year-old twin sons, engaged in a ball game across the street, would complain loudly when I called them in for a bath. (Maybe tonight, I would say yes when they begged for ten more minutes.)

Our sixteen-year-old daughter smiled slightly and waved goodbye to me from her boyfriend's car as they headed for the skating rink. (Could skating at a sophisticated rink, to the latest music, possibly be more fun than gliding on your skates down a sidewalk full of cracks that you could jump over?)

My cat rubbed, contentedly, against my knee. Looking down, I noticed some new touch-me-nots had come up by the steps. So many more than last year. A neighbor waved from across the street and I waved back enthusiastically.

Then, just for a few moments, I saw my world and family as though they were a uniquely woven tapestry that I hadn't realized was of such dear workmanship—or so nearly completed. I marveled at each child and at my husband, bent over the sprinkler.

Contentment surged through me.

Suddenly, I became aware of the presence of God and he seemed to say to me, *Remember when you couldn't understand how all of this would happen? When you were even afraid of it and wanted to turn back? Remember when this very moment was in the faraway future and you were a little girl sitting up in a tree, afraid—wondering how it would ever really happen?*

"Yes, yes, Lord," I almost shouted. "I remember." (He knew about that day in the chinaberry tree!) Now my childhood seems as incredible and as faraway as the future once did.

Somehow, I've entered this impossible world of grown-ups. I'm really here, and yet, I'm not aware of ever having let go of my childhood. My devotion to Gene Autry and paper dolls hasn't completely faded. I still like to skate and feed stray animals. I love to pick blackberries—and now I can whip up a cobbler with them. Being a child isn't very different from becoming an adult. I never knew that until this moment. Crossing over wasn't frightening or even definite. I don't know when it happened!

I laughed softly to myself and my cat looked up at me wide-eyed. Surely, by now I've crossed over. My fortieth birthday had just passed.

And then I became aware of a startling thought, so profound that my heart beat rapidly and tears stung my eyes. *Someday, you'll leave this world and enter into My everlasting Kingdom. There's no need to be anxious now or try to figure it out. You can't. But it will happen just as surely and gently as you've moved from that world of childhood into the world of adults. My child, you can't imagine how wonderful it's going to be!*

PUTTING AWAY CHILDISH THINGS

Recently I found myself back in the neighborhood where I grew up. I'd just left there when I was a teenager and now I was fifty-three. I stood just a few feet from my house and suddenly felt as though I were being pulled fiercely and rapidly back to my childhood. I heard my mother calling me for supper. I saw my yellow bicycle lying in the yard. Cats I had loved sat on the back step in the late afternoon sun. My best friend hollered from her back yard to "Come on over and play." A Christmas tree shone gloriously through our living-room window. A date said good night at my front door. My girl-friends and I laid out on an old quilt and watched falling stars. Sweet smelling flowers burst through the ground and their spring-like aroma filled our home.

Tears stung my eyes and I was afraid for a split second that I might not be able to come back to the present. Of course I could, and did. All grown up again, I was a wife, mother, and grand-mother. The house was really quite small—the yard unbeliev-ably tiny. The bedroom window wasn't high at all. The back steps weren't very steep. Oh, but the memories were tender and amazingly fresh. Staring at my childhood home, I thought God spoke to me: *Remember; drink it all in. Savor it. Cry if you need to. Laugh. Hold it to your heart. But use this experience to re-member to respond to situations in life now with maturity—putting away such things as revenge, jealousy, unforgiveness, self-centeredness, lying, belittling, pouting....*

❦

CHAPTER TWENTY-SEVEN

HOPE COMES IN DIFFERENT SHAPES AND SIZES

RESCUE ON THE CIMARRON TURNPIKE

*J*f there was anything in the world that my husband and I didn't need, it was another problem. And there it sat—just up ahead on the Cimarron Turnpike. I screamed, "Look, Gene! There's a dog in the middle of the road."

In the short time we'd been married my husband had become grimly aware of my obsession with rescuing stray dogs. "I'm not stopping, Marion. I mean it this time." He whizzed by the red puppy. So did dozens of other cars.

I looked back immediately. Of all the cars on the turnpike, the dog had selected our blue station wagon to follow. "Pleeeeeeease, oh, please stop! We're his only chance. I'll find a home for him, I promise." And then I started to cry.

Gene's voice told me that he was very angry, but he turned around. "I'm sure he'll be gone."

"No. Look. He's waiting for us by the road." Gene eased our car onto the grassy median and I jumped over into the back seat and opened the door. Cars sped by, inches away. The red puppy scampered into our car, whimpering gratefully. He crawled onto my lap and locked his front paws around my neck. He encircled my waist with his rear legs. His cold nose pressed into my neck, and he clung like a small child. I tried to peel him off, just to look at him, but he clung too tightly.

It would take an hour to get to the farm and I knew Gene wasn't going to talk to me. I didn't blame him. I decided to use the silence to examine our problems.

I sorted them out, one by one as though I were hanging out a basket of clothes on a line. First I "hung up" the problem that we had so far been unable to sell Gene's farm. It had been for sale nearly six months—not a nibble. Next to that problem, I "hung up" my home in Lilburn, Georgia. Right now my twenty-year-old twin sons lived there. But I would need to put it up for sale as soon as Gene's farm sold. In Oklahoma's depressed economy, it wasn't likely that Gene's farm would sell any time soon.

There was another enormous problem. Gene had taken early retirement from Oklahoma State University shortly after we married. He'd also resigned from pastoring a small, rural church where he'd been for twenty-five years. But now he'd discovered that he wasn't ready for retirement at all! He desperately wanted to teach or preach again somewhere. Where? How? When?

Like mismatched socks, I added straggling problems to the sagging line. Gene loved his farm. Suppose he couldn't be happy without cows, pasture, and land? Where would my sons live? They'd lived where they now were since they were four. And what kind of ministry would there be for a couple in their mid-fifties! Especially, when they didn't even know what they were supposed to be doing. Finally, I dealt with the problem of all of our furniture and junk accumulated from both our previous marriages. Pulling up stakes from homes where we'd lived with beloved spouses until their deaths would be like reopening old wounds, wouldn't it?

I mentally looked at the long line of problems. They seemed to flap and struggle in the ever-present, Oklahoma wind.

As we turned into the driveway of Gene's farm, I squinted and pretended that we'd found *our* home at last. The one we were trying to believe for. There would be a front porch, rocking chairs, hanging ferns, flowers—plenty of room inside for our antique furniture to blend together. It was, however, becoming more and more difficult to believe for "our" home. In fact, my hope was nearly gone.

I phoned the Humane Society and listened to a depressed man tell me about the twenty-eight dogs he was trying to place. I arranged for a local radio station to broadcast a description of Puppy, but no one called. None of my new friends even smiled when they said no. I phoned the newspaper and placed an ad that would run on Sunday. It read: "Rescued on the Cimarron Turnpike, red, female puppy about five-months old. Looks like Old Yeller. Very happy, trusting, obedient. Must have immediate home to survive."

Gene had told me that if no one adopted the puppy we would have to have her put to sleep. Sunday morning at church I asked everyone I saw if they wanted a puppy. No one did. As the congregation stood and sang praise songs, I sang, but my heart was cold, crammed full of unbelief. I stopped singing finally and just stood there wondering why we had this added problem of Puppy.

Suddenly, in my mind I saw Jesus. I hadn't expected to. He seemed to ask: *Why can't you worship Me?*

I have too many problems.

Would you like to give Me your problems?

I'd never done anything quite like this before, and wasn't certain exactly what to do. Mentally, with my eyes shut, I put Puppy into the arms of Jesus. I was surprised when Puppy licked Jesus' face and beard. Jesus laughed! *Is that all?* He seemed to ask.

Well, no. We have two houses a thousand miles apart... and want "our" home... with a front porch.

Would you like to give Me your two homes also?

Just like with Puppy, I surrendered our two houses into the arms of Jesus. He took them quickly and comfortably and seemed to ask once more: *Is there anything else?*

Silently, I handed Him our future—whatever it was that He

wanted Gene and me to do for Him. Our unknown future looked like a dark silhouette of Gene and me kneeling. Jesus held them all in His arms. Funny thing—the houses and our future didn't appear any larger than Puppy. But I didn't feel anything warm or wonderful. I didn't even feel spiritual. Doubt tried ever so hard to convince me that I'd made up the entire episode.

No one phoned that afternoon in response to my ad. I really didn't want to go to church that night, as was our custom. As we entered the sanctuary an Associate Minister, Johnny Cawlfield, shook hands and asked, "How are Gene and Marion tonight?"

Gene smiled and said, "Fine." Then he headed for a seat.

I lingered and blurted out, "I have to find a home for a stray dog.... "

Johnny kept right on smiling and said matter-of-factly, as though all he ever did was find homes for unwanted dogs, "That's no problem." Those marvelous words zoomed right to my doubting heart and instantly awakened a sleeping giant of hope inside me. I stood by Johnny as he spoke to people about Puppy.

Suddenly, I noticed a young man separate himself from a group and make his way toward us. Tall, easy-going, dark hair and beard, kind eyes, smiling. He wore a brown pullover sweater, jeans, and boots. He explained quickly that they didn't really want another dog, but he never stopped smiling and told us that he and his wife would come out to the farm after church to look at Puppy.

Gene and I hurried home from church, turned on the front lights, and then stood by the window looking for Don and Shirlann Bishop. Doubt didn't surrender easily. *They won't come*, it insisted.

Then car lights flooded our dark driveway and the Bishops were at the front door. Don picked Puppy up and she flopped her head over on his chest, her tail wagging hopefully. "We'll take her," he said simply.

Monday morning I picked up Sunday's paper from the den floor. It was opened to my ad. I read it once again. But another message altogether seemed to be there for me: "Rescued on the Cimarron Turnpike; a wife, probably middle fifties. Looks like a worrier. Not very happy, trusting, or obedient. Must have immediate hope to survive."

None of our circumstances had changed, with the exception of finding Puppy a home. Yet, hope was alive and expectant again in my heart. Still holding the paper these words came to my mind: *I sent the dog just for you. You only thought she was a problem. She was really a solution.*

The farm didn't sell the next day, as you might expect. It took nearly a year, but hope is a rugged thing and it survived. Gene and I both cried when the moving van pulled up. We moved to my home in Georgia and put it on the market. Amazingly, we had three contracts within ten days. Both my sons found nice apartments. We cried together again when the "Sold" sign went up and the boys moved out.

Both homes had finally been sold. For over two years, anytime we were in Georgia we had felt drawn to a small, rural church which we frequently passed by. We never attended it, but often, when no one was there, we'd park in front of the church and talk about what it would be like for Gene to pastor it. The whole idea seemed impossible, but hope urged us on and we prayed about the church.

One day the Chairman of the Board from Mount Vernon Christian Church in Monroe called Gene. They'd heard of us and wanted him to preach a trial sermon. Several weeks later, they officially invited Gene to be their new minister.

There weren't many problems left to solve. We just needed "our" home. The one we'd dreamed about for the three years we'd been married. We had looked at over a hundred houses. We couldn't find the one we knew we were suppose to have. One night we asked God to give us a sign—so we'd know that He had selected our home.

The next day we set out in our car on what seemed to be just one more of our innumerable, house-hunting trips. Suddenly, though, I screamed from the car, "Oh, Gene, look at that beautiful green sign. That's the color of the wallpaper I want in our home." He pulled off the road to look at the attractive sign. He knows color is very important to me. It was a sign for a rather new sub-division. It's name: *Bond Crossing*. How interesting that it bore my name. In smaller letters we read: "The fear of the Lord is the beginning of knowledge. Proverbs 1:7."

Hope jumped up and down and cheered inside us. Words weren't necessary. God had given us our sign. We *knew* our house was down this street! We drove right up to a brick and beige country home—as though we'd been doing this for years. We later discovered that construction on the house had begun the very week we were married. God had known all along that He would not only bring us together, but would give us, *together*, a new ministry.

We moved in three weeks later.

I love to sit on the front porch and rock and water the hanging ferns and marvel at what an amazing thing hope is. Romans 5:5 sums it up: " ...hope does not disappoint." Of course hope comes in all kinds of shapes and sizes... and often waits for us in odd places, like turnpikes.

C

THE DESPERATE STRAY

After moving to the country, it wasn't long before I spotted a rather strange looking dog—reddish, long-legged, with alert ears which never seemed to relax. He moved with the speed of a deer. Thin, but sure footed. All attempts I made to feed him, failed. I couldn't get close enough to him. "Will you help me figure out how to feed him?" I asked my husband, Gene.

"Absolutely not. He's a feral dog. Completely wild. Stay away from him." We saw the dog from time to time, usually near the edge of the woods by our home. I'd roll down the car window and call out, "Hi, boy. Good dog." But he would dash away before I could make eye contact. One sunny, fall day I drove by his hangout, and there he was, asleep in the warm sun. I stopped the car inches from him. "Hi, boy." He didn't move a muscle, but his eyes flashed open. We stared at one another silently. Then I drove off. In the rear view mirror I saw him bound into the road and stare long and hard at my car. The next day Gene announced, "Your beast is lying in our yard. He knows the car." I went out with food, but he dashed off into the woods.

Early one dark, rainy morning our headlights shone right on the dog. He stood in the middle of a country road, as though he'd been waiting for us. He hardly noticed the pounding rain. He must be desperately hungry, I thought. Gene turned the car around and drove back home. Without a word spoken between us, I understood.

Joyfully, I ran inside and grabbed all the food I could find—half of a roast. I hurried back to the car. Still in total silence we drove back, both of us hunching forward, wondering if he'd still be there. He was! He had waited! Gene drove close to him, and I rolled the window down and gently dropped the roast at his feet. Only when we were nearly out of sight did the dog move to devour the food.

I knew just how he felt. I remembered how I ran from God, terrified for years at what He might require, and wondering if He really would provide for my needs. But it was in those times of deep, spiritual hunger—even desperation—that I learned most quickly to call on Him for help to meet all my needs.

Notes

Chapter Ten
Listening

1. "In the Garden," by C. Austin Miles, ©1912, 1940 by the Rodenheaver Company.
2. *My Utmost for His Highest* by Oswald Chambers, © 1935 by Dodd, Mead & Company.

Chapter Eleven
Fear Versus Faith

1. From "No One Ever Cared for Me Like Jesus" by Charles Weigle. Copyright © 1932. Renewal 1959 by John T. Tenson, Jr. Assigned to Singspiration Division of the Zondervan Corporation. All rights reserved. Used by permission.

Chapter Eighteen
Restoration

1. From *The Nevertheless Principle*, by Marion Bond West, published by Fleming H. Revell Co., Old Tappan, NJ, © 1986.